FINANCIAL ADMINISTRATION

Financial Administration

An Introduction

M.K. Sharma

ANMOL PUBLICATIONS PVT. LTD.
NEW DELHI - 110 002 (INDIA)

ANMOL PUBLICATIONS PVT. LTD.
H.O.: 4374/4B, Ansari Road, Darya Ganj,
New Delhi-110 002 (India)
Ph.: 23278000, 23261597

B.O.: No. 1015, Ist Main Road, BSK IIIrd Stage
IIIrd Phase, IIIrd Block,
Bangalore - 560 085 (India)
Visit us at: www.anmolpublications.com

Financial Administration

First Published, 2006

ISBN 81-261-2910-7

PRINTED IN INDIA

Printed at Mehra Offset Press, Delhi.

Contents

Preface

"Financial Administration" as a paper is being taught at M.A., M.B.A. and other Management Courses at various universities and institutions. This book is designed as an introductory text to the above paper, encompassing vital information on all pertinent aspects. Thus the material presented here would be of interest as well as of great use to the students, teachers and professionals of Management Courses. This book will provide complete knowledge of financial administration, its introduction, ministry of finance and its working, union-state financial relations, organisation of financial committees, financial control over executives, the execution of budget, union and state budget, zero base budgeting, performance of budget, budgeting for economic development, tax administration in India, role planning commission, role finance commission, Government audit and accounts etc. to the students.

The major topics dealt in this book are—Financial Administration—An Introduction; Ministry of Finance—Working; Union-State Financial Relations; Organisation of Financial Committees; Financial Control over Executives; The Execution of Budget; Union and State Budget; Zero Base Budgeting; Performance of Budget; Budgeting for Economic Development; Tax Administration in India; Planning Commission; Finance Commission; Government Audit and Accounts etc.

It is hoped that all those will benefit from the contents of this book for whom it is meant. The author will feel amply rewarded, if motive is achieved.

Editor

1

Financial Administration—An Introduction

The origin of the Finance Ministry in India goes back to the year 1810 when a separate Finance Department was created out of the Public Department. But a separate Secretary for the Finance Department was appointed only in 1843. From 1810 to 1816 it remained under the charge of the Secretary of Public Department, from 1816 to 1830 under the Secretary of the Territorial Department, and from 1830 to 1843 under the Secretary of the General Department. In 1879 the Finance Department was redesignated as the Department of Finance and Commerce which designation continued up to 1905 when it was renamed as the Department of Finance. With the constitutional changes brought about by the Government of India Act, 1919, the Finance Department was reorganised into seven branches, viz., General Finance, Revenue, Currency and Banking, Salaries and Allowances, Civil Accounts, Army Finance and Military Accounts. The Auditor-General was assigned a statutory status. Though the Finance Department was given a measure of control over the Indian finances, yet the Secretary of State for India had full power to exercise control over the entire revenue and expenditure of the Government of India. He was assisted at the India office by a full-fledged Finance Department. The Government of India Act, 1935, did not relax the control of the Secretary of State over Indian financial matters.

On the attainment of Independence, the office of the Secretary of State for India was abolished. The Department of finance was now designated as the Ministry of Finance. It was organised into three wings, viz., Expenditure, Economic Affairs and Revenue. In 1949 it was organised into two Departments of Revenue and Expenditure and of Economic Affairs. In 1955 it was reorganised into four Departments:

(i) Department of Economic Affairs;

(ii) Department of Revenue;

(iii) Department of Expenditure;

(iv) Department of Company Law Administration.

In September, 1963, a new Department of co-ordination was set up in the Finance Ministry. In November, 1964, the Department of Company Affairs and Insurance was set up which took over the work relating to 'Company Law Administration'. In January, 1966, the Department of Company Affairs and Insurance was abolished. In June, 1967, the Department of Co-ordination was abolished. Now there remained only three Departments under the Ministry of Finance, viz., the Department of Revenue and Insurance, Department of Expenditure and the Department of Economic Affairs. In August, 1969, a Department of Banking was added in the Ministry of Finance. Thus, the Ministry of Finance at present is organised into the following four Departments:

(i) Department of Revenue and Insurance;

(ii) Department of Expenditure;

(iii) Department of Economic Affairs; and

(iv) Department of Banking.

Functions of the Ministry of Finance

The Ministry of Finance is responsible for the following functions:

(i) The administration of the finances of the Central Government and dealing with financial matters affecting the country as a whole.

(ii) Raising the necessary revenues for carrying on the administration and regulating the taxation and borrowing policies of the Government.

(iii) The administration of problems relating to banking and currency, and in consultation with the Ministries concerned arranging for the proper utilization of the country's foreign exchange resources.

(iv) Controlling the entire expenditure of the Government in co-operation with the administrative Ministries and departments concerned.

Organisation of the Ministry of Finance

The Ministry of Finance is under the charge of a Minister of Cabinet rank. He is assisted by a Minister of State and a Deputy Minister. As said earlier, the Ministry at present is organised into four departments;

(1) Department of Revenue and Insurance. This Department is responsible for all matters relating to Central Board of Revenue, Customs, Income Tax, Central Excise, Sales Tax, Insurance, Opium, Stamp Duties on bills of exchange, cheques, promissory notes, bills of lading, letters of credit, policies of insurance, transfer of shares, debentures, proxies and receipts and Foreign Exchange. It also advises the Government on fiscal matters, reviews tax structure, examines fresh proposals of taxation, promotes legislation for the modification of tax law and administers Gold Control regulations.

In respect of revenue matters, the Department is assisted by two statutory Boards, *viz.*, the Central Board of Direct Taxes, and the Central Board of Excise and Customs. Each of these Boards consists of a chairman and three members. The chairman of the Board holds ex-officio status of Additional Secretary and other members of ex-officio Joint Secretaries to the Government of India.

The administration of the Gold Control Rules is the responsibility of the Gold Control Administrator, who is also Joint Secretary in the Department.

The Department has under it seven attached offices and a large number of subordinate offices. The attached offices are: Department of Insurance, Simla; Enforcement Directorate, New Delhi; Directorate of Inspection, New Delhi, Directorate of Inspection (Income Tax), New Delhi; Directorate of Inspection (Income Tax). Investigation Wing. New Delhi; Directorate of Inspecton (Customs and Central Excise), New Delhi; Directorate of Intelligence, New Delhi.

The subordinate offices are: Offices of Collectors of Customs, Bombay, Calcutta, Madras, Visakhapatnam and Kandla. Offices of the Collectors of Central Excise Bombay, Calcutta, Madras, Bangalore, New Delhi, Shillong, Hyderabad, Allahabad, Baroda, Patna, Poona, Nagpur, Cochin, Kanpur, Panjim and Pondicherry; Income Tax Department; Statistics and Intelligence Branch; Central Revenues Control Laboratory; Office of the Narcotics Commissioner; Directorate of Emergency Risks Insurance Scheme.

The Department looks after all the affairs relating to Insurance and for this purpose the Life Insurance Corporation has been set up.

(2) Department of Expenditure. This Department is responsible for financial rules and regulations, delegation of financial powers, financial sanctions relating to all Ministries and offices of the Government of India, advice to Ministries and government undertakings on Cost Account matters, expenditure proposals relating to the Delhi Administration, Indian Audit and Accounts Department, Defence Accounts Department, Local Taxation, State Finance, Capital Budget, Planning and Development Finance, Bureau of Public Enterprises.

The Department consists of following Divisions:

(i) **Establishment Division** is responsible mainly for the administration of the various financial rules and regulations including those relating to the conditions of service of the Central Government employees, administrative matters relating to the Indian Audit and Accounts Department, financial work relating to the Departments of the Ministry of Finance and administration of the Department of Expenditure.

(ii) **Civil Expenditure Divisions.** There are ten Divisions each headed by an Additional Secretary or a Joint Secretary. In addition to rendering financial advice to the Ministries/ Departments of the Government of India/Officers of these Divisions also function as financial representative of Government on Boards of Directors of various public sector undertakings and on the governing bodies of autonomous organizations which receive substantial financial assistance from Government.

(iii) **Defence Division.** This Division is constituted with the Financial Adviser at the head assisted by four Additional Financial Advisers and a number of Deputy Financial Advisers attached to the various Principal Staff Officers of the Army, the Chief of Naval Staff, the Chief of the Air Staff and the Director General of Ordnance Factories. This Division renders financial advice to the Defence Headquarters, the Defence Ministry and to the officers directly subordinate to the Ministry. The Financial Adviser (Defence) is also a Member of the Board of the Border Roads Development. The Division is responsible for scrutiny, sanction and accounting of the expenditure of the Defence Ministry.

(iv) **Bureau of Public Enterprises.** It was set up in March, 1955, to provide a central point of reference on importance aspects of management of public undertakings. It also explores avenues for economy in capital cost and devises steps to increase the profitability and productivity of these undertakings. It reviews the working of public enterprises and presents these reports to Parliament and other government agencies.

(v) **Staff Inspection Unit.** The function of the Staff Inspection Unit is to keep the staffing position in Ministries/Offices under the Government of India under constant review in accordance with pre-determined programmes of work measurement studies. The Unit also undertakes ad hoc reviews, by special request, of Ministries/Offices not included in the programme as well as of the public sector undertakings. The other aspects of work study, such as procedures and methods simplification, etc. are the responsibility of the Department of Administrative Reforms under the Ministry of Home Affairs.

(vi) **Cost Accounts Wing.** It deals with all cost accounting work arising in the various departments. It also undertakes, on request, cost and economic studies and investigations into accounts of both private and public sector undertakings.

(vii) **Plan Finance Division.** It deals with State plans for economic development. It advises on proposals of states for investment in industrial enterprises, irrigation, power and flood control projects. It is also associated with the scrutiny of proposals of Central Ministries for large projects involving heavy capital outlays.

(3) Department of Economic Affairs. The Department of Economic Affairs of the Ministry of Finance, headed by a Secretary, is one of the most important Departments of the Ministry. It prepares the Government's Budget, makes periodic assessments of foreign exchange needs and resources and takes necessary steps to mobilise and allocate resources, both internal and external, in keeping with the country's Plans and development needs. The Department is also responsible for policies regarding currency, banking, financial corporations and foreign exchange, including private foreign investments. Control over capital issues is also under the administrative charge of the Department. Recently, the work relating to the administration of Securities Contracts (Regulation) Act, 1956, and regulation of stock exchanges has been transferred to this Department.

The Department of Economic Affairs has the following Divisions:

(i) Budget Division. This is one of the most important Divisions in whole of the Ministry of Finance. It prepares the Central Government's Annual Budget (other than that for Railways) and Supplementary and Excess Grants for presentation to Parliament. It deals with questions of Public Debt-market loans, small savings schemes, the Compulsory Deposit Scheme and other investments in Government securities. It also looks after the ways and means position of the Central and State Governments and their market borrowings and administers the Contingency Fund of India and deals with the implementation of the recommendations of the Finance Commission and matters of audit and accounting. The fixation of rates of interest on loans given by the Central Government, the administration of the Central Treasury Rules and the submission of reports of the Comptroller and Auditor-General to Parliament are also handled by the Division.

(ii) Internal Finance Division. This Division deals with all matters connected with currency and coinage, banking, industrial finance and control of capital issues. It is also responsible for the administration of Mints, Assay Offices, the Silver Refinery Project, the India Security Press, the Security Paper Mill Project and the Kolar Gold Mining Undertakings.

(iii) External Finance and Foreign Aid Division. This Division is concerned with all matters relating to foreign exchange including exchange control, foreign investments and economic, financial and technical assistance received by India or rendered by her to foreign countries. All proposals in regard to trade and payments agreements with foreign countries as well as broader questions of policy in regard to foreign trade are examined in this Division.

(iv) Economic Division. The Economic Division advises the Department on questions of economic policy. Its important functions include analysis of events of economic importance and research and study on economic problems. The Economic Survey, the Economic Classification of the Central Budget and the Pocket Book of Economic Information are prepared annually. The Division also prepares briefs on economic matters for consultation with the International Bank for Reconstruction and Development and the International Monetary Fund and for the Indian Delegations to the United Nations General Assembly, the Economic and Social Council, the Economic Commission for Asia and Far East, Colombo Plan and other International Conferences.

The work of the Division is organized under five units:

(a) Internal Economics unit keeps under constant review developments in the money, capital and commodity markets. Trends in agricultural and industrial production, stocks, prices, controls, money supply, bank advances, etc., are reviewed periodically.

(b) Public Finance and Planning unit looks after the analysis and consolidation of Central and State Budgets, the relcassification of transactions of Government and their departmental and non-departmental undertakings, review of budgetary trends and assessment of resources for the Plan.

(c) International Economics unit reviews trends in balance of trade, foreign aid, foreign exchange resources and economic developments in other countries.

(d) Tax Research unit works in close collaboration with the Central Board of Direct Taxes, the Central Board of Excise and Customs, the Finance Departments of state Governments, the Planning Commission, the Central Statistical Organization and other Divisions of the Department.

(e) Briefing Unit prepares briefs and submits material on financial and economic questions relating to India's participation in the United Nations and Allied Organizations.

(v) **Administration Division.** This Division looks after the administrative matters of the Department. The work relating to the Administration of grants for the Indian Institute of Public Administration, the National Council for Applied Economic Research and the Indian Economic Association is also looked after by this Division.

(4) Department of Banking. This Department was created in August, 1969, as a follow up to nationalisation of the 14 major commercial banks in the country. It is responsible for *(a)* all Indian banks, whether nationalised or not; *(b)* all foreign banks so far as their operations in India are concerned; *(c)* all matters relating to the Reserve Bank of India except those which remain directly the concern of the Economic Affairs Department; *(d)* all long-term financial institutions; *(e)* chit funds and other non-banking companies accepting deposits; *(f)* other matters relating to banking in India and *(g)* all matters relating to cooperative banking.

Role of the Ministry of Finance

The importance of the Ministry of Finance as an agency of financial control springs from two factors:

(1) It is charged with the responsibility of raising the resources for the over-all expenditure of the Government of India. Thus, it is an agency which exists more for others than for itself; and

(2) It has to see to the desirability of the demands of other departments, taking into consideration the interest of tax-payers. In this case, it acts as an outside Tribunal free from external and internal pressures.

The control exercised by the Ministry of Finance over other spending departments finds ample justification in the remarks of

Royal Commission on Civil Service: "On the whole, experience seems to show that the tax payer cannot be left to the spending departments, that those interests require the careful consideration of each item of public expenditure in its relation to other items and to the available resources of the State, as well as the vigilant supervision of some authority not directly concerned in the expenditure itself and that such supervision can be most naturally and effectively exercised by the department, which is raising the revenue required". The Ministry of Finance, working as an independent agency, acts as an "extended arm" of the Parliament and ensures that the wishes of the Parliament are fulfilled by the executive. The control exercised by the Ministry of Finance, particularly by its Department of Expenditure, can be divided into three parts;

(a) Control Exercised during the Preparation of the Budget. During the preparation of the budget, it has to scrutinise all proposals emanating from the spending departments in so far as they have financial implications. This enables the Ministry to have a hand in the formulation of policies of other departments. Generally, the scrutiny exercised by the Ministry of Finance is "very broad in nature....and is more concerned with the overall financial implications of the proposal and its impact on the expenditure'. Thus every proposal or policy having financial implications has to be scrutinised by the Finance Ministry and the Cabinet attaches considerable weight to the opinion of the Ministry. After all the proposals have been received from the spending Ministries, it proceeds to determine priorities of the schemes and suggests economies, where possible, taking into consideration the standing and continuing charges. "To secure a uniform standard in the measurement of the financial sacrifice involved in the activities of all departments", says Prof. Hawtrey, "the general criteria adopted" in the selection of new proposals are:

1. Is the proposal a proper one, *i.e.*, does it merit an expenditure from Public funds?
2. Has the Ministry the authority to propose such an expenditure?

3. Is there enough of justification to show that the expenditure is necessary or desirable?

4. Have all parties substantially interested in it been consulted?

5. Are the costs of individual items excessive? and

6. Are the financial arrangements proposed the most desirable and economical having regard to the circumstances, or are alternative arrangements possible?

It is on the answers given to these questions that the Ministry of Finance formulates its opinion. The importance of its control lay in seeking justification for every proposal from the departments proposing it and what Lord Goschen once said about the English practice holds equally good as applied in the Indian context. He said; "The first object of the treasury must be to throw the departments on their defence and to compel them to give strong reasons for any increased expenditure and to explain how they have come to demand it. This control helps to make the departments careful in what they put forward". Equipped with these answers, the Ministry of Finance proceeds to review the total estimates in the light of likely revenue for the year. At this stage, it can suggest reduction or as technically known 'cuts' if it finds the estimates too high or 'inflated'.

(b) Control Exercised during the Execution of the Budget. After the budget has been passed by the Parliament, the responsibility for the control of expenditure from thereon lies on the administrative Ministry and each Head of the department, who is aided and advised by an Internal Financial Adviser—again a representative of the Ministry of Finance—in the discharge of his responsibilities. During the execution of the budget, it is the responsibility of the Ministry of Finance to ensure that the amounts are spent properly and economically. It has also to see that the achievement is in accordance with the plans included in the budget of the other departments. Besides, there are certain matters which still require of other departments to keep themselves in touch with the Ministry of Finance. Prior consultation of the Ministry of Finance is sought whenever any department wants to spend on schemes whose estimate exceeds a particular limit. This is technically known as 'expenditure sanction'. Similarly, prior approval of the Finance Ministry is essential before amounts can be transferred form one sub-head to another, technically known as 're-appropriation'. Besides, the Ministry of Finance, through its accredited Financial Adviser, conducts financial reviews after every quarter in order to know the progress of expenditure.

(c) Control on Miscellaneous Matters. The other matters on which the Ministry of Finance exercises control arise in the various specified fields of expenditure such as grants-in-aid write-off of losses, waiving of recoveries, contracts, inspection of establishment of other Ministries through Staff Inspection Unit, etc.

Thus we find that the control exercised by the Ministry of Finance helps in promotion a financial order in the country. In almost all fields where risk is involved in spending huge amounts, the shadow of the Ministry of Finance is always present though it minimizes the effect of financial delegation of powers already granted to several Ministries. This function is performed by our Ministry of Finance.

Criticism of Financial Control

The financial control as exercised by the Ministry of Finance has been a subject of great controversy. It is alleged that its control extends even to trivial matters, it is too-detailed and born out of financial mentality. The policy of the Ministry is of saving "candleends" and that it betrays an attitude of "cheese-paring" and "woodpacking". Its motto, in the words of Dr. Appleby, is 'acceptance of precedence and refusal of risks". The Ministry, because of its irrevocable habit of imposing 'cuts' or reductions in estimates, makes other departments to unusually 'inflate their estimates'. This results in 'false economy' being effected by the Ministry of Finance. Further, the Finance Ministry also examines the technical details of the developmental schemes—a function for which it is ill-suited. In the words of Asoka Chanda, 'This not only acts as an irritant but is also time—consuming. Ultimately these objections mostly come to be waived, but often only after interminable discussions; and control becomes effective only over establishment proposals, the expenditure on which forms but an insignificant fraction of the total cost. The Finance Ministry, therefore, while straining at the gnat, has often to swallow the camel'.

No doubt control by the Finance Ministry is a delicate affair "comparable only to tight-rope walking' but much is to be lost than gained by relaxing this control. Late John Mathai (former Finance Minister) observed: "I think the control that the Finance Ministry exercises even in certain matters of detail has a deterrent effect which is not entirely to be disregarded...On the whole I think more is to be lost than gained if I issue instructions to the Finance Ministry to relax its present method of control". Of course, things have changed since John Mathai made this statement and the Ministry of Finance has already relaxed much of its control in favour of other departments but the kernel of the problem still stands unsolved: 'How much of control' It is very difficult to determine the degree of control as too much of it may prove a hindrance and too little of it may create financial disorder. Dr. Appleby rightly stated: "The first concern of financial administration is frugality. The enthusiasm of those charged with special functions have a high value; to damp them unduly is wasteful; not to discipline them is to open wide the door to extravagance and imbalance.

Before we close this chapter, we may briefly review the Organisation and functions of the British Treasury and the American Bureau of Budget, the two institutions concerned with budget-making in Great Britain and the U.S.A. respectively.

Nature and Importance of Financial Administration

Having completed the structure of the administrative vessel and provided it with a well-trained crew, we have now to supply it a motive power' so as to enable it to move. Such a motive power is 'finance' without which not a limb of this vessel can move.

Public finance is, in fact, an integral part of administration. Every administrative act, says Dr. White, "has its financial implications, either creating a charge on the treasury or making a contribution to it. Nothing can be done without the expenditure of money at the very minimum for the payments of the salary or wages of the official or employee who acts. Available financial resources set a maximum limit on administrative activity as a whole and on each of its separate parts. The management of finance is, therefore, one of the first and one of the inescapable responsibilities of administrators." As a matter of fact, financial operations affect the very structure of the government and the nature and scope of its policy. That is why the movements for self-government have always and everywhere been a movement of controlling the treasury of the government.

But public finance has several aspects, such as, public revenue and public expenditure, public debt, balancing the budget, fiscal policy, financial administration, etc. Our chief concern here is with financial administration, that is, how public revenue is collected and how it is spent, and who collects it and who spends it.

Financial administration, broadly speaking, has three objectives, namely, fiscal policy, accountability and management. Fiscal policy, though one of the most important factors in financial administration, falls outside the scope of our study, as it involves highly technical questions like the tax theory, the debt theory, the social implications of taxes etc. Accountability and management, therefore, remain for our study the two important aspects of financial administration.

Accountability is the central principle of democratic administration. But in financial administration, it acquires added importance because, firstly, one who controls the strings calls the tune, and secondly, democracy requires its officers not only to act honestly but also to show that they did act honestly. Kautilya, the celebrated statesman of ancient India said, "Just as it is impossible not to taste a bit of the honey but happens to be on the tip of one's tongue, similarly, it is impossible for government servants not to taste a bit of the money that passes through their hands." Democracy has to apply all sorts of mechanical and human means to safeguard public money from this susceptibility of its officials.

The accountability of the public official is not only fiduciary, it also refers to his conformity to the Appropriation Acts and other executive and departmental rules and procedure and also to the general principles of 'wisdom, faithfulness and economy. Hence accountability in Public Administration cannot be effected merely by the traditional devices of bonding, book keeping, accounting and reporting. It 'goes farther than custody and stewardship and enlists the dynamic policy determining qualities of management." Its effectiveness, therefore, is not only a matter of developing a few internal and external controls but of devising an integrated administrative machinery which, in collaboration with the general planning machinery may prepare a work plan and so manage the flow of the fuel (*i.e.* finance) as to accomplish the targets of the plan with the minimum expense of money and energy within the specified time limits. Thus, a sound fiscal management is at the root of the financial administration. In a welfare state, it functions not merely as an instrument of administrative control but also as to regulator of the flow of funds to vital centres of economic and social activity and also as means of coordinating the activities of operating agencies and determining priorities in public activities.

Fiscal management is a dynamic process involving a continuous chain of operations which may be indicated as:

(1) Estimates of revenue and expenditure need, technically called 'Preparation of the budget'. *(2)* Securing legislative sanction for these estimates, technically called 'Legislation of the budget, *(3)* Execution of the revenue and 'expenditure operation' called 'Execution of the budget'. *(4)* Legislative accountability of these operations, called Audit. According to Dr. White, "Fiscal management includes, as its principal sub-divisions, budget making followed by the formal act of appropriation, executive supervision of expenditure (budget execution), the control of the accounting and reporting system, treasury management and revenue collection and audit."

So far the best known machinery for fiscal management is the Budget system.

2. The Budget System. The nineteenth century witnessed the growth of the problem of public finance on a gigantic scale. The problem arose owing to the growth of the functions of the State in all directions, the establishment of parliamentary control over public finance, the necessity of check in financial administration to prevent fraud and waste, and to secure the highest possible results from public expenditures, and the growth in credit operations which resulted in the creation of central banks as the bankers of the government. To solve this problem, there arose a new system in England, called Budgetism or the Budget system, which was wholly unknown until 1803.

The term 'budget' is derived from a French word bougette, meaning a leather bag or wallet. This word came in England by the year 1733. The Chancellor of Exchequer used to have a leather wallet to carry his papers etc., to the house of Commons. So when he set off to place his financial plan before the House of Commons, he used to open his "budget", that is the bag. The term was used in its present sense for the first time in 1733 in a satire entitled 'Opened the 'Budget' pointed against Walpole's financial plan for that year. Since then, the term began to be used for a financial scheme or statement. And gradually, it developed into an elaborate system of financial management which today includes not only a plan of public revenue and expenditures but "thc entire condition of material finances as disclosed in the ministerial statement placed before the legislature and the orderly administration of the financial affairs of the government". It "not only gives an account to the year's house keeping and of the year to come so far as the State is concerned, but it is the basis of control of the financial affairs of the State regarded as a household. It sets in motion a continuous chain of events of great importance in the every day work of government."

Budget today has become one of the principal tools of financial administration. A number of other management tools depend upon it. In the words of Stephen Story, it may be "compared to a lathe or to a drill press which can perform the major operations upon wood or metal stock but which operations may be amplified or improved by attachments of other tools to accomplish further operations." It is not merely a statistical statement of the year's income and expenditure and an estimate of the proposed revenue and expenditure for the next year, but "a proposed work programe, with estimates of the funds necessary to execute it." The execution of the general plan depends upon the amount of money available and the manner in which it is made available. Therefore, it will have to be split up into smaller work plans devised by taking into consideration the order of priority and availability of money, material and skill. A budget so drawn would really become an useful instrument of management in general.

But to be an effective instrument of financial and work management, a budget must conform to certain budgetary principles. A loosely compiled statement of rough and less-though-out estimates of income and expenditure cannot serve this purpose. A sound budget must conform to the following principles:

(a) **Planning.** A budget after enactment becomes the work programme of the government. It must, therefore, be based upon proper planning of the resources and activities of the government. Of course, plans are long-term, while budget is short-term, yet it must reflect, even if in part, all the governmental responsibilities and activities in their social, economic and even cultural aspects. Thus budgetting and programming are two sides of the same coin. Lack of planning is the main defect in our budget system in India. Prof. Appleby said, "Under the present system 'schemes' or projects of various kinds are presented to the Finance Ministry throughout the year, some for early clearance and apportionment of funds, some as a hostage to later budgets. These schemes are usually not much more than policy ideas; they are almost never actual administrative or expenditure projections ready for serious consideration as such...As time for making the budget is approached, all of these schemes on file are examined, and some are selected, and these, in addition to normal establishment expenditures, become the budget of a particular Ministry.'

(b) **Research.** Such planning must be based upon the thorough research not only of the national needs and resources but also of the world conditions. Economically, the world today is a single composite unit. A slight change in the economy of one country has far-reaching repercussions in other parts of the world. "Hence much of the budget planning of the future will flow, from statistical machines which constantly tabulate the flow of information from the remote corners of the world."

(c) **Balanced Budgets.** "The balancing of the budget" says P.K. Wattal, an experienced Accounts Officer of India, "is the first requisite of financial stability, and occupies the same place in financial administration as the maintenance of law and order in the executive administration." On the other hand, "unbalanced budgets are bound sooner or later to weaken the faith of in estors and to lead to monetary inflation, which if uncontrolled, will terminate in national disaster." By balancing the budget, however, is not meant that public expenditure should balance public income from year to year. There may be deficit, and in fact there are bound to be deficits in periods of intense economic development, but the deficits should be planned in advance.

(d) **Treasury Control.** The legislature authorises the government to spend money, but it cannot direct them how to spend it. That is the business of the government itself. The best system of direction and internal control so far devised by human ingenuity is that of the British Treasury. The Treasury Department is responsible not only for preparing the budget of the government but also for exercising day-to-day supervision over the flow of finance to the operating agencies.

(e) **Executive Discretion.** If the executive is to exercise supervision over the activities of the spending departments, it must be vested with sufficient discretion in allotting appropriation. M. Reue Stourum has rightly said, "The pilot incharge of steering a vessel is the only competent judge of the position and of the speed he has need to give his sails because he alone is posted in such a way as to know the force and the direction of the winds and the currents, which may hinder or delay his movements." The appropriations, therefore, should not be to narrowly defined. The legislature should provide for broadly defined functions of the spending agencies so as to keep the appropriations of the spending in harmony with legislative determination of the current objectives of the government. To the executive should be left the determination of the precise means of operation to achieve the purpose set forth by law. It should have power to make re-appropriations from one minor head to another. It should also have the power and means to meet emergency expenditure. The constitution of a Contingency Fund in India in the name of the President is a fine method in meeting the needs of natural calamities.

(f) **Annuality.** The principle of annuality is one of the most important elements in budgetism. The budget must be prepared for a year. That means that the Legislature should grant money to the Executive for one year and that no money be spent by the Executive unless it is authorised for that year. Money left unspent during the year for which it was sanctioned must lapse to the public treasury and the government cannot spend it unless re-sanctioned in the next year's budget. Public expenditure and income must be planned for neither too long periods, as it may make it difficult to know the actual financial position of the government, nor for very short periods, as that would make planning impossible. The system of biennial budgets or supplementary budgets is wrong. Similarly, the system of having separate called "Extraordinary", budgets for separate items is wrong. The important rule in budget-making is that it must reflect the complete and true picture of the country for a particular year. The system of supplementary and extraordinary budgets obsecures the true financial position of the country and makes it difficult to assess the real surplus or deficit of the government as a whole.

(g) Lastly, a well established principle of budgetism is that no demand for grant is made except on the recommendation of the Executive. This principle implies two things; firstly, that it is the function of the Executive, and the Executive alone, to prepare the budget and place it before Parliament and secondly, that Parliament can decrease or refuse the demands presented to it by the Executive but cannot increase them, this for the simple reason that the Executive cannot be made responsible for the money it does not need. But the last principle is not strictly followed in U.S.A.

The Budget System in India

In India, the budget is called the "Annual Financial Statement". Unlike France and the United Kingdom, India does not have one budget for the whole country but has a number of budgets. The State Governments have their own separate budgets, and the Union Government its own. But, the Union Government itself has two budgets, viz., the General Budget and the Railway budget. The Railway Budget deals with the estimate of Railway Ministry, while the General budget deals with the estimates of all other central agencies. The former is prepared by the Railway Ministry and is submitted to Parliament by the Railway Minister. The General budget is prepared by the Finance Ministry and is introduced in Parliament by the Finance Minister. The General Budget is introduced first and the Railway budget follows it after a week or so. The separation of Railway finance from General Finance was made in 1924 to safeguard the stability of the General Budget of Government, as railway estimates were subject to violent fluctuations by their very nature. Under the separation convention, railway revenues have to pay an annual contribution to the general revenues, which is now fixed at 4 per cent on the capital invested on the building of railways as computed annually. The railway estimates provide for the cost of replacements, and renewals of railway assets, expenditure on passenger amenities, labour welfare and rail projects which are necessary but not always remunerative.

Yet another feature of our financial system is the complete centralisation of the Audit and Accounts functions. Firstly, audit and account are united in one and the same department called the Indian Audit and Accounts Department and secondly, this Department is responsible for the audit and accounts of the Union as well as State Governments. It is placed under the control and supervision of the Comptroller and Auditor—General of india who is a constitutional authority independent of the Executive branch. Thus the Audit and Accounts Department actually falls outside the Executive branch of the Government, Central or State.

Further, besides the Consolidated Fund in which are deposited all the incomes of the Government of India, the Constitution also provides for the establishment of a Contingency Fund of India. Accordingly, Parliament has built up this fund to which money is provided from different sources from time to time. This Fund is put under the direct control of the President for purposes of meeting unforeseen expenditure pending parliamentary authorisation. The need of such a provision was great in India due to the fact that the economic condition of the country as a whole, as well as of the people individually, depends upon the success or failure of the monsoons and that the budget is prepared much before the advent of the monsoons. Therefore, one cannot forecast with certainty the future of the income and expenditure of the Government. The Government might have forecast in the budget a very large income by way of land revenue but actually the Government may have to incur huge expenses in order to give relief to the flood-stricken people. The Constitution provides that no tax shall be levied or collected or no expenditure shall be incurred except by the authority of Parliament. The Government may find itself in a very great predicament in cases of emergency. It is, therefore, to meet such contingencies that the Constitution has authorised Parliament to establish a Contingency Fund in the nature of an imprest and to place it at the disposal of the Government.

Such a Fund exists at the Centre as well as in the States.

Machinery for Fiscal Management

The process of fiscal management is, as we saw above, a continuous chain of operations beginning from preparation of estimates by each organisational unit, their review and scrutiny by the heads of the agencies and then by the central agency, their legislation by Parliament, the collection, custody and disbursement of the funds, their accounting, auditing and reporting. The organisation for such activities is necessarily all pervasive. It runs all the way from the Cabinet, ministers and departmental heads through the middle management to the rank and file. It takes in its purview all the governmental agencies, political as well as administrative and line staff as well as auxiliary agencies. These agencies which have a part in the fiscal management fall under the following categories:

(1) The Operating Agencies.

(2) The Finance Department.

(3) The Executive.

(4) The Legislature.

(5) The Audit and Accounts Agency.

(1) Operating Agencies. The operating agencies perform two types of functions in fiscal management: first with regard to budget preparation and second, budget execution. Budget estimates always emanate from the operating agencies, as they alone know what their needs or sources of income are. The officers who prepare the estimates are known in India as 'Heads of the Offices' or 'Disbursing Officers'. The task of preparing the estimates is perhaps the most important one. In the words of Mr. Wattal, "It is not a simple arithmetical exercise in striking out averages of previous years' actuals and putting in a safe figure which would not look exactly like a repetition of the last year's performance. Behind figures lie the insistent realities of administration. The circumstances of no one year are exactly similar to those of the previous year and yet they are not quite dissimilar. One has, therefore, to use his judgement in estimating the similarities and dissimilarities and making due allowance for each." If the budget is to serve as an instrument of work programme, then far more attention must be paid to the preparation of the estimates. The officer's judgment and experience supported by cumulative intelligence and research must be given to this function. Deficiency in an estimate plan cannot be made up by a type of fiscal control. Dr. Appleby has observed with regard to our budgeting that "in some part the present system of expenditure control conceals a serious inadequacy in the development of the Government's budget. The expenditure control is used to far too great an extent as a substitute for good budgeting."

These two authorities are also concerned with the execution of the budget. As soon as the budget is passed by Parliament, the 'Controlling Officer' who is usually the head of the department of agency, allocates funds to the disbursing officers who are responsible for the disbursement of the money. The Controlling Officer has to keep constant watch upon the funds. It is his duty to see that firstly, no expenditure exceeds the amount voted by the legislature, secondly, no amount is spent by any officer in excess of his authority, and thirdly, the amount is being economically, honestly and efficiently used.

(2) The Finance Department. The Finance Department performs three different types of functions, *viz.*; *(a)* preparation of the budget, *(b)* management of government finances and *(c)* control over finances. For this purpose, the Finance Department usually comprises of two agencies—a budget agency and the revenue and expenditure agency. In the U.S.A., the Bureau of Budget falls outside the treasury Department and is part of the President's Office. In India, the Finance Ministry is divided into two Departments, *viz.*, the Budget and Economic Affairs Department and the Revenue and Expenditure Department.

The Budget and Economic Affairs Department consists of the following divisions:

(a) **The Budget Division.** It receives budget estimates from various Ministries and Departments and then prepares the annual budget of the Government except the Railway Budget and the budget estimates of the Defence Services and the Posts and Telegraph Department which prepare their own budgets. It also deals with all questions relating to audit, accounting procedure, classification of transaction in Government accounts and compilation of Treasury rules. It places the Appropriation Accounts and Audit Reports before the Parliament.

(b) **The Internal Finance Division.** It is responsible for policy-formulation in all matters relating to coinage and currency, Reserve Bank and general banking, Rehabilitation Finance Administration, Industrial Finance Corporation, State Financial Corporations, Stock Exchanges, Mints, Central Treasuries and other Financial Agencies of the Government.

(c) **External Finance Division.** It administers the Foreign Exchange Regulation Act and deals with the foreign exchange resources of India, foreign investments in India, sterling balances, Common—wealth economic co-operation, import and export policy and its bearing on foreign exchanges, foreign assistance, both economic and technical, and administration of the Finance Ministry Library.

The Indian Statistical Institute, although an autonomous body, is attached to this Division for administrative purposes.

(d) **The Planning Division.** It delas with Financial Assistance to States including loans and grants for development purposes, grants for the development of Scheduled Areas and Welfare of Scheduled Tribes, assistance for natural calamities, capital budget consisting of allotment of funds on capital account for capital civil works and control over capital expenditure and policy matters relating to the National Income unit and Multi-purpose National Sample Survey. It also scrutinises State budgets with regard to matters requiring President's assent and also analyses their expenditure and income position.

(e) **Economic Wing.** This was established in 1953. It is headed by the Economic Advisor for economic research. It carries on research and study of important economic, financial and monetary problems and the preparation and maintenance of statistics relating to balance of payments, balance of trade, currency and coinage.

(f) **The Administration Branch** deals with the house-keeping activities of the Department. The branch is also the main channel of communication between the Comptroller and Auditor-General and the Government of India for all administrative and business matters.

The Revenue and Expenditure Department

This Department divided into three main Divisions, *viz.*; *(a)* Revenue Division, *(b)* Civil Expenditure Division and *(c)* Defence Expenditure Division.

(a) The Revenue Division. It is headed by the Central board of Revenue and deals with all matters of taxation policy and with assessment and collection of all central revenues.

(b) Civil Expenditure Division. It consists of three different units, viz. Establishment Division which deals with regulations regarding pay, allowances, leave, pensions etc., and with rules relating to conditions of service of the various categories of the Government of India employees and also with the general problems of administration and co-ordination in the Finance Ministry.

Expenditure Divisions. The expenditure control within all the Central Ministries and departments, except Defence Ministry, exercised by eight Expenditure Divisions of this Department. Finance officers, now called 'Financial Advisors', are accredited to the various Ministries. These officers exercise treasury control over the expenditures of these Ministries. They also deal with expenditure proposals which require the scrutiny and concurrence of the Finance Ministry.

(c) Defence Expenditure Division. This division occupies a unique position in the Central Government organisation. It is headed by a Joint Secretary of the Finance Ministry but is also accredited to the Defence Ministry where he is called the Financial Advisor and his status is above that of a Joint Secretary. He has three main functions to do. *Firstly*, as official of the Finance Ministry he exercises treasury control over Defence Expenditure, just as the Civil Expenditure Divisions control the Civil Departments. *Secondly*, he has advisory functions in regard to Defence Minister, the three Chief of Staff and the Defence Secretary. *Thirdly*, he is also the Chief Accounting Officer for the Defence expenditure and has direct responsibility for internal audit and accounting of military expenditure.

This Division is responsible for scrutiny and sanction of all expenditures debitable to Defence Services Estimates and is closely associated with the administrative authorities in the examination of proposals from the beginning till their final approval by the Government.

This Division also prepares and controls the Defence Budget.

For the administration of its functions like revenue collection, minting, assaying etc., the Ministry has the following attached and subordinate offices: *(1)* Customs Department, *(2)* Central Excise Department, *(3)* Income Tax Department, *(4)* Opium Department, *(5)* Defence Accounts Department, *(6)* Currency Notes Press, *(7)* India Security Press, *(8)* Mints, *(9)* Company Law and Investment Department, *(10)* Departments of Insurance, *(11)* national Savings Organisation, *(12)* Assay Department, and *(13)* National Sample Survey.

Thus, the main functions of the Finance department are preparation of the Budget, collection, custody and disbursement of public money, control of public expenditure, framing and interpretation of Financial Rules and Regulations, and regulation number, pay, pensions, gratuities and other financial conditions of public employees.,

(3) Executive. The Executive is responsible for formulation of the financial policy of the government. Questions of policy may arise at any time in the day-to-day administration, but they specifically arise when the budget is under preparation. After the budget estimates of the spending agencies have been consolidated by the Finance Ministry, they are placed before the Cabinet which now has to decide as to what new schemes, proposed by the operating agencies should be admitted, how funds to meet these expenditures are to be obtained, which taxation policy is to be followed and so on.

(4) The Parliament. According to the democratic principle, no tax can be levied or collected and no expenditure can be incurred by the government except with the previous consent of the Parliament. Therefore, before the government can work on its budget plan, it has to get it passed by the Parliament. This is known as the enactment of the budget.

(5) The Comptroller and Auditor-General. Even after the money has been sanctioned by the Parliament it has to see that the government does not misuse the money or does not go beyond the sanctioned limits. For this purpose, there is appointed a Comptroller and Auditor-General who exercises external control over expenditure and audits the government accounts.

Role of the Ministry of Finance as an Agency of Financial Control

The importance of the Ministry of Finance as an agency of financial control springs from two factors;

(1) It is charged with the responsibility of raising the resources for the over-all expenditure of the Government of India; and

(2) It has to see to the desirability of the demands of other departments, taking into consideration the interest of the tax-payers, In this case, it acts as an outside Tribunal free from external and internal pressure. The control exercised by the Ministry of Finance over other spending departments finds ample justification in the remarks of Royal Commission on Civil Service : On the whole, experience seems to show that the tax-payer cannot be left to the spending departments, that those interests require the careful

consideration of each item of public expenditure in its relation to other items and to the available resources of the State, as well as the vigilant supervision of some authority not directly concerned in the expenditure itself and that such supervision can be most naturally and effectively exercised by the department which is raising the revenue required." The Ministry of Finance, working as an independent agency, acts as an "extended arm" of the Parliament and ensures that the wishes of the Parliament are fulfilled by the executive. As Durell stated: "The Public and the Parliament should be satisfied that somewhere or other in the government there is a guarantee for financial order; that there is some authority which will watch the progress of expenditure, the obligations which the different departments are incurring and will give timely warning if the expenditure of those obligations are either outrunning the revenue provided for the year or engaging the nation too deeply in future years."

The control exercised by the Ministry of Finance, particularly by its department of Expenditure, can be divided into three parts:

(a) Control Exercised during the Preparation of the Budget. During the preparation of the budget. It has to scrutinise all proposals emanating from the spending departments in so far as they have financial implications. This enables the Ministry to have a hand in the formulation of policies of other departments. Generally, the scrutiny exercised by the Ministry of Finance is "very broad in nature....and is more concerned with the overall financial implications of the proposal and its impact on the expenditure." Thus every proposal or policy having financial implications has to be scrutinised by the Finance Ministry and the Cabinet attaches considerable weight to the opinion of the Ministry. After all the proposals have been received from the spending ministries, it proceeds to determine priorities of the schemes and suggests economies where possible taking into consideration the standing and continuing charges. Its main concern is to obtain "proper balance of expenditure between services, so that greater value could not be obtained for the total expenditure by reducing the money spent on one service and increasing expenditure on another". "To secure a uniform standard in the measurements of the financial sacrifice involved in the activities of all departments", says Prof. Hawtrey, "the general criteria adopted' in the selection of new proposals are:

1. Is the proposal a proper one, *i.e.*, does it merit an expenditure from Public funds?
2. Has the Ministry the authority to propose such an expenditure?
3. Are the costs of individual items excessive?
4. Are the financial arrangements proposed the most desirable and economical having regard to the circumstances, or are alternative arrangements possible?
5. Is there enough of justification to show that the expenditure is necessary or desirable? and
6. Have all parties substantially interested in it been consulted?

It is on the answers given to these questions that the Ministry of Finance formulates its opinion. The importance of its control lies in seeking justification for every proposal from the departments proposing it and what Lord Goschen once said about the English practice holds equally good as applied in the Indian context. He said: "The first object of the Treasury must be to throw the departments on their defence and to compel them to give strong reasons for any increased expenditure and to explain how they have come to demand it. This control alone helps to make the departments careful in what they put forward." Equipped with these answers, the Ministry of Finance proceeds to review the total estimates in the light of likely revenue for the year. At this stage, it can suggest reductions or as technically known 'cuts' if it finds the estimates too high or 'inflated'. It may also reject proposals which its scrutiny may reveal as technically 'unsound'.

(b) Control Exercised during the Execution of the Budget. After the budget has been passed by the Parliament, the responsibility for the control of expenditure from thereon lies on the administrative

Ministry and each Head of the department who is aided and advised by an Internal Financial Adviser—again a representative of the Ministry of Finance—in the discharge of his responsibilities. During the execution of the budget, it is the responsibility of the Ministry of Finance to ensure that the amounts are spent properly and economically. It has also to see that the achievement is in accordance with the plans included in the budget of the other departments. Besides, there are certain matters which still require of other departments to keep themselves in touch with the Ministry of Finance. Prior consultation of the Ministry of Finance is sought whenever any department wants to spend on schemes whose estimate exceeds a particular limit. This is technically known as 'expenditure sanction'. Similarly, prior approval of the Finance Ministry is essential before amounts can be transferred from one sub-head to another, technically known as 'reappropriation'. Besides, the Ministry of Finance, through its accredited Financial Adviser, conducts financial reviews after every quarter in order to know the progress of expenditure. This enables the Ministry to get a review of the performance of other departments in monetary terms.

(c) Control on Miscellaneous Matters. The other matters, on which the Ministry of Finance exercises control, comprise various specified fields of expenditure such as grants-in-aid, write-off of losses, waiving of recoveries, contracts, inspection of establishment of other Ministries through Staff Inspection Unit etc. Thus we find that the control exercised by the Ministry of Finance helps in promoting a financial order in the country. In almost all fields where risk is involved in spending huge amounts, the shadow of the Ministry of Finance is always present though it minimises the effect of financial delegation of powers already granted to several Ministries. Durrell has aptly stated: "It is the risk of public loss where the amount involved is considerable that calls for the intervention of the Treasury, for it is important that under such circumstances the responsibility should be assured by an outside imperial tribunal."

Criticism of the Financial Control

The financial control as exercised by the Ministry of Finance has been a subject of great controversy. It is alleged that its control extends even to trivial matters, it is too detailed and born out of financial mentality. The policy of the Ministry is of saving "candle ends" and that it betrays an attitude of "cheese paring" and "wood-pecking". Its motto, in the words of Dr. Appleby, is "acceptance of precedence and refusal of risks." The Ministry, because of its irrevocable habit of imposing 'cut' or reductions in estimates, makes the other departments to unusually 'inflate their estimates'.

No doubt, control by the Finance Ministry is a delicate affair "comparable only to tight-rope walking" but much is to be lost than gained by relaxing this control. John Mathai (Formar Finance Minister) so observed: "I think the control that the Finance Ministry exercises even in certain matters of detail has a deterrent effect which is not entirely to be disregarded....On the whole I think more is to be lost than gained, if I issue instructions to the Finance Ministry to relax its present method of control". Of course, things have changed since John Mathi made this statement and the Ministry of Finance has already relaxed much of its control in favour of other departments but the kernel of the problem still stands unsolved: 'How much of control?' It is very difficult to determine the degree of control as too much of it may prove a hindrance and too little of it may create financial disorder. Dr. Appleby rightly stated: "The first concern of financial administration is frugality. The enthusiasm of those charged with special functions have a high value; to dump them unduly is wasteful; not to discipline them is to open wide the door to extravagance and imbalance. True economy, consequently, results from the interaction of the drives of enthusiasm with the restraining disciplines of review."

MEANING OF THE ADMINISTRATIVE RESPONSIBILITY

In every democratic country the administration is expected to work in accordance with the will of the people which is discovered and formulated in the form of laws. The Legislature constituted as it is of the representatives of the people, not only lays down the broad policy and makes necessary provisions for the money and personnel for its execution but it is also to see that the administration carries it out faithfully. There exists, therefore, in every country some means whereby it may be ascertained whether the administrative officials are treading the laid out track or deviating from it, whether they are using their powers or discretion in conformity with the wishes of the people or abusing them. The administrative officials are to be held responsible for their official actions. Administrative responsibility can, therefore, be defined as the liability of the official to give a satisfactory account of the exercise of the power or discretion vested in them to some one to which it is, due, failing which some kind of punishment may follow.

Difference between Responsibility and Accountability. Prof. Pfiffner makes a distinction between Responsibility and Accountability. He writes that Accountability refers to the formal and specific location of responsibility while responsibility is a highly personal moral quality and is not necessarily related to formal status or power. He further says that, responsibility refers to the public servants responsiveness to public will while Accountability denotes the specific method and procedure to enforce the public servant's responsibility. Responsibility, therefore, is subjective and works from within. On the other hand, accountability is objective and works from without.

Types of Controls of Administration

Broadly speaking there are two main types of administrative control: *(i)* The internal control and *(ii)* The External control. Internal controls are those which are fitted into administrative machinery itself and work automatically with the movement of the machinery. In other words, Internal control is a self-regulating device within the administrative machinery and it controls its movement. The External controls on the other hand, are those which operate from outside. They are fitted outside the Administrative machinery and the Constitution of a country invariably makes a provision for them. The External controls may be in the form of accountability of the administration to the Legislature, the Executive, the Judiciary and the people themselves. Either of these two types of control is not sufficient by itself to exercise effective complete control over administration.

INTERNAL CONTROLS

Internal controls are of the five kinds *viz*:

(1) Budgetary Control,

(2) Personnel Management Control,

(3) Efficiency Survey Control,

(4) Professional Morality Control,

(5) Administrative Leadership. They may be briefly discussed as follows:

(1) Budgetary Control. One of the effective ways of controlling the administrative branch in a democratic Government is the passing of the budget by the Legislature. The budgetary system is not only the method of apportioning available resources among various branches of administration, but it is also a very effective means of keeping the administration on the proper track. The budget is passed by the Parliament before the commencement of the financial year. The administration is thereby authorised to collect the taxes and incur expenditure for the various services as soon as the financial year begins. Even when the budget has been passed, the Finance Ministry and the Comptroller and Auditor-General exercise on behalf of the Parliament continuous control over the financial activities of the spending ministries. No money can be withdrawn from the public funds without the previous sanction of the Finance Ministry and the Auditor-General. When money has been spent on items for which it was sanctioned and that there is no misappropriation or embezzlement.

(2) Personnel Management Control. Administration is internally controlled through personnel management also. The hierarchical structure of the administrative machinery provides the internal control automatically. According to this system authority is exercised through a chain of command from the top to the bottom. The legislature controls the ministers who in turn control the Heads of Departments who control the next lower in rank and thus everyone is bound up in a single chain of command. In such a system one controls and supervises the work of the others and thus none is outside the chain of command. If there is any negligence where the official concerned is immediately held responsible by his immediate superior officer and is pulled up or even reprimanded and if the negligence is very serious it may lead to issuing of a strict warning, loss of increment, demotion, dismissal or even prosecution.

Another means of control under personnel management is the recruitment of the personnel of the various departments by a Central agency. Their terms and conditions of service, grades and salaries are determined by this agency. In Great Britain it is done by the Treasury and in our country by the Home Ministry of the Government of India. This control over the establishment activities of the ministries becomes in fact the effective control over their operational activities.

(3) Efficiency Survey Control. Carrying an efficiency survey of the work of an administrative unit is an effective means of internal control. The officers of the various departments visit the field stations in order to ensure that administration is being carried out according to the rules and regulations. The system of inspection and touring by the higher officials keeps the subordinate officers on the laid out track.

In some countries scientific standards of efficiency measures are employed for determining promotions etc. There is no universal standard of measuring efficiency which could be applied to all the jobs equally. Still the quantity, quality and system of work could constitute some of the guiding principles.

(4) Professional Morality Control. Every profession has its code of morality which it builds up in due course of time, and which is observed by every member of the profession. The code of morality may be said to be consisting of those traditions, precedents and standards which a profession has built up and which has to be kept up by one and all of that profession. There are some professions like Law and medicine which have formal and legal means also of enforcing these standards upon their members. Any person found guilty of unprofessional conduct is taken a task by other members of the profession and for a more serious offence unbecoming of the profession, he may be even debarred to practise the profession any longer. The civil service has also developed, a code of morality, which may be more appropriately called as "Administrative Ethics" which consists of high traditions of loyalty to the nation, devotion to the work, a very high sense of integrity and public good. The British Civil Service in particular has been called the envy of the world for its traditions of honour, patriotism and integrity. The code of morality is followed by the Civil Service automatically for the pride of it. This form of control is most effective of all the formal checks described above, because no member dare go against the professional code of ethics for fear of ostracism and ridicule. Moreover, this form of control is based on one's own conscience and is self-cultivated. No formal punishment can be effective as the condemnation of an employee by his own conscience, his own sense of dignity and pride and by persons of his own class.

(5) Administrative Leadership. Administrative leadership is another effective means of Internal Control. If the Officers at the top provide right type of leadership to their subordinates by their personal examples of hard work, devotion to duty, honesty and integrity, there is no reason why there should be any slackness or inefficiency in the administration. The superior officers should not behave like commanders or 'big bosses', they should on the other hand transform themselves into good leaders and instead of being authoritative, they should be able to inspire and guide their subordinates dare not resort to corruption, negligence etc.

❐

2

Ministry of Finance—Working

FINANCE DEPARTMENT IN THE PRE-INDEPENDENCE DAYS

It was under the Government of India Act of 1919 that the legislature in India was granted the power of voting of supplies. But this right excluded certain estimates like the Defence Estimates which were treated as non-votable. The Finance Department was, therefore, to begin with an organ of executive control charge with the functions of wise house-keeping and economy in expenditure consistent with policy of the Government. As more powers came to be granted to the legislature, the Finance department was made responsible for the imposition and regulation of taxation subject to legislative approval, the collection of revenue through the Central Board of Revenue, the supervision and co-ordination of departmental budget estimates and the control of Public expenditure and of public Debt, Currency and Banking. It may be noted that the legislature did not then possess the right to disapprove the executive policies by refusing the supplies the Governor-General had the legal power to certify the estimates.

Finance Department has been however, one of the most important departments of the Government concerned with the maintenance of financial stability of the country. For political reasons this department has been headed by a British official till 1946, who was chosen from the higher ranks of British Home Civil Service.

Until 1947, the Finance department was organized in three wings:

(i) The ordinary Branch to control civil expenditure,

(ii) The Military Finance Department to control defence expenditure and

(iii) The Central Board of Revenue administrating income-tax, Customs and Central Excise departments. In addition there was a Financial Commissioner for Railways who was personally responsible to the Finance Member for economic administration of the Railways.

Ministry of Finance

Since the formation for the interim National Govt. in 1946 the Finance Department has been under the charge of Finance Minister, who has been assisted sometimes by a Minister of State and sometimes by a Deputy Minister and sometimes by both the Minister of State and Deputy Minister. In the absence of the constitutional provision or convention with regard to the number of junior Ministers their number has been varying from time to time. At present the Finance Minister is assisted by only one Deputy Minister.

Besides the Ministry of Finance originally consider of four departments *viz. (i)* Department of Finance Affairs; *(ii)* Department of Revenue, *(iii)* Department of Expenditure, (iv) Department of Company Law Administration. In September, 1963 Department of Coordination was added. In 1964 (Nov.) Department of Company Affairs and insurance was set up. In January, 1966 the Department of Insurance and Company Affairs was abolished. In June 1967, Department of Coordination was abolished. In August 1969, Department of Banking was added. Thus now again there are four departments as under:

The Ministry of Finance is now organized into four departments:

(1) Economic Affairs,

(2) Expenditure,

(3) Revenue and Insurance and

(4) Department of Banking

This department was created in August 1969. The composition and functions of these departments are as under:

1. The Department of Economic Affairs consists of six divisions:

(1) Insurance,

(2) Budget,

(3) International Finances,

(4) Planning and Co-ordination,

(5) Capital Issues and Stock Exchange and

(6) Economic Division

The work of the department as is clear from the names of its above mentioned divisions was of diversified nature and is mainly concerned with banking currency, Capital issue, Foreign Exchange, balance of Payments, Consolidated and preparation of Central budgets, Review of State budgets, technical Assistance programme, Control of life insurance etc. The functions of two divisions of this department namely—The budget division and Economic Division deserve special mention particularly those of the first one as we are most concerned with it. The budget Division is concerned with the preparation and consolidation of the budget except the Railway Budget. It also deals with all questions relating to Public Debt, Audit, According procedure, Classification of Transactions in Government Accounts and Compilation of Treasury rules. It also places the appropriation accounts and audit reports before the Parliament. The Economic division (Economic Advisor's Office) was established in 1953. It is headed by the Economic Adviser for Economic Research who is assisted by economic advisers on Public Finance and Planning, Monetary and banking problems, inflation, deflation, production etc.

2. The Department of Expenditure. is arranged in nine divisions, most important of which are the Civil Expenditure Division and the Defence Expenditure Division. The Civil Expenditure Division is concerned with the scrutiny and the sanction of expenditure of the various administrative ministries. Its establishment unit deals with regulations regarding pay, allowances, leave etc. and unit rules relating to conditions of government employees. The Defence Expenditure Division is concerned with the scrutiny and control of Defence Expenditure. Its head is of the status of an Additional Secretary and is designated as Financial Adviser (Defence). This division prepares and control the Defence Budget. The Financial Adviser exercises Treasury control over Defence expenditure and has advisory function in regard to Defence minister, the three Chiefs of Staff and the Defence Secretariat. He is also the Chief Accounting Officer for the Defence Expenditure and has direct responsibility for internal audit and accounting of the Military expenditure.

3. The Revenue Department is arranged in five wings *viz.*, *(1)* Estate Duty *(2)* income-Tax *(3)* Customs *(4)* Central Excise and *(5)* Administration. It is headed by the Central board of Revenue and is responsible for taxation policy and assessment and collection of all Central revenues.

4. Department of Banking. This Department was created in August, 1969 when fourteen major commercial banks were nationalized. It is responsible for :

(a) all Indian banks whether nationalists or not;

(b) all foreign banks so far as their operations in India are concerned

(c) all matters concerning Reserve Bank of India except those which remain directly the concern of Economic Affairs Department;

(d) all long term financial institutions;

(e) chit funds;

(f) other matters concerning Banking in India;

(g) all matters related to cooperative banking; and

(h) administration of all statutes regulations and other laws linked with items referred above.

The Finance Ministry has a Principal Secretary and four departmental secretaries. There are beside about 18 Joint Secretaries and 17 Deputy Secretaries in the Ministry. So much strength of the administrative staff of the Ministry may look to much but this strength would be perhaps justifiable when we take into consideration the wide range of functions performed by the Ministry.

The main functions of the Finance department as would be revealed from the above discussion are those of preparation of the budget; collection, custody and disbursement of Public money; control of public expenditure, framing and interpretation of financial rules and regulations and rules regarding pay, leave, pension and other conditions of service of Government employees.

Assessment of the Working of the Finance Ministry

The regulations provide for the control of the Finance Ministry over other departments. Unless and until specially provided by the Ministry no department can issue any order, without the permission of the Finance Ministry. This has led to the concentration of bulk of powers in the hands of the Finance Ministry. This situation was brought to the surface by the Administrative Reforms Commission. It stated:

Ministry of Finance did not share this responsibility with any other Department of the government. It acted as a sole repository of financial wisdom. The result was delay in the execution of Projects and delays of funds.

However, a suggestion was made by A.R.C. in its Report on, Finance, Accounts and Audit (January 1968) to solve this dilemma.

"The control of Finance Ministry over Public expenditure is exercised in the main at three stages: *(i)* approval of programme or policies in principle, *(ii)* acceptance of provision in the budget estimate, and *(iii)* prior sanction to incurring of expenditure subject to such powers as have been delegated to the administrative ministries. It is the control at the first and third stages that generally engaged much of the time of the Finance Ministry and that impinges on the day-to-day working of the administrative ministries. A control at these stages, if too rigid or detailed involving much time and effort can slow down the speed of work, delay the implementation of projects—particularly development commercial or industrial ones and thereby cause loss of national effort or income. While the need for control or scrutiny is not denied, it must be constructive, purposeful, imaginative and not narrow in outlook or cramping in effect."

The Indian Government responded to the suggestion brought out by the commission and following steps were taken:

(i) Appointment of Financial Advisors in the different Ministries.

(ii) Scrutiny by the Finance Ministry not required for the sanctions amounting upto Rs. fifty Lacs. This change was brought in August, 1952.

(iii) Delegation of financial powers to the Ministry of Commerce and Industry, Ministry of Community Development and Co-operation and Department of Food. This change was brought in September, 1961.

(iv) Preparation of detailed budget to negate the post-budget limitations and checks.

A suggestion was given by Paul H. Appleby for shifting to better budgeting. He stated:

"The Ministry of Finance needs to shift more of its attention to better budgeting and away from detailed expenditure control after budgeting. Expenditure control in the proper terms which relate to programme objectives can only be closely and usually achieved in the programme agencies. It is only when these agencies have had experience in this superior kind of financial management that they will being to be able to make budget submissions of a proper sort. It is only after the ministries are thus doing an improved job of budgeting that the Ministry of Finance can produce the kind of budget appropriate to its responsibility."

ORGANISATION OF MINISTRY OF FINANCE

Ministry of Finance of the Government of India is headed by the Union Minister of Finance (having cabinet rank) and is added by State and Deputy Ministers.

The Ministry of Finance discharges its function through following departments:

I. Department of revenue,

II. Department of Economic Affairs.

III. Department of Expenditure.

The subjects for which these departments are responsible are explained below:

I. Department of Revenue

This department is responsible for following subjects:

1. All matters relating to Central Board of Direct taxes and Central Board of Excise and Customs.

2. All questions relating to Income tax (except questions relating to the Income tax Appellate Tribunal which is under law Ministry) corporation tax, capital gains tax, excess profits tax, business profit tax and estate duty, wealth tax, expenditure tax and gift tax, companies (Profit) Sur-tax Act, 1954 super income tax, 1953, Interest Act, 1974, Voluntary disclosure of Income and Wealth Act, 1976, and Compulsory Deposit (Income tax payers) Act, 1974.

3. All matters relating to customs including Custom Tariff Act, 1975 and matters relating to Customs nomenclature and duties on goods imported or exported.

Tariff valuation and valuation under the Customs Act, prohibitions and restrictions on the import and export of goods under the Customs Act.

Customs Cooperation Council.

4. All matters relating to Central Excise Administration.

5. Administration of the Gold Control Act.

6. International agreements relating to dangerous drugs and their implementation.

7. Medicinal and Toilet Preparations containing alcohol or Opium, India hemp & Narcotic drugs and narcotics.

8. Stamp duties on bills of exchange, cheques, promissory notes, bills of lading, letters of credit; policies of insurance, transfer of shares, debentures, proxies and receipts.

9. Opium, as regards cultivation, manufacture and sale for export.

10. Supply and distribution of all kind of stamps.

11. Administration of excise in the Union Territories, all questions relating to:

    (a) Alcoholic liquors for human consumption.

    (b) opium, Indian hemp & Narcotic drugs and narcotics.

12. Sales tax.

    (i) The Administration of Sales Tax Laws (Validation) Act, 1956.

    (ii) Levy on tax on sales in the course of inter-State trade or commerce problems arising out of the administration of the Central Sales Tax Act, 1956.

    (iii) All questions relating to replacement of sales tax by additional excise duty including administration of the additional duties of Excise.

(iv) All bills etc. relating to sales tax levied in States coming up for the previous instructions, recommendations or assent of the president.

(v) Declaration of goods as of special importance in inter-State trade or commerce under Article 286(3) of the Constitution laying down the conditions and restrictions to which the State Laws providing for the levy of tax on them would be subjected.

(vi) Legislative matters concerning sales tax in the Union Territories.

(vii) Problems arising out of the invalidation of sugarcane cess levies of States including validation of such levies.

(viii) All matters relating to Regional Council for sales tax and State Excise duties set up under Article 263 of the Constitution.

(ix) All matters relating to levy of tax on consignment transfers, hire purchase transactions, work contracts etc.; and

(x) All matters arising out of refugee relief levies which were imposed in 1971 for relief of refugees from Bangla Desh and which were withdrawn in 1973.

13. All matters relating to pre-partition duty refund claims on salt.

14. Subordinate Organisations:

(a) Income Tax Department.

(b) Customs Department.

(c) Settlement Commission.

(d) Appellate Tribunal for Forfeited Property.

(e) Central Excise Department.

(f) Narcotics Department.

(g) Regional Office of the Gold Control Administration, and

(h) Gem and Jewellery Museum.

15. Preventive detention for reasons connected with the Conservation of foreign Exchange or Prevention of Smuggling, persons subjected to such detention.

16. Directorate of Enforcement and its subordinate formations (Legislative Work under the Foreign Exchange Regulation Act is handled by Economic Affairs department and Appellate work under Foreign Exchange Regulation Act by the law Ministry.)

Functions: Investigation, adjudication & prosecution of cases arising out of breaches under the Foreign Exchange Regulation Act, 1973.

II. Department of Economic Affairs

This department is responsible for following subjects:

(i) Exchange Control

1. Administration of the Foreign Exchange Regulation Act, other than enforcement work mentioned under the Department of Personnel Administrative Reforms in the Cabinet Secretariat.
2. Foreign Exchange budgeting.
3. Control of the foreign exchange resources including scrutiny of proposals for imports from the foreign exchange point of view.
4. Foreign Investment.

5. Import and Export of gold and silver.

6. Approvals for Commercial Borrowings Abroad.

(ii) Foreign Aid for Economic Development

7. Technical and economic assistance received by India under:

   (a) The Technical Co-operation Scheme of the Colombo Plan.

   (b) The United Nations' Technical Assistance Administration Programme.

   (c) Ad hoc offers of Technical Assistance from various foreign countries.

   (d) The United States Point Four Programme.

8. Technical Assistance given by India to the Member countries of the Colombo Plan under Technical Assistance from various cooperation Scheme of the Colombo Plan.

9. All matters relating to the Meetings of Colombo Plan Council and the Consultative Committee of the plan and Council of the plan and

   (i) U.S. Technical Cooperation Mission.

   (ii) U.S. Development Loan Fund.

   (iii) Colombo Plan.

   (iv) Food Foundation and Rockfeller Foundation.

   (v) Loans and Credit from IBRD and IMF Export-Import Bank.

   (vi) Norwegia Aid, etc.

9A. All matters relating to the Indian Consortium.

9B. All matters relating to grant of Loans and Credits to other countries except Nepal, Bhutan and Bangladesh.

9C. Policy issues relating to the United Nations fund for Population Activities (UNFPA) and contributions to the specialised Agencies of the United Nations and other UN Bodies.

9D. All matters relating to the Foreign Volunteers programme in India including the United Nations volunteers (except outgoing Volunteers.)

9E. Technical Assistance received by India or given to foreign governments; International Institutions and Organizations, except such as are relatable to subjects allocated to any other Department.

(iii) Internal Finance

10. Currency and Coinage, that is to say, question relating to:

(a) The security Press and the Mints including the Assay Department and Silver Refinery Project.

(b) Coinage

(c) Note issue.

11. Functions of the Treasurer of Charitable Endowments for India.

12. Investment Policy including Investment Policy of LIC, UTI & GIC.

12A. Investment pattern for Employees Provident Fund and other like Provident Fund

(iv) Economic Advice

13. Advice on matters which have a bearing on international external aspects of Economic Management including prices.

13A. Credit, Financial and monetary policies.

(v) Budget

14. Ways and Means.

15. Preparation of central Budget other than Railway Budget including Supplementary Excess grants and when a proclamation by the President as to failure of constitutional machinery is in operation in the relation to a State or a Union Territory, preparation of the Budget of such State or Union Territory.

16. Fixation of Interest rates, including borrowing rates, productivity Test Rates; etc.

17. According to Audit procedure including classification of transactions.

18. Financial Matters relating to partition, Federal Financial integration and re-organization of States.

19. Contingency Fund of India and Administration of Contingency Fund of India Act, 1950.

20. Borrowing and Flotation of Market Loans by the Central and State Government.

21. Borrowing of Public bodies such as Corporations, Municipalities, etc.

22. Administration of the public Debt Act.

23. Treasury Bills including ad hoc to replenish the Central balances.

24. Sterling pensions transfer of responsibility to U.K. Government and actual calculation of the liability involved.

25. Taxation Inquiry Commission.

26. Small savings, including the administration of the National Savings Organisations.

27. Conspectus of Central and State Government Budgets.

28. Finance Commission.

(vi) Stock Exchanges

29. Administration of Securities Contracts Act, 1956.

30. Regulation of Stock Exchanges.

(vii) Stock Issues

31. Control over the Issues of Capital by Joint Stock Companies.

(viii) Miscellaneous Acts

32. (a) Government Savings Bank Act, 1873.

(b) Section 20 of the India Trusts Act, 1862.

(c) Metal Tokens Act, 1889.

(d) Charitable Endowment Act, 1890.

(e) Finance Commission Act, 1951.

(f) Government Savings Certificates Act, 1959.

(g) Unit Trust of India Act, 1963.

(h) Compulsory Deposit Scheme Act, 1963.

(i) Legal Tender Act, 1964.

(j) Asian Development Bank Act, 1966.

(k) The public Provident Fund Act, 1968.

(l) Small Coins Act, 1971.

(m) Indian Coinage Act, 1906.

(n) Indian Securities Act, 1920.

(o) Currency Ordinance, 1940.

(p) International Monetary Fund and Bank Act, 1945.

(q) Capital issues Act, 1947.

(r) Comptroller and Auditor General Act, 1971.

(s) Additional Emoluments Act, 1974.

(ix) Insurance

33. Policy relating to General Insurance; Administration of the Insurance Act, 1933, Insurance Companies Association Pool; Subsidiaries of the Life Insurance Corporation.

34. Policy relating to life Insurance, Nationalisation of the Life Insurance Business; Administration of the Life Insurance Corporation Act, 1956; Life Insurance Tribunal.

35. Office of the Controller of Insurance.

36. The responsibility of the Central Government relating to matters concerning centrally administered areas in respect of any of the entries from 32 to 35 above.

(x) Banking

37. All India Banks, whether nationalised or not.

38. All foreign banks so far as their operations in India are concerned.

39. All matters relating to the Reserve Bank of India.

40. All matters relating to Long Term Financial institutions excluding Unit Trust of India, Life Insurance Corporation and General Insurance Corporation.

41. Chit Fund and other non-banking in India.

42. Other matters relating to banking in India.

43. All matters relating to Cooperative Banking which are the concern of this department.

44. Administration of all Statutes, regulating and other laws connected with entries from 37 to 43 above.

III. Department of Expenditure

This department is responsible for following subjects:

1. Financial Rules and Regulations as follows:

(i) proposals relating to revisions of pay structure of employees;

(ii) proposals for revisions of pay scales of Central Government employees;

(iii) pension structure and relief to pensioners;

(iv) any new facility to Government employees by way of service conditions or fringe benefits which involve significant recurring financial implications;

(v) appointment of Pay Commission procession of the recommendations and implementation thereof;

(vi) dearness allowance and other compensatory allowances and travelling allowances;

(vii) matters relating to amendments to service rules having a predominantly financial character.

2. Delegation of Financial Powers.

3. Financial sanctions relating to all Ministries and offices of the Government of India, which are not covered by powers delegated or conferred by the rules or by any general or special orders.

4. Review of the staffing of Government establishments with a view to securing economy.

5. Defence Accounts Department.

6. Release of Grants and Loans for the State plans including advance Plan assistance towards expenditure on relief measures in the event of natural calamities.

7. Advice to Ministries and Government undertakings on Costs Accounts matters and attending to cost investigation work on their behalf.

8. Indian Audit and Accounts Department.

9. State Finance.

10. Plan Budget.

11. Planning and developing finance.

12. Bureau of Public Enterprises, Including industrial Management Pool.

13. Scrutiny of Central and State Legislation having financial and economic implications.

14. Grants to the Indian Institute of Public Administration.

15. The Organization of the Comptroller General of Accounts; the issue of instructions about the system and form of account and procedures for accounting of receipts and payments and reconciliation of Government cash balance with Reserve Bank, maintenance of requisite technical standards of accounting in the departmentalised Accounts Offices; cadre management of Group 'A' and Group 'B' officers of the departmentalised Accounts offices monitoring of the flow of receipts and expenditure in relation to overall budgetary estimates and presentation of a consolidated review to the Finance Minister, covering the trends of revenue, significant features of expenditure and its impact on surplus; deficit projected in the budget, consolidation of monthly accounts of Government of India, compilation of union Finance and Summary Appropriation Accounts (Civil) and their presentation to Comptroller and Auditor General of India, updating and publication of Central Treasury Rules and Accounts Codes, co-ordination and assistance in the introduction of management accounting system and organizing/conducting training and departmental examinations for staff belonging to Groups 'C' and 'D'.

IMPORTANCE OF FINANCE

Finance occupies a very important place in the study of Public Administration. Of the several factors that enter into the problem of efficient administration, none is of greater importance than that of financial administration. Finance is the fuel for the engine of Public Administration. It is the life-blood of a Government. It keeps the administrative machinery on its wheels. No administration can function without finance. The success of administration depends upon the availability of finance. In India the lack of adequate finance is a major cause of the failure of the Government to improve the standard of living of the people and implement the various welfare projects. Public finance is, in fact, an integral part of administration. No act of the Government can be performed without money. The Government requires money for every activity it performs. Mr. Lloyd George once remarked thát Government is finance. This is quite correct because the governmental machinery will come to a halt unless funds are available to pay the personnel and purchase the equipment and materials required.

"Every administrative act', says Dr. White, "has its financial implications, either creating a charge on the treasury or making a contribution to it. Nothing can be done without the expenditure of money, at the very minimum for the payment of the salary or wage of the official or employee who acts. Available financial resources set a maximum limit on administrative activity as a whole and on each of its separate parts. The management of finance is therefore one of the first and one of the inescapable responsibilities of administrators." As a matter of fact, financial administration and public administration are closely inter-twined. Firstly, most administrative acts have their financial implications. They either spend money from the public exchequer or bring money to it. Secondly, financial operations may be designed to develop and promote particular public policies *e.g.*, tariffs may be so levied as to provide protection to the home industries, or taxation may be so imposed as to bring economic equality. Thirdly, financial administration raises important issues of administrative organization and relationships, *e.g.*, what machinery of financial administration there should be, or what should be the relation between financial machinery and administrative machinery, or what should be the proper sphere of jurisdiction of the financial officers and the administrative officers. It is not going too far to say that the government which has worked out and is employing a satisfactory system of financial administration has gone a long way towards putting the administration of its affairs upon an efficient basis. And the one which has failed to do so cannot possibly give to its citizens what they are entitled to.

Agencies of Financial Administration

The term 'financial administration' is used in a broad sense to include all the processes involved in collecting, budgeting, appropriating and expending public money; crediting income and expenditures and receipts and disbursements; accounting for assets and liabilities and for the financial transactions of the government and reporting upon income and expenditures, receipts and disbursements, and the condition of funds and appropriations. It has three objectives, namely, fiscal policy, accountability and management. Fiscal policy is the technical aspect of financial administration and includes matters like the taxation theory, the debt theory, the social implications of taxes, etc. It does not form a part of our study as it falls under economics. But a student of Public Administration is very much concerned with its two other aspects of accountability and responsibility. Public Administration requires the administrators not only to act honestly but also to show that they did act honestly. They are supposed to follow the prescribed rules and procedures. The financial officers should maintain the accounts in proper forms and follow the rules of expenditure without any departure. Public money is a trust and it should be spent cautiously. But accountability does not end with proper maintenance of accounts and strict adherence to financial rules, it also involves the principles of wisdom, faithfulness and economy. It "goes farther than custody and stewardship and enlists the dynamic policy-determining qualities of management.' Financial administration thus involves the management of finance in such a way as to accomplish the targets with the minimum expense of money and energy within the specified time limits.

Fiscal management is a dynamic process involving a continuous chain of operations which are:

(i) preparation of the budget, *i.e.*, of the estimates of revenue and expenditure for the ensuing financial year;

(ii) securing legislative sanction for these estimates;

(iii) execution of the budget, *i.e.*, regulation of the expenditure and raising of revenue;

(iv) treasury management, *i.e.* safe custody of the funds raised and due arrangements for the necessary payments to meet the liabilities; and

(v) rendering of the accounts by the executive and the audit of these accounts.

According to Dr. White, "Fiscal management includes as its principal sub-divisions budget making; followed by the formal act of appropriation; executive supervision of expenditure (budget execution); the control of the accounting and reporting system; treasury management and revenue collection and audit.'

The above operations are carried out by:

(i) the central department or departments concerned mainly with financial administration;

(ii) the legislature;

(iii) the principal financial officers in the administrative departments;

(iv) the audit organization; and

(v) the committees of the legislature.

A brief discussion of the above agencies follows:

(1) The Executive. The chief executive is responsible for formulation of the financial policy of the Government and the preparation of the estimates of expenditure and revenue for the ensuing financial year. He is assisted in this job by a central department which in Britain is called the Treasury and in India is known as the

Ministry of Finance. The budget estimates originate from the operating agencies as they alone know their sources of revenue and needs. The estimates prepared by the disbursing officers are reviewed by the head of the department. These are then forwarded to the Finance Department which gives to these estimates final shape and puts them in the budget.

(2) The Legislature. According to the democratic principle no tax can be levied or collected and no expenditure can be made by the Government except with the previous consent of the Parliament. The executive makes the demands and the legislature grants them. The power of authorising expenditure and collection of the taxes is usually vested in the popular or lower chamber of the legislature, for example, in the House of Commons in England and in Lok Sabha in India. The upper houses in both these countries do not have much say in the matter. It may also be noted that in parliamentary countries, the legislature performs its financial functions under the leadership of the executive. Though constitutionally the legislature has the power to reduce or refuse the demands made by the executive yet this power is seldom exercised on account of the party control. The majority of the members belong to the same party to which the executive belongs. They are under party discipline and cannot vote against the financial proposals brought by their Government. However, in the U.S.A. the legislature is not subject to any such control by the executive. It may do with the budget proposals whatever it likes.

(3) Audit. A very important agency of financial administration is the Audit Department. In India the audit agency is headed by the Comptroller and Auditor-General. His function is to exercise control over the drawing of the money from the public exchequer according to the budget, to examine the accounts and ascertain and point out to the legislature the cases of expenditure contrary to the grants made by the legislature.

(4) Heads of the Departments. As soon as the budget is passed by the legislature, the 'controlling officer' who is usually the head of the department allocates funds to the disbursing officers who are responsible for the disbursement of money. The controlling officer has to keep constant watch upon the funds. It is his duty to see that firstly, no expenditure exceeds the amount voted by the legislature, secondly, no amount is spent by any officer in excess of his authority. In England the Head of a Department is also nominated as the Accounting Officer by the Treasury but in India the heads of departments are not responsible for account keeping. This work is done by the Comptroller and Auditor-General of India.

(5) Parliamentary Committees. Finally two committees of the legislature known as the Estimates Committee and the Public Accounts Committee exercise financial control on behalf of the legislature. The Estimates Committee is intended to suggest economies in the estimates of the spending departments, while the Public Accounts Committee examines the appropriation accounts in the light of the audit report of the Comptroller and Auditor-General and draws the attention of the Parliament to irregularities and makes suggestions for preventing them in future. Such committees do not exist in the U.S.A.

ACCOUNTING

Accounting has been defined as the "art of recording classifying and summarizing transactions, wholly or in part of a financial nature in terms of money and interpreting the results thereof". In simple words, it means keeping a systematic record of financial transactions. Francis Oakey defines accounting as 'the service of producing promptly and presenting clearly the facts relating to financial condition and operations that are required as a basis of management". Accounting means maintaining a proper record of the finances of the organization. It has a dual function to perform:

(1) First is the determination of the fidelity of all officers who handle the fund,

(2) Second is the furnishing of information needed regarding financial condition of and operations for policy determining and administrative purposes. In the words of Dr. L.D. White, "The

primary functions of a system of accounts are to make a financial record, to protect those handling funds, to remove the financial condition of the organisation in all its branches or purposes at any time, to facilitate necessary adjustments in rate of expenditure, to give information to those in responsible positions on the basis of which plans for future financial and operating programmes can rest, and to aid in the making of an audit." Accounting is an indispensable means of exercise of financial control. Without accounts it is impossible to know how much was received, or how much was spent and for what purpose. Only through systematic accounting can the honesty and legality of transactions be determined. Scientific budget preparation would be impossible without accounts being available for the past years.

Essentials for Public Accounting

The form of public or Governmental accounting differs from that of business and commercial accounts, because the objects of the two are different. Business and commercial accounts are so kept as to facilitate the preparation of balance sheet, showing profit or loss, assets and liabilities. On the other hand, the purpose of Governmental accounting is to furnish data to show whether the provisions of the budget as voted by the legislature have been observed or not. Hence the essentials of public accounting are different from those of private accounting. These are the following:

(1) Centralization of Accounts. One officer should be made responsible for keeping the accounts of all the agencies of the Government. This will give a co-ordinated and unified picture of all the expenditure and income of the Government.

(2) Classification of Funds. Assets, liabilities and proprietorship of every fund or group of funds should stand out as a separate balanced group of accounts. A complete balance sheet should be compiled for every fund.

(3) Double-entry Book-keeping. The Government accounts should be maintained on a double-entry basis which means that every item of expenditure is entered at two places. One entry remains with the operating service while another is sent to the Accounts Office if there is a separate department of the Government or to the controlling officer of the same service.

(4) Revenue Accounting. In the Accounts reports all items of a non-revenue character should be excluded from reports of revenue. Revenues should be classified by fund and by source.

(5) Budgetary Control Accounts. The Government accounts should follow the budgetary form, *i.e.*, they should be kept under the same heads and sub-heads as those of the budget.

Accounting in India

Generally speaking accounting is an executive function and is therefore usually vested in the executive departments of the Government. In Britain the Head of each department is nominated as the accounting officer in respect of his department, and each department keeps its own accounts. But in India, accounting has not been made the responsibility of the executive. It is vested in a separate department known as the Accounts and Audit Department headed by the Comptroller and Auditor-General of India whose office is a creation of the Constitution and who is independent of the executive control. To assist the Comptroller and Auditor-General there is in each State an Accountant-General in whose office the accounts of the transactions (union as well as State) taking place within the territorial limits of that state are kept. It may be, however, noted that the A.G's office does not maintain the accounts of the Railway and Defence Departments. These are maintained by the Financial Commissioner for Railways and the Military Accountant-General respectively.

There are four stages of accounting in India:

(1) Initial Entry. The basic unit of accounting in India is the Treasury. In each District, there is a Government treasury in charge of a Treasury officer. The treasury is maintained at the cost of the State Government, but it keeps the accounts of the Central as well as

State Governments. Where there are branches of the Reserve Bank or the State Bank of India, they perform the cash duties of the Government. Every financial transaction, revenue and expenditure is recorded in the treasury.

(2) Classification of accounts by the A.G. All accounts of the previous month reach the A.G's office by the 1st of the next month. This office classifies these accounts, *i.e.*, marks each item of receipt of payment according to the head of the account. There are four different accounts, *i.e.*, revenue accounts, capital accounts, debt accounts and remittances. Each one of these accounts is divided into major heads which constitute the main units of classification.

(3) Compilation. The next stage is compilation. Before compilation the accounts are audited by the auditor. Then they go to the Accounts officer who compile them every month and submit them to the Government concerned by the end of the following month.

(4) Lastly comes the annual compilation of all the accounts of the Government. This is done by the Auditor-General of India. He submits the Finance Accounts, Appropriation Accounts and his Audit Reports to the President or the Governor, as the case may be, sometime in January or February of the following year.

AUDIT

Audit is one of the most important instruments of Parliamentary control over the finances of the country. It is a means of enforcing accountability and is a part of the external control over administration maintained by the Legislature. Audit, in simple words, means the examination of accounts with a view to determining their correctness and of the transactions they "undertake to quickly know everything and understand the profit and loss". According to James C. Charlesworth, "Audit means the process of ascertaining whether the administration has spent or is spending its funds in accordance with the terms of the legislative instrument which appropriated the money". It is "a systematic examination of the books and records of a business or other organisation in order to ascertain or verify, and to report upon the facts regarding its financial operation and the results thereof". "An audit is an examination and verification of the accounts after transactions are completed in order to discover and report to the legislative body any unauthorised, illegal or irregular expenditures, any financial practices that are unsound, and whether the administration has faithfully discharged its responsibility."

Audit as a system of Legislative control over public finance first arose in England and it was more the result of a gradual process than a creation. In the first place, Parliament insisted during the reign of king John that they should have the control of receipts and revenues and the discretion with regard to expenditure was considered to be a prerogative of the Crown. But the Stuart autocracy made the parliamentarians more exacting and they began to claim a share in the control of public expenditure as well. As more and more powers passed from the hands of the king to Parliament, gradually the present practice was established which gave the Parliament complete control over expenditure also. To audit system was established in England under the Exchequer and Audit Department Act of 1866.

Formerly audit was conducted only in case of expenditure and that only to ensure that money had been spent in accordance with the appropriation grants. But at present it is conducted for all financial transactions, whether for receipt or payment to ensure that money which has been collected and expended is in accordance with the provisions of the Appropriation Act passed by the Legislature and that there is no fraud or embazzlement. The present audit goes a step further also, to examination of the 'faithfulness, wisdom and economy' applied by the official in making the expenditure. It is no longer sufficient that appropriations should be applied to purposes approved and should not be exceeded without parliamentary approval. It is more important that those should be wisely and economicaly expended and that extravagance and waste be avoided.

Objects of Audit

The main objects of Government audit are to ensure:

(1) that there is provision of funds for the expenditure duly authorised by competent authority;

(2) that the expenditure is in accordance with a sanction properly accorded and is incurred by an officer competent to incur it;

(3) that payment has, as a fact, been made and has been made to the proper person, and that it has been so acknowledged and recorded that a second claim against Government on the same account is imposible;

(4) that in the case of audit of receipts, (i) sums due are regularly recovered and checked against demand and (ii) sums received are duly brought to credit in accounts;

(4) that in the case of audit of stores and stock, where a priced account is maintained, stores are priced with reasonable accuracy, and that the rates initially fixed are reviewed from time to time, correlated with market rates and revised when necessary;

(5) that the charge is correctly classified, and that (as in the case of Pubic Works and Forest accounts) if a charge is debitable to the personal account of a contractor, employee or other individual, or is recoverable from him under any rule or order, it is recorded as such in a prescribed account;

(6) that the articles are counted periodically and otherwise examined for verification of the accuracy of the quantity balances in the books and that the total of the valued account tallies with the outstanding amount in the general accounts and that the numerical balance of stock materials is reconcilable with the total of value balance in the account at the rate applicable to the various classes of stores; and

(7) that expenditure conforms to the following general principles which have for long been recognised as standards of financial propriety, namely:

(i) that the expenditure is not prima-facie more than the occasion demands, and that every Government servant exercises the same vigilance in respect of expenditure incurred from public moneys as a person of ordinary prudence would exercise in respect of expenditure of his own money:

(ii) that public moneys are not utilised for the benefit of a particular person or section of the community;

(iii) that the amount of allowances such as travelling allowance granted to meet expenditure of a particular type is so regulated that the allowances are not on the whole sources of profit to the recipients;

(iv) that no authority exercises its powers of sanctioning expenditure to pass an order which will be directly or indirectly to its own advantage.

Difference between Auditing and Accounting

(1) Audit Begins where Accounting Ends. Auditing and accounting are very closely related yet there exists a great difference between the two. Accounting means keeping systematic record of financial transactions whether of a public authority or of a private concern or of an individual. Unless accounts are properly maintained it is impossible to know how much was received and how much was spent and for what purpose. In the absence of such knowledge there can be no control. It is only through systematic accounts supported by vouchers and receipts that legality and honesty of the transactions can be determined. Accounting is thus concerned with ensuring that the money requisitioned by a department is provided in the budget and that money is used by the department only up to that sum which is permitted by the budget and that the expenditure is in accordance with the law passed by the Parliament. The audit goes a step further. It has to see that the expenditure is in accordance with the Appropriation Act, that the amounts are correct and all payments and receipts of money are supported by documents and vouchers.

(2) Accounting is an executive function, Audit is the function of the legislature. Secondly, the keeping of the accounts is the function of the Executive authorities spending the amount and auditing that of the legislature. Those who spend the money must keep accounts and be responsible for the fact that what they have spent was within the grants made by the legislature. The auditors are not to keep the accounts.

(3) Auditing Guides Accounting. Thirdly, the Audit Department should have the power to prescribe the accounting system. Only then it can perform its audit duties efficiently. If the spending departments are given the discretion to adopt different methods of accounting it would make the task of audit difficult.

Audit in India

Audit of Government accounts in India is a union subject. The main features of the Indian audit system are as follows:

(1) Indian Audit is Governed not by law, but by an Executive order. The Government of India Audit and Accounts Order 1936 as adopted under the Indian (Provisional Constitution) Order of 1947. In Britain there is statutory provision for audit under the Exchequer and Audit Act 1921, and so also in the U.S.A. under the Budget and Accounting Act 1921.

(2) The Audit is Mostly Limited to the Expenditure Side Only. Its concern with receipts is limited to those items only which it may be required by the executive to undertake, or may undertake with its approval.

(3) Indian Audit is Primarily a Legality Audit. It does not usually go into the question of merits of expenditure. However, it is not precluded from investigating into or commenting upon the impropriety, wastefulness or extravagance of expenditure where there is a prima-facie case for doing it.

(4) The Audit is conducted on Behalf of the Executive and audit reports are submitted to the executive.

(5) Combination of Accounting and Auditing Functions. Though the office of the Comptroller and Auditor-General of India is organised on the British model, yet there is one substantial difference between the two. In England the Comptroller and Auditor-General is not concerned with the accounts but deals only with the Audit. But in India, audit and accounts have been organised under one and the same service called Indian Audit and Accounts Service and, therefore, the personnel of this department are concerned with accounts as well as audit.

(6) Centralisation of Audit and Accounts Services. Indian audit and accounts system has also a centralised feature which means that there are no separate audit and account Services for the Union Government and the State Governments as they are generally in a country with a federal constitution. In Indian federation there is one single agency in the form of Auditor-General. As the head of Audit and Accounts administration, he exercises control over public finance not only of the Union Government but also of the State Governments. He is, however, assisted in his functions by Accountants General in the States. This system of centralisation has both its advantages and disadvantages. The uniformity of accounts through the country, consequential facility in auditing, fairness and purity of accounts and the fact that the personnel of this department belong to a central service and they, being under independent Auditor-General, enjoy sufficient freedom from the control of the executive, are some of its advantages. Too much concentration of power in the single head of a department, pressure of work, jurisdiction over whole of the country are, however, some of its disadvantages.

Organisation of Audit in India

The power of accounting and audit is vested in the Indian Audit and Accounts Department which is headed by the Comptroller and Auditor-General of India. The office of the Comptroller and Auditor-General came into being in 1919, when the first Auditor-General of India was appointed by the Secretary of State under Montage-Chelmsford Reforms Act. We have borrowed this from England where it was established under the designation of 'Comptroller-General of Receipts and issue of His majesty's Exchequer.' Auditor-General in India was then made responsible to the Secretary of State and held office during his majesty's pleasure. He was thus made independent of the government of India whose accounts he had to audit. The Government of India Act 1935 gave him a constitutional recognition. Our new Constitution also, under Article 141, makes provisions for such officer re-designated as the Comptroller and Auditor-General of India. His office is thus the creation of the Constitution.

The Comptroller and Accountant-General is assisted by a Deputy Comptroller and Auditor-General and three additional Deputy Comptroller and Auditor-General. The Department is divided into five Classes of offices, namely:

(1) The Civil Accounts and Audit offices;

(2) The Posts and Telegraphs Accounts and Audit offices;

(3) The Railway Audit Offices;

(4) The Defence Services Audit offices; and

(5) the Commercial Audit offices.

In addition, there are two overseas offices;

(a) The Director of Audit, Indian Accounts in United Kingdom, London, whose audit jurisdiction extends to all the expenditure from the Indian revenues in-countries in Europe.

(b) The Director of Audit, Indian Accounts in the U.S.A. Washington, whose audit jurisdiction extends to all the expenditure in both the Americas, met from the Indian Revenues.

The Position and Functions of the Comptroller and Auditor-General of India

The Constitution has installed the Comptroller and Auditor-General as a high independent statutory authority. He is the dignitary who sees on behalf of the legislature that the expenses voted by them are not exceeded or varied and that the money expended was legally available for and applicable to the purpose or purposes to which it has been applied. Nothing can fetter his discretion or judgment in any manner as to matters which he may bring to the notice of the legislatures in the discharge of his duties. His oath of office under the Constitution requires him to uphold the Constitution and the laws and to discharge his duties without fear of favour, affection or ill-will. For the purpose of securing the highest standards of financial integrity of the administration and watching the interest of the tax payer and also for purposes of legislative control over the entire executive Government and its officers, the Constitution safeguards the independence and freedom of the Comptroller and Auditor-General in a variety of ways. Article 148 of the Constitution provides that the Comptroller and Auditor-General shall be appointed by the President under his hand and seal and shall only be removed from office in like manner and on the like ground as a Judge of the Supreme Court. It also provides that after retirement he would not be eligible for any other office either under the Government of India or the Government of any State and that the administrative expenses of his office, including all salaries, allowances and pensions payable to or in respect of persons serving in that office, shall be charged upon the Consolidated Fund of India.

The Comptroller and Auditor-General is the administrative head of the Indian Audit and Accounts Department. The Constitution states that: "The Comptroller and Auditor-General shall perform such duties and exercise such powers in relation to the accounts of the Union and of the States and of any other authority or body as may be prescribed by or under any law made by Parliament and until provision in that behalf so made, shall perform such duties and exercise such power in relation to the accounts of the Union and of the States as were conferred on or exercisable by the Auditor-General of India immediately before the commencement of this Constitution in relation to the accounts of the Dominion of India and of the provinces respectively".

Later on, through Comptroller and Auditor-General (duties, powers and conditions of service) Act 1971, such powers of 'C and AG' were defined. On March 1976, President of India issued an ordinance relieving him of the responsibility of compiling the accounts of the Union and the states at once or through stages. The ordinance was replaced by Comptroller and Auditor-General Act 1976.

Accounting functions

(1) Maintenance of Accounts. The duties and powers of the Comptroller and Auditor-General in relation to accounts of the Union and State governments are laid down in Article 150 of the Constitution, in paragraphs 11, 12, and 15 to 17 of the Audit and Accounts Order, 1936, as adapted, and in the Initial and subsidiary Accounts rules issued thereunder. Article 150 of the Constitution empowers the Comptroller and Auditor-General with the approval of the President to prescribe the form in which the accounts of the Union and the States are to be kept. It has been held that the power to prescribe the form includes the power to prescribe classification and to give any directions with regard to the methods or principles in accordance with which any accounts are to be kept. This provision is designed to secure the maximum degree of uniformity in accounting amidst the immense volume and variety of financial transactions of different Governments of India. The Comptroller and Auditor-General also derives the power to prescribe the form of the initial and subsidiary accounts directed from Article 150 of the Constitution. Sub-paragraph (1) of paragraph (1) of paragrpah 11 of the Audit and Accounts Order, 1936 as adapted makes the Comptroller and Auditor-General statutorily responsible for the keeping of the accounts of the Union and of each State, other than the accounts relating to the Defence and railways and accounts relating to transactions in the United Kingdom. The Initial and Subsidiary Accounts Rules which relieve the Comptroller and Auditor-General of the responsibility for keeping initial accounts kept in treasuries and departmental office including accounts of stores and stock, trading, manufacturing and profit and loss accounts that may be required to be kept in any particular office or department, but this does not impair his authority, also specifically empowers him to prescribe the form in which accounts are to be rendered in his office and the forms in which initial records on which such accounts are based are to be kept.

(2) Preparing Each Year's Account. The Comptroller and Auditor-General has also the duty of preparing each year's accounts showing the annual receipts and disbursements for the Federation and the states and to submit the same to the respective governments. These accounts are designated the Finance accounts. Besides the accounts, the Comptroller and Auditor-General has also to submit annually to each Government in respect of accounts kept by him. Appropriation Accounts, that is, accounts relating to expenditure brought into account during a financial year to the several items specified in the schedule to Appropriation Acts passed in accordance with the provisions of Articles 114 and 204 of the Constitution.

(3) Submitting Annual Financial Statement to the President. Under paragraph 12 of the Audit and Accounts Order, 1936, as adapted, the Comptroller and Auditor-General has to prepare annually in such form as he, with the concurrence of the President, may determine and to submit to the president a General Financial Statement incorporating a summary of the accounts of the Union and of all the States for the preceding financial year and particulars of their balances and outstanding liabilities and containing such other information regarding their financial position as the President may direct to be included in the statement.

(4) Miscellaneous. Under the provisions of paragraph 15 of the Audit and Accounts Order, 1936, as adapted, it is the duty of the Comptroller and Auditor-General (so far as the accounts for the compilation of which he is responsible enable him so to do), to give to the Union Government and to the Government of every State such information as they may from time to time require and such assistance in the preparation of their annual financial statements as they may reasonably ask for. Paragraph 17 of the Order empowers the Comptroller and Auditor-General to inspect any office of accounts which is under the control of the Central Government or of a State, including treasuries and such offices responsible for the keeping of initial or subsidiary accounts as submit accounts to him.

Auditing Functions

Paragraph 13 of the Audit and Accounts Order, 1936, as adapted, contains the fundamental provisions relating to audit and runs as follows:

(1) It shall be the duty of the Auditor-General ;

(i) to audit all expenditure from the revenues of the Union and of the States and to ascertain whether moneys shown in the accounts as having been disbursed were legally available and applicable to the service or purpose to which they have been applied or charged and whether the expenditure conforms to the authority which governs it;

(ii) to audit all transactions of the Union and of the States relating to debts, deposits, sinking funds, advances, suspense accounts and remittance business;

(iii) to audit all trading, manufacturing and profit and loss accounts and balance sheets kept by order of the president or of the Governor of a State in any department of the Union or of the states;

and in each case to report on the expenditure, transactions or accounts so audited by him.

(2) The Auditor-General may with the approval of, and shall, if so—required by, the President or the Governor of any State audit and report on:

(i) the receipt of any department of the union or as the case may be, of the State;

(ii) the accounts of stores and stock kept in any office or department of the Union or, as the case may be, of the state.

The President or the Governor of a State may after consultation with the Auditor-General make regulations with respect to the conduct of audits. The Comptroller and Auditor-General has to prepare an annual report for each of the governments whose accounts are audited. The audit report contains the comments of Audit authority on the correctness or otherwise of the expenditure and other financial transactions. The report particularly points out the more important financial irregularities like cases of budgetary grants being exceeded, failure to obtain the necessary sanction for expenditure, non-compliance with rules and regulations, cases of improper and wasteful expenditure and of misappropriation and embezzlement. He submits this report in the case of the Centre to the President and in case of States to the Governor who are required by the Constitution to cause them to be laid before their respective legislatures.

One point more need be mentioned here. Because of the fact that Parliament has not been able to pass legislation defining the powers and duties of the Comptroller and Auditor-General, the word 'Comptroller' has continued to stand just an appendage to his title. His counterpart in Great Britain exercises what is known as "Exchequer control" in the capacity of an officer of the house of Commons. It is the responsibility of the Comptroller and Auditor-General in Great Britain to ensure that the total issues from the Exchequer do not exceed the amounts prescribed by the Parliament. The object behind making our Auditor-General as 'Comptroller' was that he, too, should exercise the same type of control as his counterpart in Great Britain in regard to the control of expenditure.

Limitations of Audit

There are certain fields which are outside the purview of audit. Important among such fields are:

(i) Secret Service expenditure (A certificate from the Ministry of Home Affairs that the amounts have been utilised is admitted in audit and is deemed adequate for audit purposes).

(ii) contributions to International Organisations.

(iii) Contributions to independent institutions receiving grants-in-aid of amount less than Rs. 1 lakh per annum recurring and Rs. 5 lakhs non-recurring.

(iv) Grants given to local authorities are audited by Examiner, Local Fund Accounts, who is a provincial employee and not a member of the Audit Department.

Role of Comptroller & Auditor-General

The Comptroller and Auditor-General plays a very important role and acts as an 'extended arm' of the Parliament in controlling public expenditure. His report is most impartial and based on factual data. This is so because he is free from any kind of pressures. In the words of Sitaramayya; "The C & A.G. today has been installed as a Supreme master who has his own judgment to look to and who has no frowns or favours to be guided by from outside". The role of the Comptroller and Auditor-General has been described in glowing terms by Durell who says, "the C. & A.G. is the agent of the Parliament. He is Parliament. Parliament only works through him". This is certainly a flattering view of his role. T.G. Bowles calls him the "acting hand of the Committee" of Public Accounts and Osber Peake as the 'guide, philosopher and friend".

THE PROBLEMS OF ECONOMY AND RETRENCHMENT

The word economy is used in a double sense. Firstly, it is used as a synonym for wise or efficient expenditure. In this sense, economy may involve not a reduction but an increase in the existing expenditure with a view to obtain the best possible results from it. When we talk of 'true economy', or 'higher economy' or 'economy in the long run', it is this meaning of the term we have in mind. Economy in this sense is 'financial statesmanship' and the opposite of 'penny-wise pound-foolish', policy.

The other and more common meaning of economy is reduction of expenditure as far as possible consistently with the requirements of safety and efficiency. In this sense, economy involves retrenchment. The present discussion relates to economy in this sense.

Need and Scope for Economy

In spite of the checks to which it is subjected, governmental expenditure has a way of increasing, as it were, of itself. There are several reasons for it. In the first place, a certain amount of increase in the expenses of administration takes place from year as a result of salary increments, better conditions of service demanded by the changing social standards of the time, etc. Secondly, many of the services and projects are undertaken on rather imperfect information or appraisal of the ultimate cost involved. As time goes on, items unforeseen before, reveal themselves and the expenditure goes up. Thirdly, even when current information is available, decision may not be based on it. A policy of expenditure is more popular than a policy of economy, because it may support certain ideals and offer direct benefits to individuals, while benefits of economy, spread as they are over the whole of the community, arouse no enthusiasm. Fourthly, political parties while biding for the support of the voters during election campaigns put forward programmes of new expenditure for their benefit and thus, on coming, into office, they find themselves already heavily committed to increased expenditure. This limits financial control to the secondary questions of devising most economical methods of carrying out the pledges already given. Lastly, investigations of commissions and committees of enquiry also often result in recommendations involving additional expenditure and the government find themselves committed to the carrying out of the recommendations because these have behind them the prestige of the Commission or Committee and have already aroused expectations in the minds of the people.

In view of these factors working towards progressive increase in expenditure, it is impossible to keep it down unless deliberate attempts are made to do so. Expenditure has many advocates in the various organized interests and pressure groups, but economy and retrenchment have few supporters. The case for reduction in expenditure, therefore, goes by default, unless there is some specific machinery and procedure to review the national expenditure from time to time with an eye to economy and retrenchment.

The scope for reduction of governmental expenditure is rather limited. Over a large part of it, *e.g.*, the public debt, pensions, grants, etc., there is hardly any room for economy. Also, the state is not free to curtail its services without causing unemployment, stagnation in industry, and consequent adverse repercussion on its own revenue, and suffering a loss of prestige. Commitments by politicians are beyond the control of administration. Even so, there is always some room for economy. Even in a well managed state or department, careful investigation may reveal cases of waste, duplication of services, more costly methods and equipment than is really needed, superfluous or under-worked personnel, etc., which taken singly may be insignificant but which in their aggregate go to swell the cost by large amounts.

The Machinery for Suggesting Economics and Retrenchment

Apart from the Treasury or Finance Ministry and the executive authorities which are responsible for the day-to-day financial control, the machinery for suggesting economies in expenditure consists usually of Retrenchment Committees appointed from time to time, and Estimates Committees which exist in countries like Britain, India, and others following the British Parliamentary system.

Retrenchment Committees

Retrenchment committees are ad hoc devices to meet special circumstances. They are not a regular part of the financial machinery of the state and do not function continuously. They are usually appointed during periods of crisis caused by unforeseen economic depression, to make suggestions for retrenchment. In Britain retrenchment enquiries have been made by committees of 3 types

(a) by Select Committees of the House of Commons *e.g.*, in 1918-19,

(b) by Committees appointed by Government, *e.g.*, the Geddes Committee of 1921-22, and

(c) by Cabinet Committees. In India a Retrenchment Committee was appointed by the Government during the economic depression of 1930-31 and an economy committee of the Cabinet functioned during 1948-49.

The Estimates Committees

Estimates Committees represent a permanent and continuously functioning Machinery for the investigation of the scope for economy in expenditure and for recommending concrete steps for it.

In Britain an Estimates Committee of 20 to 30 members has existed since 1912. It is an annual Select Committee of the House of Commons for the detailed examination of the estimates of the various Ministries and departments. Its work is, however, outside the normal financial Procedure, *i.e.*, the examination of estimates by it need not precede and usually does not precede their voting and passing in Parliament. The Estimates Committee is assisted in its work by a representative of the Treasury and can call departmental officials. Its reports are made to the Treasury. Questions of policy are excluded from its purview, *i.e.*, it cannot criticise policy or suggest alterations in it. Such recommendations for economy as it has to make, must be made within the framework of existing policies.

In view of this limitation, the effectiveness of the work of the Estimates Committee has been doubted. To be effective, it is said, the committee must encroach on the region of the executive which the latter cannot allow. The estimates are subjected to a searching scrutiny and criticism by the Treasury before they are submitted to the House of Commons. Can the criticism of the Estimates Committee be more searching and informed? What expert guidance other than that of the Treasury has the Committee got to assist it?

The Indian Estimates Committee

Following the British model, Estimates Committees had been established in India too both at the Centre and in the States. The Central Estimates Committee consists of 30 members who are elected by the House of People from amongst its members according to proportional representation by the single vote so that all the parties may find due representation on it. The Chairman of the Committee is nominated by the Speaker from among its members, but if the Deputy Speaker is a member, he has to be appointed by the chairman. So far the Deputy Speaker has, in fact, been chairman. The term of office of the members is only one year, but they are frequently re-elected and thus experience of some old members is made available for every new Committees.

The Estimates Committee has the following functions:

(a) to report what economies, improvements in organization, efficiency and administration, consistently with the policy underlying the estimates, may be effected;

(b) to examine whether the money is well laid out within the limits of the policy implied in the estimates;

(c) to suggest the form in which the estimates shall be presented to the Parliament; and

(d) to suggest alternative policies in order to bring about efficiency and economy in administration.

To begin with, it was assumed that the Estimates Committee would concern itself mainly with the suggestions for economy and the forms of estimates and would not meddle with matters of policy, but the committee has always interpreted its duties in broad terms and held that policy cannot always be separated from economy and efficiency. The speaker in the course of his address to the committee in May, 1959 said. 'The fundamental objectives of the committee are economy, efficiency in administration and ensuring that money is well laid out; but if, on close examination, it is found that large sums are going to waste because a certain policy is followed, the committee may point out the defects, and give reasons for the change in policy for the consideration of the House."

The Estimates Committee has often commented on questions of policy in connection with the reforms it has suggested from time to time. Among other things it has dealt with the reorganization of the Secretariat and the departments of the Union Government (2nd report), working of river valley projects with special reference to the Damodar Valley Corporation (4th report), certain important administrative, financial, and other reforms (9th report), organization and administration, of the nationalized undertaking (116th report), a common pattern for reports of public enterprises of the Union Government, the importance to be given to the question of unemployment in the 3rd five year plan (88th report) etc. In dealing with these and similar other matters the estimates committee often made strictures on the existing policy and suggested alternative courses which caused a flutter in the official dovecotes. The greatest controversy arose when the committee criticised the existing organization of the Planning Commission, particularly the Prime Minister being its chairman. The point was that with the Prime Minister as its chairman, the Planning Commission became virtually irresistible so that the Cabinet and Parliament had merely to register its decisions, which derogated from the responsibility of both these bodies. Vociferous criticisms arose that the Estimates Committee should not delve into the matters of high policy.

Typical of such criticisms is that by Ashok Chandra, the ex-Comptroller and Auditor-General of India. His criticism may be summarized as follows:

(1) The committee's emphasis on review of the policies of the government and of the structure of the departmental organization has substantially altered the character and purpose of the committee whose main function is and should be a detailed scrutiny of the estimates.

(2) Since its membership is floating, it cannot be sufficiently familiar with the details of administrative process and problem to be able to suggest fruitful lines of administrative reorganization or reform.

(3) The manner of its functioning is fast making it an inquisitorial body like the congressional committees in the U.S.A. Instead of a fact-finding body, it is converting itself into a fault-finding mechanism.

(4) The committee is arrogating to itself a role which constitutionally belongs to the House of People.

(5) The committee makes many recommendations on administrative reorganization and redistribution of functions.

These may have a publicity value, but since they are hardly of much practical utility, the government has often to reject them. This creates an embarrassing situation, detracting the prestige of both the Governmental and the committee.

These criticisms are not without their force specially when we remember that the estimates committee is essentially a Layment's committee, and though it can call for papers and summon the departmental officials to make enquiries, it has no expert assistance as the Public Accounts Committee has of the Comptroller and Auditor-General. But, much of the glamour and usefulness of the committee would be gone if it were excluded from the questions of policy. Even in Britain the Estimates Committee does encroach sometimes on questions of policy, because policy and finance are inextricably interwined. There can be no question of its encroaching on the functions of the House, because it is a committee of the House and the house is the ultimate judge of the propriety or otherwise of its activities and recommendations.

Every year the Estimates committee examines the estimates of one or more ministries and reports to Parliament suggesting the directions in which economy could be effected or efficiency improved. So far (till 1957) it has made more than 30 reports on the various ministries, including two, on the reorganization of the secretariat and departments of the Government of India (Second) Report (1950-51) and on Administrative Financial and other Reforms (9th report 1953-54) respectively. As in Britain, estimates do not wait for the examination by this committee for being considered and voted by the House of the People.

The recommendations of the Estimates Committee are forwarded to the Government also which considers them and implements them as far as feasible.

Estimates Committees in the states function along similar lines.

Ways and Means of Effecting Economics. There are three principal ways of effecting economies in expenditure, namely:

(a) reduction in the cost of carrying out existing policies without any material alteration in the methods of carrying them out,

(b) modification or partial abandonment, temporary or permanent, of certain objects of policies,

(c) adoption of less expensive methods, the objects of policies remaining the same, and

(d) cost can be reduced without alteration in the existing policies and methods in three ways, namely :

(i) by the elimination of wastes,

(ii) by economies in the use of personnel, and

(iii) by postponement of capital expenditure not immediately needed.

As regards *(i)* the wastes are of two kinds—the crude and obvious ones and the subtler and less obvious ones. Examples of crude waste are unnecessary use of fuel, light, stationery, etc. Such waste can be eliminated by careful attention to detail such as shutting out the light when not needed, cutting down lighting in the corridors, writing on both sides of the paper, leaving narrower margins on writing sheets, closer typing the same envelopes a number of times by attaching flaps for writing the address and closing etc. etc. Less obvious wastes arise from use of more costly material and equipment than is necessary and economy can be effected by the substitution of articles of cheaper kind equally good for use. Considerable savings may result from not insisting on too high a quality of paper, printing, office furniture, machinery, etc.

As regards *(ii)* the question of the optimum quality of staff which will do, is not easy to determine, because it involves the human element. Variations of aptitude occur even within the same grade of service. Even so, as an organization grows older and its administration gets systematized and simplified it may be possible to assign many categories of work to less highly paid staff. To meet the needs of economy during a temporary period of economic difficulty, a reduction in salaries and wages or in the size of the staff by extension of the hours of work may be tried. Reduction in salary or wages may be confined only to the new entrants, or it may be applied to all. If it is confined to the new entrants only, it is slow to produce results and causes complications due to the rise of two sets of conditions for the same service. An all round reduction is simpler, but if it is for a prolonged period or out of line with salaries and wages prevailing outside the service, it leads to discontent.

Finally, economy can be effected for the time being, by postponement expenditure on capital work, repairs, renewals, decorations, etc. Care has, however, to be taken that such postponement does not result in the deterioration of property.

❒

3

Union-State Financial Relations

According to Indian Constitution our States enjoy considerable financial autonomy. These have right to collect taxes and also to spend money in the way approved by the state legislature. But as compared with their sources of income their sources of expenditure are many more, with the result that the states are required to financially depend on the centre. It is, therefore, essential to discuss centre-state financial relationship.

Financial Pattern

There are certain types of taxes which are levied by the Union government but collected by the State *e.g.* Stamp Duty, Excise Duty etc. These will be collected by the state government of the state in which the tax is levied but collected on behalf of central government. On the other hand, there are taxes which are collected by the Union government and assigned to the States. In such cases, the pattern of distribution is however, decided by the Parliament *e.g.* duties in respect of succession to property; estate duty; terminal taxes; railway fares and freights, taxes on sale and purchase of newspapers. There are certain types of taxes which are levied etc. and collected by the Union but shared with the state government *e.g.* income tax, excise duty etc.

Grant in Aid to States

But our states cannot have their fullest development unless they are extended financial assistance by the centre. Before, we discuss that, let us have an idea about the sources of income of our states as well as the central government. Land revenue, taxes on agricultural income, taxes on lands and buildings, excise duty, taxes on sales of electricity, vehicles, entertainment etc. are some of the main sources of income of our state governments. Customs duty, excise duty, corporation tax, estates duty, income tax, taxes on sales and purchase of newspapers etc. are some of the main sources of income of central government. It will be observed that the income of state governments is, therefore, very much limited as compared with the income of the central government. Therefore, the state governments are required to depend on the grant-in-aid of the central government. This grant-in-aid can be on the basis of special programmes that might be assigned to a state by the Union Government; for the development of scheduled castes and scheduled tribes, and also on the basis of their population and with the object of removing regional imbalance that might come during the course of development.

Finance Commission. In establishing financial relations between the centre and the states finance commission plays a very important role. The President is empowered to appoint a finance commission after every five years to

(a) decide basis of net distribution of proceeds realised through income tax;

(b) distribution of other divisible central taxes.

(c) principles governing grant-in-aid of the revenues of the States and also the basis of deciding shares of state governments about property tax etc. So far the president has set up eight finance commissions. The first commission was set up in 1951 and the fifth one was set in 1968. Eighth Finance Commission submitted its report on 30.4.1984.

Transferring of Sources

The central government has regularly been transferring resources and tax revenues to the states, in order to make them self-sufficient.

Conclusion

In spite of the fact that our states are weaker partners in centre-State relationship. Yet it will be observed that there is no desire to keep the states financially weak. In financial relationship it appears to be the policy of the centre that gradually the states should become self-sufficient. No doubt the difficulties are there and the states realise and appreciate these in true spirit.

Resources and Tax Revenues Transferred to the States

(Rs. in Crores)

Period	*Taxes and Duties*	*Grants*	*Loans*	*Totals*
First Plan Period	326.7	387.7	798.5	1412.9
Second " "	711.1	746.2	1410.8	2867.9
Third " "	1995.9	1303.1	3101.4	5600.4
1966-67	372.6	410.5	915.4	1698.5
1967-68	415.7	460.8	869.2	1745.7
1968-69	491.0	499.1	890.6	1880.7
1969-70	621.7	530.7	1029.3	2181.7
1970-71	755.4	568.4	1012.0	2335.8
1971-72	850.3	733.7	946.5	2530.5
Fourth Plan Period				
1978-79	1952.8	2472.7	2361.4	6786.6
Fifth Plan Period				
1979-80	3407.0	2083.1	1865.8	7356.7
1980-81	3791	2652	3087	9530
1981-82	4274	2727	3522	10523
1984-85	5739	4819	5214	15722

ORGANISATION OF FINANCE DEPARTMENT

Finances are most important for the development of state. Since these are also scarce in the states, therefore, every care is taken to ensure that finance department is very rationally and reasonably organised.

Minister. At the head of the Finance Department is Finance Minister, who is invariably a senior cabinet minister. He holds a very high and senior position in the cabinet. He is political head of the department.

The State Legislature. All the financial activities, policies and programmes in the state are initiated by the Finance Minister, but these must be approved by the State Legislature. Unless state legislature approves the budget of the state, no financial activity can get going. The state legislature has a very elaborate system of passing finance bill or the budget, which may briefly he described as under.

Money Bills. A money bill can originate only in the Legislative Assembly and not in the Legislative council. When passed by the assembly, it is sent to the council which must return in to the assembly with its recommendations within fourteen days of its receipt. The assembly may then accept or reject the recommendations. The Bill will be considered to have been passed in the form finally adopted by the assembly. But if the Bill is not returned to the assembly by the council within fourteen days, it is also considered to have been passed by both the Houses, in the form in which it was originally passed by the assembly, and after receiving the assent of the Governor shall become an Act.

Organisation of Finance Department. Finance Department in every state is headed by a Finance Secretary, who is also called Commissioner for Finance Planning. The Finance Secretary has staff working under him. The Deputy Finance Secretary (Administration) usually deals with Treasury and Accounts Loans, Small Savings and matters dealing with Tax Evasion. Then comes Deputy Secretary (Finance planning). He deals with planning of finance Economic and

Statistical problems and plan evaluation. There is Deputy Secretary (Finance Regulation) who deals with regulating financial matters in the State. In the department, then come Assistant Secretaries. Under Secretary (Budget) may deal with budget, loans, financial ways and means. Under Secretary (Finance Regulations) deals with Public Accounts Committee, Assurance Committee and Budget Estimates Committee. Under Secretary Finance (Works) deals with General Finance Branch. Irrigation and Civil Works etc. Under Secretary (Finance Development) handles branches dealing with Financial Development in the State.

In some cases the work among the Deputy Secretaries can be as follows. In the State Deputy Secretary Finance (I) deals with budget, loans, small savings, ways and means, planning and regulations. Deputy Secretary (Finance II) deals with Finance in general Irrigation and Civil Works. Deputy Secretary (Finance III) deals with Treasuries and Accounts, Finance Development, Regulation Work, Tax Evasion, Delegation of Powers and Pension matters. More or less this pattern has been adopted by Haryana State Government.

Functions of Finance Department. In a State usually this department is required to perform the following functions:

1. It suggests measures for small savings.
2. It takes measures for recovery of state revenues.
3. It collects and disburses public money.
4. It decides borrowing and lending policies.
5. It permits creation and retention of posts.
6. It prepares and presents budget to the legislature.
7. It helps the minister in satisfying legislature about financial policy of the state.
8. It controls public expenditure.
9. It supervises treasury and accounts.

10. It sanctions expenditure for the implementation of schemes.
11. It controls Contingency Fund.
12. It frames pension regulations.
13. It co-ordinates important economic matters.
14. It frames and interprets financial rules.
15. It deals with central financial assistance and matters relating to grant-in-aid.
16. It supervises centrally sponsored schemes.

Board of Revenue. In some states there are Boards of Revenue, which help in the running of financial administration. There is no fixed number of members of the Board. Usually senior officers of the State are nominated as its member. Main functions of the Board are: *(a)* to advise the government; *(b)* to hear appeals in revenue cases; *(c)* to exercise general control over the state revenues; *(d)* to inspect revenue departments; and *(e)* to supervise district financial administration etc.

Revenue Tribunals. In some states instead of Revenue Boards, there are Revenue Tribunals. Each Tribunal has a chairman and also members, whose strength is not fixed. Divisional Commissioners are ex-officio members of the Tribunals. These Tribunals perform judicial functions and have both official and non-official members.

Financial Commissioners. Some states have financial commissioners of Boards of Revenue. These commissioners perform the same duties as the Board of Revenue. Usually a state has three Financial Commissioners one each dealing with Revenue, Planning and Taxation. Each Financial Commissioner is head of a department and final court of appeal in revenue matters and is revenue collecting authority in the state.

State Financial Corporations. In financial administration of states. State Financial Corporations are also playing a big role. There are several such Corporations which give financial support to small and medium industries. These can stand a guarantee for the loans raised by industrial concerns from the scheduled banks and state co-operative banks. These also stand guarantee for deferred payments due from any industrial concern in connection with the purchase of capital goods within India.

Assessment of Finance Departments

Finance Departments in almost all the states have come under severe criticism. Some of the important points of criticism raised are as under:

1. The officers in the department usually have neither vision nor courage to make it dynamic.

2. The departments doubt the integrity of other departments which is absolutely unhealthy.

3. The officers of Finance Department unnecessarily suffer from superiority complex.

4. By their stagnant approach the departments have created frustration and inefficiency.

5. A Finance Department usually follows the policy of penny wise and pound foolish.

6. Many a time inexperienced officers are required to man high and responsible posts in the Finance Department.

7. Finance Departments in the states have usually failed to ensure that the funds are spent not for a single constituency or faction but for the state as a whole.

8. Finance Departments have also failed to effectively check over spending tendency of other departments.

9. When the proposals and programmes have already been scrutinised at many important levels, their scrutiny by the finance department is annoying and irritating.

10. Finance Department in a state cannot act independently because it is always subjected to political pressures.

11. Usually Finance Department is un-reasonable in raising objections.

Role of Finance Department in State Administration

Finance Department plays a very important role in the state administration. It is evident from the fact that it is said that 'Finance is State'. For the development and growth state finance comes forward. Administration and administrators are obliged to adjust themselves according to the availability of funds. Similarly the administrative policy and personnel policy of the state must be approved and O. Kayed by the finance department. Finance department is the key to the state administration. It scrutinises all proposals before these are submitted for the approval of the cabinet. It supervises the work of all departments and ensures that no administrative head exceeds the limits of budgetary allocations. It examines justification for the creation of all new posts and retention of all existing posts. It can make the administration both dynamic as well as static.

One cannot deny that there is some justification in the criticism laid against Finance Department in the states. The departments usually work under heavy political pressure. But many healthy trends have already been set in the states and many more will be set with the passage of time.

FINANCIAL RELATIONS BETWEEN THE CENTRAL AND THE STATES

Turning to the financial relations it may be firstly noted that the Constitution does not enumerate separately the heads of taxation. The power to tax is included in the power to legislate. Thus the subjects which are numerated in the Union List are in the purview of Central Government for purposes of taxation and similarly the State Governments have the power of taxation in respect of subjects enumerated in the State List. The three lists of powers given in the Seventh Schedule divide the sources of revenue between the Union and the States as follows:

(A) The Union Sources:

(a) Taxes on income other than agricultural income.

(b) Custom duties including export duties.

(c) Duties of excise on tobacco and other goods manufactured or produced in India except alcoholic liquors for human consumption and opium, Indian hemp and other narcotic drugs and narcotics.

(d) Corporation tax.

(e) Taxes on capital value of assets, exclusive of agricultural land of individuals and companies; taxes on capitals of companies.

(f) Estate duty in respect of property except agricultural land.

(g) Terminal taxes on goods or passengers carried by sea, air or railway.

(h) Taxes other than stamp duties on transactions in stock exchanges and future markets.

(i) Rates of stamp duty in respect of bills of exchange, cheques, promissory notes, bills of lading, letters of credit, insurance policies, transfers of shares, debentures, proxies and receipts.

(j) Taxes on sale or purchase of newspapers and on advertisements published therein.

(k) Fees in respect of any of the matters in the Union List except fees taken in any court.

(B) The State Sources:

(a) Land revenue.

(b) Taxes on agricultural income.

(c) Duties on succession to agricultural land.

(d) Estate duty in respect of agricultural land.

(e) Taxes on land and buildings.

(f) Taxes on mineral lights subject to limitations imposed by law.

(g) Excise duties on alcoholic liquors for human consumption and opium, hemp and other narcotic drugs.

(h) Taxes on the entry of goods into a local area for consumption, use or sale therein.

(i) Taxes on consumption or sale of electricity.

(j) Taxes on sale or purchase of goods other than newspapers.

(k) Taxes on advertisements other than those published in the newspapers.

(l) Taxes on goods and passengers carried by road or inland water-ways.

(m) Taxes on vehicles for use on roads.

(n) Taxes on animals, and boats.

(o) Tolls.

(p) Taxes on professions, trades, callings and employments.

(q) Capitation taxes.

(r) Taxes on luxuries, entertainments, betting and gambling.

(s) Rates on stamp duty on documents other than those subject to Union stamp duty.

(t) Fees in respect of any of the matters in the State List.

The Concurrent List does not contain any subject in respect of which taxation may be levied.

The division of the resources as given above does not mean that the party to which a tax is assigned is the sole authority to determine it and is entitled to all the proceeds of that tax. So far as the taxes in the State List are concerned, they go entirely to the Sates but it is different with the Union taxes, the proceeds of many of which are assigned to or shared with the States. The Constitution distinguishes for categories of Union taxes which are available, whole or in part, to the States:

(i) Duties levied by the Union but collected and wholly appropriated by the State: Stamp duties in respect of bills of exchange, cheques, promissory notes, bills of lading, letters of credit, policies of insurance, transfer of shares, debentures, proxies and receipts and excise on medicines and toilet preparations containing alcohol.

(ii) Taxes levied and collected by the Union but whose proceeds are shared between the union and the states. The tax which comes under this category is income tax.

(iii) Taxes levied and collected by the Union but wholly assigned to the States: duties in respect of succession to property other than agricultural land; terminal taxes on goods and passengers carried by rail, sea or air; taxes on railway fares and freights; taxes on the sale or purchase of newspapers and advertisements published therein.

(iv) Taxes which are levied and collected by the Union but whose proceeds may be distributed between the Union and the States if Parliament by law so provide. Union duties of excise other than such duties of excise on medical and toilet preparations fall under this category.

Grants in-aid

The Constitution also provides for Grants in-aid to the States. Thus Assam, Bihar, Orissa and West Bengal receive grants-in-aid in lieu of export, duty on jute and jute products. Apart from the Union Government's constitutional obligation to provide grants-in-aid to the States for financing approved schemes for the welfare of the Scheduled Tribes and for improving the standard of administration in tribal areas, article 275 of the Constitution makes a general provisions for Union grants-in-aid to the states. It is for the Union Government to fix the extent of these grants and lay down the conditions under which they are to be administered. It need not be stated that grants-in-aid are potent instrument, for the extension of Central control and direction on the states.

Borrowing Powers

The Constitution also makes certain provisions in respect of the borrowing powers of the States. A State can borrow only within India and it cannot raise a new loan without the consent of the Union Government if there is outstanding any part of a previous loan and guaranteed by the Union or owed to it. The Government of India may, subject to such conditions as may be laid down by or under any law made by Parliament, make loans to any state provided that the limits set by parliament to union loans are not exceeded.

Financial Emergency

During the Proclamation of financial Emergency the President may empower the Union to give directions controlling state's financial activities and require state Money bills to be reserved for his consideration. Besides salaries of state employees also can be slashed to meet the situation.

It will be clear from the above description of Union State relations that every effort has been made to make the union government much stronger than what central governments are usually found to be in other federations. The emphasis is more on the authority of the centre than on the autonomy of the state. As a matter of fact interference and dictation by the centre is not only so prohibited, but authorized as a normal procedure of the functioning of the constitution. The absence of equal representation to the States in the Council of States; the power given to that chamber to declare by a two-thirds majority any subject to be of national importance, and then to enable the Union to give directions to make a law thereupon; the power of the Union to give directions to the State Governments; and the power given to the president practically to suspend the state Constitution in times of emergency—are some of the exceptional features of the Indian Federation which have led the critics to describe the Indian federation as being only a quasi-federation or as a unitary federation. Hence some states like Assam, Punjab and Kashmir are in open revolt against the centre. They seek fully autonomous status. The Sarkaria Commission made 247 recommendations to improve centre state relations besides suggesting 12 amendments to the constitution and 20 new legislations. But the past experience reveals that states demands carried weight when centre was on a weak wicket and they were ignored the moment the centre became powerful. The Sarkaria Commission was the outcome of the states' demands for more powers but when the ruling party at the centre got a massive mandate it was forgotten. Now again the issue has been raked up perhaps because Narasimha Rao's government is in minority & many states are ruled by the non congress governments. A committee has been set up to review the Gadgil formula under the chairmanship of Pranab Mukherji. It has also been decided to revive inter state council. The Home Minister has assured that the centre will be consulting states in matters other than those in concurrent list. It appears the present govt. has been the writings on the wall. It is willing to review the centre-state relations. This is apt to strengthen the federal situation. India in fact can remain a federal state—a union of federating states by providing full autonomy and self respect to the states.

CRITICISM OF THE INDIAN AUDIT SYSTEM

Dr. Paul H. Appleby, an American expert on Public administration, severely criticised our audit system in his second report on the Indian administration. He said: "the function of the Comptroller and Auditor-General in India is in large measure an inheritance from the colonial rule. The function did not impede British rule; it upheld that rule and was an integral part of it. It greatly restricted the Indians who served the government. These restrictions were sought by the government, in situation of provincial administration largely concerned with police and taxation functions and not engaged in rapid pursuit of welfare state objectives."

"In the first flush of independence Indian ministries were disposed to disregard the Comptroller and Auditor-General, and abuses became vivid. This situation has been fully corrected, but in the process the old restrictive effects have been restored and strengthened at the very time that new policies were calling for more flexibility and more use of responsible discretion.

"This repressive and negative influence is in considerable part indirect, impinging on the bureaucracy by way of Parliament because of the exaggerated and unselective attention given by Parliament to the petty exceptions and the inflated pretensions built around the pedestrian function of auditing. About two years ago there were signs of a more progressive approach in the office of the Comptroller and Auditor General. Indeed, not very long ago he soundly recommended the transfer of the accounting from his jurisdiction to that of the Ministries. But latterly he deems to be falling deeper into some of the conventional ruts, and even digging them deeper. On his own motion, he has extended his review to "all existing undertakings in which the Central or State Governments have substantial financial stakes and such other as may be established hereafter" and "in addition to such audit as is required to be carried out under Company Law."

This audit by the Comptroller and Auditor-General will be generally directed towards a review of the decisions by the Board of Directors to ascertain to what extent their powers have been exercised in the best interest of the undertakings (and) to see whether the powers delegated to the Chief Executives have been exercised properly.

"Nothing could be more calculated to stop the Plan in its tracks, to undermine responsible government and to establish government of, by and for auditors. What special competence for appraising objectives and appraising administrative performance in general has the Comptroller and Auditor-General? What is Cabinet for, what is the Prime Minister for, what is Parliament for, what are the individual ministers for, what is Secretariat for, and what is a bureaucracy for?"

'Parliament is surely at fault in this. It has a greatly exaggerated notion of the importance of auditing to 'Parliamentary responsibility', and so has failed to define the functions of the Comptroller and Auditor-General as the Constitution contemplated it would do.

"Beyond legal definition confining his whole function, however, the Comptroller and Auditor-General can make his function most useful by confining himself further. Too many of his reports are mere substitutions of hindsight for the kind of judgment possible and necessary and proper at the time of action.

Summing up the criticism, Dr. Appleby says: "First, the members of Parliament greatly exaggerate the importance of the function of the Comptroller and Auditor-General, and pay far too much attention to his reports. So doing, Parliament increases the timidity of public servants at all levels, making them unwilling to take responsibility for decisions, forcing decisions to be made by a slow and cumbersome process of reference and conference in which everybody finally shares dimply in the making of every decision, not enough gets done and what gets done is done too slowly". Dr. Appleby feels that "the Comptroller and Auditor-General's function is not really a very important one. Auditors don't know, and can't be expected to know, very much about good administration; their prestige is highest with others who don't know much about administrtation. What auditors know is auditing—which is not administration; it is a necessary but highly pedestrian function with a narrow perspective and very limited usefulness. Any Deputy Secretary knows vastly more about significant problems in his ministry than the entire staff of the Comptroller and Auditor-General can discover by auditing. In close observation of various governments during many years the writer has never known of a really important insight produced by governmental comptrollers. Yet here the Comptroller and Auditor's reports presume to speak as an authority on administration in general.

In short, the main points of Appleby's criticism are;

(i) The system is in a large measure an inheritance from colonial rule;

(ii) The Parliament and public give undue importance to the audit report;

(iii) Auditing is a highly pedestrian function with a narrow perspective and very limited usefulness;

(iv) Audit of public undertakings is not done in a fashion which may fit the nature of operations of each enterprise;

(v) Auditing is strictly negative and aggressive. It does not suit the needs of a Welfare Administration.

Mr. Chanda's defence

Mr. A.K. Chanda, Comptroller and Auditor-General (Retd.), in a statement on August 15, 1956 at Lucknow, defended the office of the Auditor-General against the criticism levelled by Dr. Appleby. He said: "I do not know the historical basis for such an observation (that the functions of C. & A.G. is an inheritance of colonial rule). I do not know of any colonial system which had, or has, any analogous post, independent of the Executive with freedom to criticise administrative lapses. The conception of such a post runs counter to that of a colonial or autocratic system. Any student of constitutional history would be aware that this post was an essential one in a democratic form of government, as its functions were so defined as to secure public accountability of the administration."

As for the 'pedestrian function' of audit, Mr. Chanda said: "Dr. Appleby seems allergic to audit which he describes as 'a highly pedestrian function with a narrow perspective and very limited usefulness". This attitude of mind has obviously coloured his observations on the Indian Audit Organisation". Emphasising the importance of the Auditor-General's office, Mr. Chanda referred to the ever-widening scope of its functions in every democratic country. He said: "In the U.S.A., the Comptroller-General's audit covers banking institution and other corporations in which the Government had any financial interest, even when it was not a majority. The U.S. Comptroller-General had also been given the power to issue surcharges against corporation and individual officers to effect recovery of expenditure which, in his opinion, was illegal". He further added: "The powers of the Comptroller and Auditor-General in the U.K., as defined in the Exchequer and the Audit Act, were not also different from the present powers of his counterpart in India, except that they were more comprehensively defined. The audit of the U.K. Comptroller and Auditor-General extended beyond the formulae of expenditure to an examination of its 'wisdom, faithfulness and economy. In the continental democracies, there was a constituted court of accounts with a president who fulfilled analogous functions as the Comptroller and Auditor-General.

Mr. Chanda, commenting on Dr. Appleby's disapproval of auditing of public enterprises by the C. & A. G. said, "this suggestion ignores the basic differences between the structure of public and private enterprises'. "While, in the case of private enterprises, those in control have a significant financial stake in the concern and are also vitally interested in its financial operations, there is no such incentive in the case of State undertakings. These are managed by officials without any direct financial interest..." There is a basic difference. Mr. Chanda said, between the functions of the Auditor-General and a professional auditor. In his words, "A public auditor responsible for the audit of commercial enterprises is primarily concerned with the certification of the profit and loss account and the balance sheet. So long as any expenditure is concerned by a sanction of the appropriate authority and it does not contravene the provisions of the company Law, he is precluded from commenting on the propriety of such sanctions or on the manner of exercise of discretion by the authorities concerned.

Its functions are not merely to ensure that the appropriations made by Parliament have not been exceeded without a supplementary vote or that the expenditure conforms to rules, but also to be satisfied as to its 'wisdom, faithfulness and economy. These words are comprehensive in their scope and have led to a broader and newer approach, with greater attention to efficiency and to development of a discretionary audit directed towards discovering waste and matters beyond accounting, which, though intra, vires, are apparently unwise of extravagant. According to Mr. Chanda, the Auditor-General's office is "one of the essential ingredients of a parliamentary democracy" whose rule is to "uphold the Constitution, and the laws in the field of financial administration".

Mr. Chanda, however, recognises the need of reorienting our audit system so as to meet the requirements of the social ideology and objectives of the national government. "In the past, audit and administration", he says, "have functioned in watertight compartments. There has been little inclination to get together to understand each other's points of view and what is more important to clarify issues and take remedial measures. Objections are raised, technical in character, even in respect of schemes and projects which have been executed with competence and expedition. It must be recognised that the purpose of a plan or project and the manner in which it is being implemented, are far more important than mere technicalities".

Separation of Accounting and Auditing Functions

In the earlier paragraphs we have seen that a peculiar feature of our account and audit system is the combination of the accounting and audit functions in the same agency, viz., Auditor-General. This combination of accounting and audit functions in hands of the same agency has been severely criticised for some time past. To combine both these functions in the same organisation is incompatible with the present constitutional set-up of the country under which the Parliament has been given the supreme powers of control over national finances. The Parliament can exercise effective control over public finance only through an independent audit of the accounts kept by the Executive. The accounts should therefore be maintained by the spending departments and they should be audited by an independent authority as is done in England. There every department has its own Accounting officer who works under a minister and is charged with the function of making payments, scrutiny of claims and keeping of accounts. The Audit Department is separate and it has nothing to do with the accounting. Shri P. K. Wattal has emphasised the desirability of separating these two functions by remarking:"Accounting is essentially an executive function and must be under the control of the executive head of the department. Auditing is a quasi-Parliamentary function, which involves a checking of the works done by the executive authorities for report to the Parliament. A combination of these two essentially distinct functions in a parliamentary officer is good neither for the executive administration nor for the parliament. It is almost as bad as a combination of executive and judicial functions. In every modern administration, accounting and auditing functions should be kept distinct and separate from each other. It is only then that the auditor's certificate regarding the correctness of the accounts has any meaning.

This glaring defect of the Indian system of combination of auditing and accounting functions in the same person has been spotlighted by many a Commission also, like the Simon Commission and Welley Commission. In some States and in some departments, the two functions were once separated but the separation could not last long due to reasons of economy. After the advent of freedom, this issue has become so prominent that even the various Comptrollers and Auditors-General have themselves condemned this system from time to time and advocated for the separation of the two functions. Mr. Narahari Rao, the first Comptroller and Auditor-General of free India, in a note submitted to the Public Accounts Committee had written : "The present arrangement under which the spending authorities are not responsible for the maintenance of complete and up-to-date accounts relating to the transactions for which they are responsible and the duty of compiling and maintaining these accounts rests upon an outside authority, namely, Indian Audit Department is wholly inconsistent with the various responsibility to the parliament to keep within the budget grants and appropriations. Indeed existing arrangements blur the responsibilities and are highly defective. The separation of audit from accounts organisation of the necessary accounting machinery under the administrative departments with a view to removing these serious defects and the enforcement of effective executive control are essential and overdue and I, as Comptroller and Auditor-General, attach the greatest importance to these reform being carried out after the minimum interval required to introduce the necessary organisational changes." An Introduction to Indian Government Accounts and Audit puts the problem as follows:

"In 1924 an experimental scheme of separation of Account from Audit was introduced on the civil side in the United provinces (now Uttar Pradesh) and also in certain departments of the government of India. This experiment was amended in 1931 expressly on financial grounds, as the separated Accounts system was found to be more expensive. The system of combined Accounts and Audit is, however, unsound in theory, and it tends to undermine the independence of audit by combining with it the functions of accounts, which are entirely those of the executive authorities. Man-power problems now stand in the way of this very necessary reforms which will have to be seriously taken up when the man-power position improves."

The Public Accounts Committee in its third report (1952-1953) expressed itself in very strong terms in favour of separating accounting from auditing and recommended to the Government to do the needful. An abstract from the observations made by the Committee on the point in question is reproduced as follows: "The function of payment and maintenance of initial accounts is that of the executive authority, and it is well known and universally accepted that the agency which has to audit payments should be separate from the independent of the agency which has to make disbursements, as a combination of these functions is likely to facilitate frauds and embezzlements and prevent their coming to light. This places the Auditor-General in a most embarrassing and anomalous position. It is fundamentally wrong in principle, therefore, to make Indian Audit Department responsible for making payments. The Comptroller and Auditor-General has informed the Committee that he as well as his predecessors have been protesting to Government from time to time against the impropriety of his department being made responsible for pre-Audit and treasury payment work and pressed for its being relieved of this work. This work is constitutionally entirely outside the duties of his department.

As a statement of an abstract principle the separation of accounting from auditing is unassailable, but many problems will arise if accounts are transferred to spending departments. "The departmentalization of accounts will require arrangements for the consolidation of these accounts and their compilation into the combined Finance and Revenue Accounts of the Union and State Governments as a whole. It will be necessary to ensure that uniformity in accounting principles and procedure is observed in the Ministries. Co-ordination between the Union and the State will have to be provided for ... The question whether adequate and efficient audit can be provided by an agency, unfamiliar with the departmental structure of accounts and of rules and regulations of special application, also becomes relevant and important in this consideration. The formation of linguistic states where the business will be conducted in the regional language, is likely to create yet another problem."

The discussion can be summed up by explaining the case for and against separation of Accounts from Audit.

Case for Separation

(1) Separation will lead to efficiency of Audit Department as it will have ample time to devote itself to more important enquiries and investigations.

(2) Frauds and embezzlements can be prevented if the two are separated as the officer authorizing the payment is not made responsible for admitting the charge in audit.

(3) The keeping of the two together places the Auditor-General in a very embarrassing position as he is expected to audit the accounts compiled by himself. Hence in many other democracies, the two have been bifurcated. It speaks of the popularity of the move to keep the two separate from each other.

(4) Accounting, being an Executive function, should be entrusted to the executive head of the department, whereas Auditing, being a quasi-parliamentary function, should not be combined with the Accounting.

(5) Separation is in consonance with the sound financial administration. Accounting responsibilities must be entrusted to the

spending departments so that they may not exceed the appropriations passed by the Parliament.

(6) The transfer of accounting responsibilities to departments will mean opting for a logical pattern of administration. Asok Chanda correctly remarked. "...In Government...authority is diffused and financial control and accounting responsibilities vested in organisations outside the administrative departments. The malaise of India's administration has been this divorce of authority from responsibility."

(7) The separation will facilitate close budgeting and more effective preparation of revised estimates. With the bifurcation of the Pay and Accounts departments, a close understanding between the two can develop. Such an understanding will help in preparing their budget and Revised Estimates more effectively."

Case Against Separation

(1) Experience speaks otherwise. In the Departments of Defence and Railways where the accounting responsibilities have been entrusted to the Departments, there is no positive indication of increase in efficiency or effective budgetary control.

(2) It is more economical to maintain status quo as the same manpower can be utilized for the both in accounting and auditing. Separation would mean more expenses as two sets of persons will be required.

(3) It is apprehended that separation may lead to decline in competence. Already administration in the country is facing an eclipse.

(4) The accounting staff if separated from the audit and placed under the general control of the respective departments of the State Government will not be able to indulge in criticism of the executive freely and restrain extravagance, as it can do now.

(5) The present system is working on satisfactory lines. Why should it be changed at all? The theoretical excellence of the separation can hardly prove useful.

(6) Separation of audit from accounts hardly guarantees keeping of appropriations within the sanctioned limits, U.K. system is the instance worth quoting to support this contention.

(7) The separation will mean centralising the payments under the Pay and Accounts Officer. Such centralisation is apt to cause difficulties in our country where banking facilities are comparatively inadequate.

(8) It is further maintained that even under the present system the Accountant-General's staff renders adequate help and assistance in the preparation of budget and revised estimates. Whey then the separation be envisaged?

(9) The present system can easily detect discrepancies as accounts are maintained both by the Accountant-General and the Heads of the Department. This may not be possible if separation is effected.

An appraisal of the arguments on both the sides makes us conclude that a thorough study of the pros and cons of such a step is essential before it is actually taken.

The Government however accepted the separation of audit and accounts in principle and steps are being taken to separate audit from accounts gradually. The central accounting was discontinued with regard to three Departments of Supply, Food and Rehabilitation with consequent departmentalisation of accounts on April 1,1955 to begin with. The Railway Accounts and Defence Accounts have always been kept by the Financial Commissioner for Railways and the Financial Adviser, Defence, respectively.

❐

4

Organisation of Financial Committees

In all parliamentary democracies parliament is the supreme body. The members of the Parliament reflect the will of the people and it is essential that the parliament should have effective checks on the national purse. It has rightly been said that without parliamentary control there will be no effective check for checking financial improprieties. In India, our Parliament too is the sovereign body and it enjoys very effective powers in controlling expenditure. Our Parliament is the sovereign body to authorise the executive government to levy taxes and also to collect money. Without parliament's approval the executive government cannot draw money from the treasury even for running day-to-day administration of the country. But at the same time parliament is to see that all taxes which have been collected by the executive government are properly spent and that too for the purpose for which they were authorised. For this the parliament has Estimates and Public Account Committees.

Estimates Committee. It is one of the parliamentary committees through which the Parliament exercises control over public. The Committee came into being in 1950. Its term of office is only one year and includes members from all political parties on the basis of proportional representation. Usually outgoing members are re-elected to the committee. Deputy Speaker, if a member of this Committee, is ex-officio its chairman otherwise the Speaker appoints a chairman from amongst its members. The committee exercises control over executive policies and acts as a liasion between the public and the government.

The committee selects at random few ministries each years for reviewing their working. These ministries are required to send information about their policies, programmes, offices and organisations and the money which is being spent on each organisation. The information received is circulated to the members, who may even decide to divide themselves into sub-committees with a view to saving time. The members of the committee, who are usually 30, are empowered to tour the field establishments of the ministry, the work of which is being reviewed. It has also the power of summoning the public servants as well as tax payers to give their comments on the working of the ministry.

The committee is required to suggest ways and means for effective economy and promoting efficiency as well as suggesting means and methods for reforming the working of the ministries. It is also to comment on the soundness of financial policies being followed by the ministry and to suggest alternative policies, if necessary.

The committee reports on the working of these ministries to the Lok Sabha through its chairman. The House is given an opportunity to discuss these reports and thus through this committee the parliament gets an opportunity to discuss the working of executive department. The committee has so far done really very useful work.

Public Accounts Committee. Public Accounts Committee is another parliamentary committee which provides effective parliamentary control over public money. Since 1954 it has become a joint parliamentary committee consisting of 22 members, 15 from the Lok Sabha and 7 from the Rajya Sabha. The members represent different political parties in the parliament and in fact are according to their strength in their respective House. The committee is constituted for a period for one year and if Deputy Speaker is a member of the committee he becomes its chairman, otherwise the Speaker nominates a member of the committee, as its chairman.

The committee is required to suggest economy measures and administrative reforms and sees that the moneys spent were legally available and actually spent for the purpose for which these were earmarked. The committee is to see that every reappropriation has been made in accordance with the rules framed for the purpose and that this has been done by the competent authority. It is supposed to see that the expenditure conforms to the authority which governs it. The committee has been empowered to examine the balance sheets of all such commercial organisations which the President of India may direct the committee to examine.

For the purpose the committee considers the report of the Comptroller and Auditor General of India on the working of the ministries/departments. In fact these report form the basis of the working of the committees. In order to effectively carry out its obligations the committee has an authority to call for papers and persons. Usually secretary of the ministry is required to personally satisfy the committee by appearing before it. The chairman is assisted by the Comptroller and Auditor General who gives him all technical advice for examining these public servants. After the persons have been examined that report is submitted to the parliament which is usually accepted. But if there are differences between the committee and the government efforts are made to see that these are sorted out but if the differences still persist then the parliament is the final authority to decide, whose decision is final.

An assessment of the Work of the Committee. It is said that the committee cannot do any useful work because it only does the post-mortum and thus cannot have any effective checks. Once the money has been spent that cannot be got back. But the criticism does not appear to be very valid. The very existence of the committee has a great moral and psychological effect and check. Then the committee can guide about the future and sees that the mistakes once committed are not repeated. In fact during post partition period it has really done very useful work and made very useful suggestions. In 1947-48 it suggested that steps should be taken to ensure that spending departments show complete responsibility in matters of budgeting and keeping control over expenditure. It was again through the report of the committee that in 1948-49 extravagant expenditure of Rs. 150 lakhs on the construction of Barwadi Sarnath Railway came to light. It was due to the committee that irregular purchase of jeeps by our High Commission in England and deflation in Posts & Telegraphs department in 1958-59 came to light. The committee is the main instrument in getting the procedure for writing off losses codified. The committee has also suggested separation of audit from the accounts and had also recommended that audit departments should be relieved of pre audit and payment responsibilities.

Report of the Comptroller and Auditor-General. Then another method through which parliament controls the finances is the report of the Comptroller and Auditor General, which is laid on the floor of the House through the Ministry of Finance and Minister and Parliamentary Affairs. The report points out irregularities and shortcoming in the working of government departments. It will thus be seen that the parliament exercises real control over the national finance. The need and necessity of such a control is being increasingly felt, particularly because our economy is very rapidly expanding and both public and private sectors are now required to spend much more than what they used to spend only few years back. In case parliamentary control is relaxed there may be irregularities than what these are today.

ESTIMATES COMMITTEE

The system of appointing Estimates Committee in our country has been taken from England where such a committee was first created in 1912 and was charged with the function of examining such of the Estimates presented to the House as the committee may choose to examine and to report what, if any, economies consistent with those estimates could be effected. The idea of an Estimates Committee in india was first mooted in 1938 when a resolution asking for the constitution of a Retrenchment Committee to secure a reduction in the Government expenditure by 10% was moved. But during the British rule such a committee was not created because the foreign government could not allow its policies to be criticised, and their financial implications scrutinised by their subject people.

Creation of the Estimates Committee in India

The Estimates Committee was created in our country after the inauguration of our constitution in 1950 on the suggestion of Dr. John Mathai, the then Finance Minister, to scrutinise expenditure of each department of the Government and of the Government as a whole.

The Composition of Estimates Committee. The Estimates Committee is elected every year from amongst the members of the House of People only according to the principle of proportional representation by means of a single transferable vote system. Its membership was initially fixed at 25 but was later increased to 30. Its Chairman is appointed by the Speaker from amongst its own members. But if the Deputy Speaker happens to be a member of the Committee, he automatically becomes its Chairman. The Committee is renewed every year but according to convention only one-third of its members retire every year and usually the same members are re-elected year after year.

Functions of the Estimates Committee. The main function of the Committee as laid down in the Rules of Procedure and Conduct of Business in Parliament was to scrutinise the estimates and to suggest 'what, if any, economies consistent with the policy underlying the estimates may be effected therein', Shri Mavlankar, the then Speaker of the House of People, while interpreting the meaning of the term 'Policy' to the committee remarked that "it related only to policies laid down by Parliament by statute. It shall, therefore, be open to the committee to examine any matter which may have been settled as a matter of policy by the Government in the discharge of its executive functions." But in 1953 the rule was amended to expand the scope of the committee's examination. Under the new rules the committee wili "report not only what economies, consistent with the policy underlying the estimates may be effected, but it may also suggest alternate policies in order to bring about efficiency and economy in administration and examine whether the money is well laid out within the limits of the policy implied in the estimates." The committee, therefore, now devotes a great deal of attention to the organization aspect also and to measures which, in its opinion, should be undertaken to ensure that the money voted by Parliament was better spent.

Refereeing to the functions of the committee and expectations from it, the Speaker of the Lok Sabha held on July 17, 1957 "The whole country looks to the Estimates Committee to suggest ways and means of economising the expenditure."

How the Committee Functions? The procedure which the committee has adopted for its work is that it selects the estimates of any Ministry or Ministries that it may like to review. It then sets about collecting all materials relevant to an examination of the estimates selected. The information thus collected from the Ministry concerned is circulated amongst the members of the committee. When the committee meets, it may frame further questions to get such information as it may desire. The committee usually divides itself into Sub-Committees and each sub-committee is assigned one part of scrutiny work. The committee can summon officials of the Ministry or its officers to furnish such information as the committee may ask for. It may also summon non-officials to render evidence. It may also undertake tours to examine the work of field establishment of the Ministry. The committee then draws up a report and submits it to the House of People. As the Estimates Committee is a Committee of Parliament drawing its authority from it, its recommendations are naturally given due consideration by the Government. If the government feels unable to accept a particular recommendation of the committee, it makes representation to the committee for reconsideration of its recommendation.

Utility of the Committee. The Estimates Committee has done a useful work in spot-lighting the various acts of omission and commission of the Government. In the various reports, submitted from time to time, it has recommended the reorganization of the Secretariat, the reorganization of state-owned or state-controlled industries, the tightening of Parliamentary control over the various projects and so on. In its 102nd report submitted on December 22, 1960 the Committee reiterated its earlier recommendation for amalgamation of the two presses, printing stamps and currency-notes at Nasik, as it was not convinced with the explanation given by the Government against such amalgamation.

While proposing the constitution of an Estimates Committee, Dr. John Mathai had hoped that it would exert healthy influences upon the course of public expenditure. He was of the view that its suggestions and criticism would give very useful guidance to the Government, in the matter of regulating expenditure. Secondly, the knowledge that the expenditure of the Government and of every department would be examined in details by an independent authority, would work as a deterrent to extravagance in public expenditure. Thirdly, though the results of its report would not lead to the immediate modification of the expenditure which had been proposed or of the expenditure which had already been accepted by the House, it would be, however, a guide to the Treasury and the Ministry concerned with regard to the basis on which proposals for expenditure should be formed for the coming year. It is gratifying to note that the Estimates Committees both in the House of People and State Legislative Assemblies have justified their existence by discharging their functions successfully. But it is an unhealthy trend that the committees are laying more emphasis on a review of the policies of the Government and of the structure of departmental organization to the relative exclusion of a detailed scrutiny of the Estimates for which they are primarily meant. They are said to be behaving like Congressional Committees in U.S.A. and becoming a fault-finding rather than a fact-finding mechanism." It is, therefore, desirable that in order to prove more effective and useful, as a mechanism of parliamentary control, they should be more concerned with scrutiny of Estimates presented to the House with a view to suggesting possible economies in them rather than interfering with the functions of other authorities.

COMMITTEE ON PUBLIC ACCOUNTS

Function of Committee on Public Accounts : 308. (1) There shall be a Committee on Public Accounts for the examination of accounts showing the appropriation of sums granted by the House for the expenditure of the Government of India, the annual finance accounts of the Government of India and such other accounts laid before the House as the Committee may think fit.

(2) In scrutinising the Appropriation Accounts of the Government of India and the report of the Comptroller and Auditor-General thereon, it shall be the duty of the Committee to satisfy itself:

(a) that the moneys shown in the accounts as having been disbursed were legally available for, and applicable to, the service of purpose to which they have been applied or charged.

(b) that the expenditure conforms to the authority which governs it; and

(c) the every re-appropriation has been made in accordance with the provisions made in this behalf under the rules framed by competent authority.

(3) It shall also be the duty of the Committee:

(a) to examine the statement of accounts showing the income and expenditure of state corporations, trading and manufacturing schemes, concerns and projects together with the balance sheets and statements of profit and loss accounts with the President may have required to be prepared or are prepared under the provisions of the statutory rules regulating the financing of a particular corporation, trading or manufacturing scheme or project and the report of the Comptroller and Auditor-General thereon;

(b) to consider the report of the Comptroller and Auditor-General in cases where the President may have required him to conduct and audit of any receipt or to examine the accounts of stores and stocks.

(c) to examine the statement of accounts showing the income and expenditure of autonomous and semi-autonomous bodies, the audit of which may be conducted by the

Comptroller and Auditor-General of India either under the directions of the President or by a statute of Parliament; and

(4) If any money has been spent on any service during a financial year in excess of the amount granted by the House for that purpose the Committee shall examine with reference to the facts of each case the circumstances leading to such an excess and make such recommendation as it may deem fit;

(Provided that the Committee shall not exercise its functions in relation to such public undertakings as are allotted to the Committee on Public Undertakings by these rules or by the Speaker.)

Constitution of Committee : 309. (1) The Committee shall consist of not more than fifteen members, who shall be elected by the House every year from amongst its members according to the principle of proportional representation by means of the single transferable vote:

Provided that a Minister shall not be elected a member of the Committee, and that if a member after his election to the Committee, is appointed a Minister he shall cease to be a member of the Committee from the date of such appointment.

(2) The term of office of members of the committee shall not exceed one year.

COMMITTEE ON ESTIMATES

Functions of Committee on Estimates : 310. There shall be a committee on Estimates for the examination of such of the estimates as may deem fit to the Committee or are specifically referred to it by the House or the Speaker. The functions of the Committee shall be:—

(a) to report what economies, improvements in organization, efficiency or administrative reform; consistent with the policy underlying the estimates may be effected;

(b) to examine whether the money is well laid out within the limits of the policy implied in the estimates;

(c) to suggest the form in which the estimates shall be presented in Parliament; and

(d) to suggest alternative policies in order to bring about efficiency and economy in administration.

Constitution of Committee : 311. (1) The Committee shall consist of not more than thirty members who shall be elected by the House every year from amongst its members according to the principle of proportional representation by means of the single transferable vote:

Provided that a Minister shall be elected a member, after his election to the Committee, if appointed a Minister he shall cease to be a member of the Committee from the date of such appointment.

(2) The term of office of member of the Committee shall not exceed one year.

Examination of Estimates by Committee. The Committee may continue the examination of the estimates from time to time throughout the financial year and report to the House as its examination proceeds. It shall not be incumbent on the Committee to examine the entire estimates of any one year. The demands for grants may be finally voted notwithstanding the fact that the Committee has made no report.

Committee on Public Undertaking

Functions of Committee on Public Undertaking : 312A. There shall be a Committee on Public Undertaking for the examination of the working of the public undertaking specified in the Fourth Schedule. The functions of the Committee shall be:

(a) to examine the report and accounts of the Public undertakings specified in the Fourth Schedule;

(b) to examine the report, if any, of the Comptroller and Auditor-General on the public undertakings;

(c) to examine, in the context of the autonomy any deficiency of the public undertakings, whether the affairs of the public undertakings are being managed in accordance with sound business principles and prudent commercial practices; and

(d) to exercise such other functions vested in the Committee on Public accounts and the committee on estimates in relation to the public undertakings specified in the Fourth Schedule as are not covered by clauses(a), (b) and (c) above and as may be allotted to the Committee by the Speaker from time to time.

Provided that the Committee shall not examine and investigate any of the following, namely:

(i) matters of major Government policy as distinct from business or the commercial functions of the public undertakings;

(ii) matters of day-to-day administration; and

(iii) matters for the consideration of which machinery is established by any special statute under which a particular public undertaking is established.

Constitution of Committee : 312B. (1) The Committee shall consist of not more than ten members who shall be elected by the House every year from amongst its members according to the principle of proportional representation by means of the single transferable vote:

Provided that a Minister shall not be elected a member of the Committee, and that if a member, after his election to the Committee, is appointed a Minister he shall cease to be a member of the Committee from the date of such appointment.

(2) The term of office of members of the Committee shall not exceed one year.

Provided that the members of the Committee constituted for the first time shall hold office for the duration of the Third Lok Sabha.

Utility. The Committee has lessened the burden of other two committees of the Parliament. The Committee has extended help to the Parliament in having comprehensive understanding of the working of these undertakings. Its method of work is practically the same as that of the Estimates Committee.

FINANCIAL COMMITTEES

The financial committees play an important role in the system of parliamentary control over finances. These committees ensure that the objectives of Parliamentary control over finances are fulfilled. The Parliament as a general body is too big to exercise and specific control over public expenditure. It is, therefore, left to the committees to act as the 'trustees' of the Parliament in keeping a strict watch over the public purse. In India, there are three financial committees.

(1) The Public Accounts Committee;

(2) The Estimates Committee; and

(3) The Committee on Public Undertakings.

The Public Accounts Committee

As we have borrowed the system of Public Accounts Committee from Great Britain, therefore, we shall first briefly describe the Public Accounts Committee in the U.K. in order to provide background material for study of the Public Accounts Committee in India.

The Public Accounts Committee in U.K.

In the U.K. the struggle between the King and the Parliament started first over taxation and Exchequer issues, in medieval times there had been a continuous struggle for supremacy over the finances of the country. However, it was not until the decade 1857-67 that the Parliament got control over Exchequer issues. In 1857 the Select Committee on Public Moneys recommended the constitution of a Select Committee to go into the report of the expert auditor, in pursuance of this recommendation. Gladstone in 1861 appointed for the first time a Selected Committee on Public Accounts. A standing order of the House of Commons in 1862 made it an annual affair. In

1866 was set up the Exchequer and Audit Department. The accounts audited by the Department are submitted to the Committee on Public Accounts on behalf of the House of Commons. The Committee scrutinises the report and makes its recommendations to the House for its discussion and consideration.

The Committee is constituted on the eve of each session. It consists of the members of the House of Commons alone and is presided over by an important member of the Opposition. "It has been claimed that the U.K. possesses, in the Public Accounts Committee, one of the most interesting features of her whole system of financial administration, and that it is the crowning point of that system which she has built up, step by step, for securing a real control over public expenditure".

Public Accounts Committee in India

In India, the Auditor initially submitted his reports for consideration to the Secretary of State for India and not to the Indian Legislature. It was only with the inauguration of Reforms of 1919 that it was considered desirable to arm the legislature with a semblance of expenditure control. The Government of India, in a dispatch to the Secretary of State, suggested that it should be the constitutional duty of the legislature to appoint a Committee on Public Accounts, to receive reports from it and a deal with them, in so far as might be necessary, by resolutions.

The P.A.C., which came to be constituted, was partly elected and partly nominated. The Finance Minister was appointed ex-officio chairman of the Committee. From its very inception, the committee became a major force in the legislative control of public expenditure. It exercised great influence in bringing pressure to head upon Government to enforce economy in the expenditure of public moneys. In course of time very important principles and conventions were developed by the Public Accounts Committee, which survive even to this day, as mile-stones on the road to the development of parliamentary control over public expenditure.

The Constitution adopted on 26 January 1950, makes no mention of the Public Accounts Committee. The Parliament derives its power to set up such a committee from Article 118(i) of the Constitution. Similar power has been conferred on State Legislatures by Article 208(i). The Parliament has accordingly laid down in Rule 143 of its Rules of Procedure and Conduct of Business the composition and functions of the Public Accounts Committee.

Composition of Public Accounts Committee

The Public Accounts Committee is set up at the commencement of the first session of Parliament. Its strength was initially fixed at 15 members of the House of People but in 1955, it was increased to 22 to provide for the representation of the council of State. Though technically the Council of States (Rajya Sabha) is not directly concerned with the voting of supplies, yet as its members were equally interested in the efficient and economic administration of the country, it was considered desirable to associate seven members from that body also with the Public Accounts Committee. In the words of Prime Minister Nehru, "The association of the nominees of the Council of States with Public Accountant Committee was necessary because the function of the committee was purely investigatory and since under Article 151 (i) of the Constitution, Public Accounts and Audit Reports were to be presented to both Houses, it was open to the Council of States to appoint its own committee but instead of two, it would be desirable if only one committee was appointed."

The members of the Committee are elected by the Parliament every year from amongst its members according to the principle of proportional representation by means of single transferable vote so that all parties may find due representation on its Although, theoretically, the members are elected, there is hardly ever a contest in the course of an election. The selection of members is made with great care, usually from amongst those having a financial and business background. The chairman of the committee is appointed by the Speaker from amongst the members of the committee but if the Deputy Speaker happens to be a members of the committee, he is ipso facto the chairman of the committee. The chairman has a casting vote in case of a tie. Till the third Lok Sabha, the Chairman of the Committee belonged to the ruling party. In the fourth Lok Sabha, the chairmanship has been given to the opposition parties.

Functions of the Committee

Rule 145 of the Rules of Procedure and Conduct of Business in Parliament lays down that:

(1) In scrutinising the appropriation accounts of the Government of India and the report of the Comptroller and Accountant-General thereon, it shall be the duty of the Committee on Public Accounts to satisfy itself:

(a) That the moneys shown in the accounts at having been disbursed were legally available, and applicable to the service or purpose to which they have been applied or charged.

(b) That every re-appropriation has been made in accordance with the provisions made in this behalf in the Appropriation Act, or under rules framed by competent authority under the provisions of the said Act Provided that the provision made in this Clause shall not apply to any accounts prior to the year 1950-51.

(c) That the expenditure conforms to the authority which governs it.

(2) It shall be a duty of the Committee on Public Accounts:

(a) to examine such trading, manufacturing and profit and loss accounts and balance sheets as the President may have required to be prepared and the Comptroller and Auditor-General's report thereon.

(b) to consider the report the Comptroller and Auditor-General in cases where the President may have required him to conduct audit of any receipt or to examine the accounts of stores and stock.

The above rules are self-explanatory. In brief, the main function of the Public Accounts Committee is to examine the report of the Comptroller and Auditor-General in order to ascertain whether the money granted by the Parliament has been spent by the Government within the scope of the demands. In other words, it is to see whether moneys as shown in the accounts as having been disbursed were legally available and meant for the services or purposes for which they have been spent. The examination of the committee extends beyond the formalities of the expenditure to its 'wisdom, faithfulness and economy. It is the duty of the committee, among other things, to draw the attention of the Parliament to cases of improper, wasteful or extravagant expenditure.

Working of Committee. The Comptroller and Auditor-General submits his report to the President or the Governor as the case may be, who causes it to be laid before the legislature concerned which in turn refers it to the Committee on Public Accounts. The Committee examines the Government's accounts in the light of the audit report with the assistance of the Comptroller and Auditor-General. The States Public Accounts Committees are assisted by the Accountant-General concerned instead of the Comptroller and Auditor-General. As the accounts of each Ministry or Department come up for examination, the official representative of that Ministry appears before the Committee to answer any objection or explain any points raised by it. The committee demands an explanation from each Ministry for the irregularities or the improper transactions pointed out by the audit in the report. These reports contain a summary of proceedings of the meetings of the Committee and its recommendations for improvement. A copy of the report is forwarded to the Finance Department which takes up the recommendations with the various Ministries Departments concerned. In case, the Government is unable to implement them, it has to state reasons for the same.

The Committee is assisted in its work by the officers of the Auditor-General's office who help the members in understanding the audit objections and the material on which these are based. The Committee has the power to send for persons, papers and records to record evidence. The witnesses are examined. The Auditor-General intervenes if any witness tries to cloud the issue by raising irrelevant points.

The examination of the report by the committee extends 'beyond the formality of the expenditure to its wisdom, faithfulness and economy. The purpose of this comprehensive review is to ascertain whether the executive has observed the principle of prudent house-keeping in national expenditure. It also undertakes a review of the form and details in which the estimates are composed. It pays special attention to the technical accounting procedure employed. It examines the safeguards embodied in financial orders and reviews both the formulation and application and financial principles.

Utility of Public Accounts Committee

Even though the Committee conducts a post mortem examination of the accounts after their having been audited by the Comptroller and Auditor-General yet it has been serving a very useful purpose by detecting cases of misappropriation and suggesting economies. It will be worth-while to record here extracts from some of their reports to be convinced of their utility. The first report of the Committee on the accounts of 1948-49, among other things, pointed out two instances where consideration of economy had been thrown to the winds. First, in the purchase of whiskey by the Indian High Commissioner in U.K., which was made without calling for tenders and secondly an unprofitable expenditure of Rs. 150 lakhs was incurred on the construction of Barwadi Sarnath railway line in the coal fields of Bihar and West Bengal. The second report of the Committee for the same year's accounts drew attention towards the purchase of jeeps by the Indian High Commissioner in U.K. The Committee has also pointed out other instances such as those of whiskey by the Indian High Commissioner in U.K., which was extravagance and lack of proper financial control over the Indian embassies abroad. In one of its reports, on the Posts and Telegraphs Department, the Committee noted with concern the increasing incidence of defalcation and loss of public money during 1958-59. According to the Committee, the incidence during the period was the heaviest ever recorded in the Post and Telegraphs Department and its employees were responsible for high proportion of such cases in the past. It called upon the Government to take deterrent action against those guilty of laxity in supervision. In its report laid on the table of the Lok Sabha on December 7, 1962, the Public Accounts Committee urged the Government of India to expedite introduction of legislation defining the duties and powers of the Comptroller and Auditor-General as required under Article 146 of the Constitution. The Committee also pointed out that large percentage of savings in grants were a common feature observed from year to year. It was not happy over the practice of surrendering funds year after year on the last day of the financial year and hoped that with closer liaison between the indenting and supply departments and the accounts officers, better results would be achieved in future.

The Committee, in its 23rd report presented by Mr. Mahavir Tyagi, on 25th March, 1964 suggested ceiling on the profits from public sector undertakings and asked the Government to appoint a high level inquiry committee to investigate the cases of the alleged overpayment of Rs. 100 lakhs by the Hindustan Steel Limited to a firm of Consultants in respect of certain works in the Durgapur project. It also suggested inquiry into two other cases: *(a)* loss of Rs. 27 lakhs due to the supply of defective cement in the construction of certain structures in the rolling mill at Rourkela and *(b)* the circumstances in which an order of Rs. 42 lakhs for the supply of ingot moulds and tops to the Bhilai Steel Plant was placed with a firm which quoted comparatively much higher rates and also did not possess the technical facilities for executing the orders. According to the report, the Indian Airlines Corporation incurred a loss of Rs. 16 lakhs on account of "unbusiness-like manner" in which the disposal of unwanted Heron aircraft was handled. The Committee expressed surprise that Air India engaged the services of an American architect at a free of 1.5 lakh dollars for making preliminary drawings for its multi-storeyed headquarters building in Bombay, even though competent Indian architects were available for the job.

On July 27, 1966, the Prime Minister had to bow to an overwhelming demand in the Rajya Sabha that Mr. S. Bhoothalingam,

Economic Secretary, Ministry of Finance, should not be posted to Brussels as India's Ambassador to European Common Market. The Public Accounts Committee, in its 50th report, had charged Mr. Bhoothalingam, then Secretary, Ministry of Steel, with a share of responsibility for "loss of exports or consequent loss of foreign exchange" in one of the cases of export promotion scheme. This shows how the Members of Parliament value the reports of the Committee. In its 55th report presented on 5th August, 1966, the Public Accounts Committee passed strictures against former Iron & Steel Minister, Mr. C. Subramanium, for revision of `black-listing order' in 1963. This is the first case of its kind in the history of the Committee when a Minister (Mr. C. Subramaniam) appeared in person before the Committee and the first case in the history of Lok Sabha when PAC report has bee admitted for discussion in the House.

From what has been said above, it is amply clear that Public Accounts Committee is doing an extremely useful work despite the fact that it has no power to compel any administrative action to be taken on its observations. In the opinion of Mr. A. K. Chanda, "...over a period of years the Committee has entirely fulfilled the expectation that it should develop into a powerful force in the control of public expenditure".

In the words of A. Prem Chand: "One important factor that helps the implementation of the recommendations is the support that the committee gets from the Ministry of Finance. In the U.K. it is said that "an opinion expressed with judicial mildness by the Committee" is enforced with the stronger language by the Treasury in communicating it to the department, and it is said that where the Committee has roared as mildly as a suckling dove, the Treasury roars like a Libyan lion. In India also the recommendations of the Committee receive the swift attention of the Finance Ministry and even if it does not roar like the rare lions of Gir, yet it makes its opinion felt on the transaction of business by the government through the issue of circulars and other necessary orders".

THE ESTIMATES COMMITTEE

Parliamentary control over public expenditure can be fully effective only when it is comprehensive in its scope and character. It is not sufficient to ensure that the expenditure has been made economically and prudently and within the grants and for the purposes approved: it is equally necessary to provide for a detailed examination of the estimates presented to the House to secure possible economy in the execution of plans and programmes. The Public Accounts Committee, as we have seen above, carries only a post-mortem examination of public accounts. It cannot, therefore, provide sufficient checks over the excess and misappropriations done by the Executive.

The Estimates Committee in the U.K.

The Estimates Committee in India has been modelled on the British pattern. Therefore, it may be useful to know something about the Estimates Committee in England. In that country the need of an Estimates Committee was first emphasized by a Select Committee of the House of Commons in 1903 to make an examination, not involving criticism of policy, into the details of national expenditure. However, the constitution of such a committee was delayed till 1912. The Committee consists of 20 to 30 members elected by the House of Commons each year. It is assisted in its work by a representative of the Treasury. It can call departmental officers. It was delegated the function of examining such of the estimates presented to the House as may seem fit to the committee and to report what, if any, economies should be effected therein. The Committee begins its work as soon as supply is voted by Parliament.

The Estimates Committee in England, it is felt, has not been very effective. It is supposed not to criticize the existing policy. It is required to examine to estimates within the frame-work of accepted policy. This limitation has hampered its effectiveness. Moreover, it is also not provided with the expert advice and assistance of an independent authority. However, in recent years its contribution has been more impressive.

The Estimates Committee in India

The Idea of an Estimates Committee in India was first mooted in 1938 when a resolution asking for the constitution of a Retrenchment Committee to secure a reduction in Government expenditure by 10 p.c. was moved. But during the British rule such a Committee was not created because the foreign government could not allow its policies to be criticised.

The Estimates Committee was created in our country after the inauguration of our Constitution in 1950 on the suggestion of Dr. John Mathai, the then Finance Minister, to scrutinise expenditure of each Department of the Government and of the Government as a whole.

Composition of the Estimate Committee

The Committee is elected every year from amongst the members of the House of the People (Lok Sabha), according to the principle of proportional representation by means of a single transferable vote. Its membership was initially fixed at 25 but was later increased to 30. Its chairman is appointed by the Speaker and if Deputy Speaker happens to be a member of the Committee, he automatically becomes the chairman. There is no convention that the chairman should be elected necessarily from the opposition party. The Committee is renewed every year but according to convention only one-third of its members retire every year and usually the same members are re-elected year after year.

Functions of the Estimates Committee

The functions of the Committee are:

1. To report what economies, improvements in organisation, efficiency or administrative reform, consistent with the policy underlying the estimates may be effected.

2. To examine whether the money is well-laid out within the limits of the policy implied in the estimates.

3. To suggest the forms in which the estimates shall be presented to Parliament.

4. To suggest alternative policies in order to bring about efficiency and economy in administration.

As far (1) above is concerned, the term 'policy' is rather a vague one, and as Lord Campion called it, "a very indefinite word." However, the term 'policy' was considerably amplified by the then Speaker of Lok Sabha, Mr. Mavlankar, who said that it "relates to policies laid down by Parliament either by means of Statutes or by specific resolutions passed by it from time to time. It shall be open to the Committee to examine any matter which may have been settled as a matter of policy by the Government in the discharge of its executive functions".

With regard to clause (2) above, it may be mentioned that our Estimates Committee by-passes the British Estimates Committee in its power to suggest alternate policies. The British Committee does not enjoy this power. Explaining this clause which added in mid-1953, it was stated that "the Committee shall not go against the policy approved by the Parliament, but where it is established on evidence that a particular policy is not leading to the expected or desired results or is leading to waste, it is the duty of the Committee to bring it to the notice of the Parliament. The fundamental objectives of the Committee are economy, efficiency in administration and ensuring that money is well laid out, but if on close examination it is revealed that large sums are going to waste because a certain policy is followed, the Committee may point out the defects and give reasons for a change in the policy for the consideration of Parliament."

As for (3) above that the "money is well laid out within the limits of the policy implied in the Estimates", the Committee literally "goes to the heart of the matter of economy and technical branches in the administration itself which do consider the proposals for economy and efficiency but the Estimates Committee's approach is from `sound common sense' and general understanding of the problems of economy and efficiency. It brings to bear upon these administrative problems a `people's approach' rather than a technical approach. On July 17, 1957, the Speaker of the Lok Sabha exhorted the Estimates Committee thus: "The whole country looks to the Estimates Committee to suggest ways and means of economising the expenditure.

As for (4) above, the Committee is mainly interested in seeing that proper classification of the 'charged' and 'voted' expenditure has been done in the Budget Estimates and in case it is not satisfied, it refers the matter to the Ministry of Finance or to the Minister of Finance.

Working of Committee. The procedure which the Committee has adopted for its work is that it selects the subjects concerning the estimates of the Ministry or Ministries to be examined during the year under review. It then proceeds to collect the necessary information through standard forms which it sends out to the Ministry or Ministries whose activities are to be reviewed. The form is as follows:

"(a) The organisation of the Ministry and its attached and subordinate offices.

(b) The functions of the Ministry and its attached and subordinate offices.

(c) Broad details on which the estimates are based.

(d) Actual expenditure incurred under each sub-head of the estimates during the preceding three years.

(e) Reasons for variations, if any, between the actuals of the past years and the current estimates.

(f) Volume of work in the Ministry covering the period of estimates and given for the purpose of comparison, corresponding figures for the past three years.

(g) Schemes or projects which the Ministry has under-taken. (The expenditure, period within which they are likely to be completed, yield if any, progress made to date, should be stated).

(h) Reports, if any, issued by the Ministry on its working.

(i) Any other information that the Committee may call for, or the Ministry may think it necessary or proper to give."

The information thus collected from the Ministry concerned is circulated amongst the members of the Committee. When the Committee meets, it may frame further questions to get such information as it may desire. The Committee usually divides itself into sub-committees and each sub-committee is assigned one part of scrutiny work. The Committee can summon officials of the Ministry or its officers to furnish such information as the Committee may ask for. Herein, it may be mentioned that the Committee must so conduct itself as to get the necessary information from the officials without offending them. As the Speaker of Lok Sabha once pointed out, "you must get information from them without offending them, just as a bee sucks honey from a flower without destroying it. It is rather a difficult matter".

Further, it may even undertake tours to examine the work of field establishments of the Ministry. The Committee then draws up a report and submits it to the House of the People. It is open, however, to any Member to refer to the report at the time of the general discussion on the budget, and when the estimates concerned are under consideration. As the Estimates Committee is a committee of Parliament drawing its authority from it, its recommendations are naturally given due consideration by the Government. If the Government feels unable to accept particular recommendation of the Committee, it makes a representation to the Committee to reconsider its recommendation. If the Committee re-affirms its earlier recommendation the final decision rests with the Parliament. The recommendations in the 'follow up' report are categorized in four parts:

1. Recommendations that have been accepted by Government.

2. Recommendations in respect of which replies of Government have not been accepted by the Committee

3. Recommendations in respect of which final replies of the Government are still awaited.

4. Recommendations which the Committee do not desire to pursue in view of Government's reply.

Utility of the Estimates Committee

The Estimates Committee has done useful work in spotlighting the various acts of omission and commission of the Government. In its various reports submitted from time to time the Committee has suggested valuable reforms, both administrative and financial besides acting as a 'Standing Economy Committee. Its second and ninth reports (First Lok Sabha) dealt with reorganisative of the Secretariat and Departments of the Government of India and Administration and Financial Reforms. The Committee made broad surveys on the problems of 'Budgetary Reform' and 'Growth of civil expenditure', etc. It made useful studies of the various aspects of Financial Administration such as "expenditure control, revenue collection, mint management, national savings organisation", etc. The Committee has also made important studies on the general problems of public sector undertakings, such as management, forms of public enterprise and budgeting in those fields. In its report on the International Trade Wing of the State Trading Corporation as presented to the Parliament on March 26, 1964, it rapped the Corporation for earning profits to the extent of 100 to 200 per cent on some of its commodities. The Estimates Committee fifty-second Report on 'Personnel Policies of Public Undertakings' (1963-64) based on the staffing pattern of 58 public sector corporations and government companies is a great commendable work of the Committee.

The control exercised by the Estimates Committee is not always direct. It is only by its influence, by the fear and awareness that such a body is there to examine certain aspects of governmental activities, that can make its presence felt and thereby make its control effective. Unlike its counterpart in U.K., the Estimates Committee is not organised on party lines and hence it can present a better picture of economy and efficiency in administration. The control exercised by the Committee, as the late Speaker of the Lok Sabha, Shri G. V. Mavlankar, pointed out, consists essentially in being *(a)* judicial in approach, *(b)* in representing the people's approach, *(c)* in preventing the executive from being apprehensive, *(d)* in creating a training ground for the Legislators, *(e)* in influencing the policies of the government, and *(f)* in acting as a link between the people and the government.

While proposing the constitution of an Estimates Committee, Dr. John Mathai, the then Finance Minister, had expressed the hope that it would exert healthy influence upon the course of public expenditure. He had further observed that its suggestions and criticisms would give very useful guidance to the Government in the matter of regulating expenditure. It is gratifying to note that his hopes have been realised and the Estimates Committees both in the House of the People and the State Assemblies have justified their existence by discharging their functions successfully. But it is an unhealthy trend that the Estimates Committees are laying more emphasis on a review of the policies of the Government and of the structure of departmental organisations to the relative exclusion of a detailed scrutiny of the estimates for which they are primarily meant. Mr. Ashok Chanda has levied the following criticism of the estimates committee:

(i) The Committee's emphasis on review of the policies of government and of the structure of the departmental organization has substantially altered the character and purpose of the committee.

(ii) Instead of a fact-finding body, it is converting itself into a fault-finding mechanism.

(iii) The Committee is arrogating to itself a role which constitutionally, belongs to the House of People.

(iv) With its floating membership it can hardly be sufficiently familiar with the details of administrative processes and problems to be able to suggest fruitful lines of administrative reform.

(v) The recommendations of the committee on matters of administrative reorganization, reconstitution of departments and redistribution of functions may have publicity value, but in most cases have hardly and practical utility.

These criticisms are not without force. Therefore, it is desirable that in order to prove more effective and useful as a mechanisms of parliamentary control they should be concerned with scrutiny with a view to suggesting possible economies within the estimates presented to the House rather than interfering with the functions of other authorities.

❐

5

Financial Control over Executives

ROLE OF THE MINISTRY OF FINANCE

The importance of the Ministry of Finance as an agency of financial control springs from two factors:

(1) It is charged with the responsibility of raising the resources for the over-all expenditure of the Government of India ; and

(2) It has to see to the desirability of the demands of other departments, taking into consideration the interest of the tax-payers. In this case, it acts as an outside Tribunal free from external and internal pressure. The control exercised by the Ministry of Finance over other spending departments finds ample justification in the remarks of Royal Commission on Civil Service : On the whole, experience seems to show that the tax payer cannot be left to the spending departments, that those interests require the careful consideration of each item of public expenditure in its relation to other items and to the available resources of the State, as well as the vigilant supervision of some authority not directly concerned in the expenditure itself and that such supervision can be most naturally and effectively exercised by the department which is raising the revenue required." The Ministery of Finance, working as an independent agency, acts as an "extended arm" of the Parliament and ensures that the wishes of the Parliament and fulfilled by the executive.

The control exercised by the Ministry of Finance, particularly by its Department of Expenditure, can be divided into three parts:

(a) Control exercised during the preparation of the budget ;

(b) control exercised during the execution of the budget; and

(c) control on Miscellaneous matters.

(a) Control Exercised during the Preparation of the Buget. During the preparation of the budget, it has to scrutinise all proposals emanting from the spending departments in so far as they have financial implications. This enables the Ministry to have a hand in the formulation of policies of other departments. Generally, the scrutiny exercised by the Ministry of Finance is "very broad in nature.....and is more concerned with the overall financial implications of the proposal and its impact on the expenditure." Thus every proposal or policy having financial implications has to be scrutinised by the Finance Ministry and the Cabinet attaches considerable weight to the opinion of the Ministry. After all the proposals have been received from the spending Ministries, it proceed to determine priorities of the schemes and suggests economies where possible taking into consideration the standing and continuing charges. Its main concern is to obtain "proper balance of expenditure between services, so that greater value could not be obtained for the total expenditure by reducing the money spent on one service and increasing expenditure on another". "To secure a uniform standard in the measurements of the financial sacrifice involved in the activites of all departments", says Prof. Hawtrey, "the general criteria adopted' in the selection of new proposals are:

1. Is the porposal a proper one, i.e., does it merit an expenditure from Public funds?

2. Has the ministry the authority to propose such an expenditure?

3. Are the costs of individual items excessive?

4. Are the financial arrangements proposed the most desirable and economical having regard to the circumstances, or are alternative arrangements possible?

5. Is there enough of justification to show that the expenditure is necessary or desirable? and

6. Have all parties substantially interested in it been consulted?

It is on the answers given to these questions that the Ministry of Finance formulates it opinion. The importance of its control lies in seeking justification for every proposal from the departments proposing it and what Lord Goschen once said about the English practice holds equally good as applied in the Indian context. He said : "The first object of the Treasury must be to throw the departments on their defence and to compel them to given strong reasons for any increased expenditure and to explain how they have come to demand it. This control alone helps to make the departments careful in what they put forward." Equipped with these answers, the Ministry of Finance proceeds to review the total estimates in the light of likely revenue for the year. At this stage, it can suggest reductions or as technically known 'cuts' if it finds the estimates too high or 'inflated'. It may also reject proposals which its scrutiny may reveal as technically 'unsound'.

(b) Control Exercised during the Execution of the Budget. After the budget has been passed by the Parliament, the responsibility for the control of expenditure from thereon lies on the administrative ministry and each Head of the department who is aided and advised by an Internal Financial Adviser—ag ain a representative of the Ministry of Finance—in the discharge of his responsibilities. During the execution of the budget, it is the responsibility of the Ministry of Finance to ensure that the amounts are spent properly and economically. It has also to see that the achievement is in accordance with the plans included in the budget of the other departments. Besides, there are certain matters which still require of other departments to keep themselves in touch with the Ministry of Finance. Prior consultation of the Ministry of Finanec is sought whenever any department wants to spend on schemes whose estimate execeeds a particular limit. This is technically known as 'expenditure sanction'. Similarly, prior approval of the Finance Ministery is essential before amounts can be transferred from one sub-head to another, technically known as 'reappropriation. Besides, the Ministry of Finance, through its accredited Financial Adviser, conducts financial reviews after every quarter in order to know the progress of expenditure. This enables the Ministry to get a review of the performance of other departments in monetary terms.

(c) Control on Miscellaneous Matters. The other matters, on which the Ministry of Finance exercises control, comprise various specified fields of expenditure such as grants-in-aid, write-off of losses, waiving of recoveries, contracts, inspection of establishment of other Ministries through Staff Inspection Unit etc.

Thus we find that the control exercised by the Ministry of Finance helps in promoting a financial order in the country. In almost all fields where risk is involved in spending huge amounts, the shadow of the Ministry of Finance is always present though it minimises the effect of financial delegation of powers already granted to several Ministries. Durrell has aptly stated : "It is the risk of Public loss where the amount involved is considerable that calls for the intervention of the Treasury, for it is important that under such circumstances the responsibility should be assured by an outside imperial tribunal."

Criticism of the Financial Control

The financial control as exercised by the Ministry of Finance has been a subject of great controversy. It is alleged that its control extends even to trivial matters, it is too detailed and born out of financial mentality. The policy of the Ministry is of saving "candle-ends" and that it betrarys an attitude of "cheese paring" and wood-pecking". Its motto, in the words of Dr. Appleby, is "acceptance of precedence and refusal of risks." The Minsitry, because of its irrevocable habit of imposing 'cut' or reductions in estimates, makes the other department to unusally 'inflate their estimates'.

No doubt, control by the Finance Ministry is a delicate affair "comparable only to tight-rope walking" but much is to be lost than gained by relaxing this control. John Mathai (formar Finance Minister) so observed: "I think the control that the Finance Ministry exercises even in cerain matters of detail has a deterrent effect which is not entirely to be disregarded.....On the whole I think more is to be lost than gained, if I issue instructions to the Finance Ministry to relax its present method of control." Of course, things have changed since John Mathai made this statement and the Ministry of Finance has already realxed of its much control in favour of other departments but the kernel of the problem still stands unsolved: 'How much of control?' It is very difficult to determine the degree of control as too much of it may prove a hindrance and too little of it may create financial disorder. Dr. Appleby rightly stated : "The first concern of finance administration is frugality. The enthusiasm of those charged with special functions have a high value; to dump them unduly is wasteful; not to discipline them is to open wide the door to extravagance and imbalance. True economy, consequently, results from the interaction of the drives of enthusiasm with the restraining disciplines of review."

PECULIAR FEATURES OF OUR ACCOUNT AND AUDIT SYSTEM

(i) Combination of Accounting and Auditing Functions. Though the office of the Comptroller and Auditor-General of India is organised on the British model, yet there is one substantial difference between the two. In England the Comtroller and Auditor-General is not concerned with the accounts but deals only with the Audit. But in India, audit and accounts have been organised under one and the same service called Indian Audit and Accounts Service and therefore, the personnel of this department and concerned with accounts as well as audit.

(ii) Centralisation of Audit and Accounts Services. Indian audit and accounts system has also a centralised feature which means that there are no separate Audit and Accounts Services for the Union Government and the State Governments as they are generally in a country with a federal constitution. In Indian federation there is one single agency in form of Auditor-General both for the Union Government and the State Governments. The Auditor-General as the Head of the Audit and Accounts administration exercises control over public finance not only of the Union Government but also of the State Governments. He is, however, assisted in his functions by Accountants General in the States. This system of centralisation has both its advantages and disadvantages. the uniformity of accounts throughout the country, consequential facility in auditing, fairness and purity in public accounts and the fact that the personnel of this Department belong to a central service and they, being under independent Auditor-General, enjoy sufficient freedom from the control of the Executive, are some of its advantages.

Duties and Powers of Auditor-General. The duties and powers of the Comptroller and Auditor-General of India are laid down in the Audit and Accounts Orders of 1936, as adopted by the India (Provisional Constitution) Order 1947. Article 149 of our Constitution provides that the Parliament shall lay down through an Act defining the duties and powers of the Comptroller and Auditor-General of India but it has not been done so far and, therefore, he derives his powers from the above-mentioned Orders.

Audit is a Central subject and is provided in the Union List. The Comptroller and Auditor-General has, therefore, statutory duties and powers over both the audit and accounting of all the financial transactions of the Union and the States. He performs the work of audit and accounts of local bodies also in regard to all States except Madras. U.P. and Punjab who have made thier own arrangements for the performance of this work.

ROLE OF THE FINANCE MINISTRY

In India the Ministry of Finance deals with financial business of the Union Government. It has 'overall responsibility' for preparing and framing of budget. The role of Finance Minister if highly important and he is often termed as 'steward of the nation's purpose'. The duty of the Finance Ministry headed by the Finance Minister is to ensure that the Finance of the nation is managed in the most efficient and prudent way.

The supremacy of the Finance Ministry is a matter of gradual evolution. This trend towards supremacy was resented 'in the beginning by other members of the Governor-General's Council on the gorund of departmental autonomy and prestige.' The position of the then Finance Department was strengthened by the gradual but continuous development of popular control over government and also of the parliamentary government. Finally in 1919 the 'Montford Reforms', laid down that Finance Department would exercise control over other Departments. It has been rightly observed that, "the constitution of the Public Accounts Committee of the Legislature and the appointment of the comptroller and Auditor-General to scrutinise and audit the accounts of the Departments went in direction of enhancing the power and prestige of the Finance Department."

Following two reasons may be given for such a superior status to the Finance Ministry. *(1)* The Finance Ministry is not itself a spending Ministry and thus can be expected to act as the disinterested guardian of the tax-payers interests. *(2)* This Ministry nas to find out ways and means to meet the proposed expenditure. To quote the words of the Haldane Comiittee."...if he (the Finance Minister) is to be held responsible for filling the reservoir and maintaining a certain depth of water in it, he must also be in a position to regulate the outflow."

The Finance Ministry's predominant position in comparison to other spending Ministries has come in for serious criticisms. Paul H. Appleby has summed up this sitaution in the following words.

"Under the present system 'schemes or projects of various kinds are presented to the Finance Ministry throughout the year, some for early clearance and apportionment of funds, some as a hostage to later budgets. These schemes are usually not much more than policy ideas, they are almost never actual administrative and expenditure projections ready for serious consideration as such. Their shortcomings are the primary occasion for most of the delay and conclusion now rather erroneously charged against the Finance Ministry'. As time for making the budget is approached, all of these schemes of file are examined, some are selected, and these, in addition to normal establishment expenditure, become the budget of a particular Ministry. All schemes remaining in the file have been approved in principle. Those not actually included in the budget remain in the file and may be activated in any subsequent year or at any time within a year.

"This whole system requires the agencies to submit many schemes they have little hope of being able to put into action. It establishes a pattern of poor cost estimates and poor budgeting which in turn are justifications for detailed financial intervention.

"There is another element in the picture that desierves much attention. The Ministries, knowing that Finance will reduce their requests, are given to loose and extravagant estimates of cost. They are given positive encouragement to do this. When a particular Ministry submits a tightly estimated project. Finance has complained : 'You put us in a difficult position by making it so hard for us to reduce your figures.' Actually a tight and sound estimate should be encouraged in every way possible; and endoursed by quick and unmodified approval. Conversely, the loose estimate should be over-penalised. The primary responsibility of Finance should be to encourage and to stimulate good budgeting in the agencise, and its whole review should be based on a sampling analysis which constitutes a search for poor budgeting if the sample reveals good budgeting, the request should be given maximum approval."

Suggestions from Administrative Reforms Commission

The regulations provide for the control of the Finance Ministry over other departments. Unless and until specially provided by the Ministry no department can issue any order, without the permission of the Finance Ministry. This has led to the concentration of bulk of powers in the hands of the Finance Ministry. This situation was brought to the surface by the Administrative Reforms Commission. It stated:

Ministry of Finance did not share this responsibility with any other Department of the government. It acted as a sole repository of financial wisdom. The result was delay in the execution of Projects and delays of funds.

However, a suggestion was made by A.R.C. in its Report on Finance Accounts and Audit (January, (1968) to solve this dilemma.

"The control of Finance Ministry over Public expenditure is exercised in the main at three stages: *(i)* approval of programme or policies in principle, *(ii)* acceptance of provision in the budget estimates, and *(iii)* prior sanction to incurring of expenditure subject to such powers as have been delegated to the administrative ministries. It is the control at the first and third stages that generally engages much of the time of the Finance Ministry and that impinges on the day-to-day working of the administrative ministries. A Control at these stages, if too rigid or detailed involving much time and effort can slow down the speed of work, delay the implementation of Projects—particularly development of commercial or industrial ones and thereby cause loss of national effort or income. While the need for control or scrutiny is not denied, it must be constructive, purposeful, imaginative and not narrow in outlook or cramping in effect".

Government of India took following steps as a follow-up action to the above recommendations of the Administrative Reforms Commission.

(i) Appointment of Financial Advisors in the different Ministries.

(ii) Scrutiny by the Finance Ministry not required for the sanctions amounting upto Rs. 50 Lacs. This change was brought in August, 1952.

(iii) Preparation of detailed Budget to negate the psot-budget limitations and checks.

(iv) Delegation of financial powers to the Ministry of Commerce and Industry, Ministry of Community Development and co-opeartion and Department of Food. This change was brought in September, 1961.

Finance Department in the Pre-Independence Days

It was under the Government of India Act of 1919 that the legislature in India was granted the power of voting of supplies. But this right excluded certain estimates like the defence Estimates which were treated as non-votable. The Finance Department was, therefore, to begin with an organ of executive control charged with the functions of wise house-keeping and economy in expenditure consistent with policy of the Government. As more powers came to be granted to the legislature, the finance department was made responsible for the imposition and regulation of taxation subject to legislative approval, the collection of revenue thorugh the Central Board of Revenue, the supervision and co-ordination of departmental budget estimates and the control of Public expenditure and of Public Debt. Currency and Banking. It may be noted that the legislature did not then possess the right to disapprove the executive policies by refusing the supplies. The Governor-Geneal had the legal power to certify the estimates.

Finance Department has been however, one of the most important departments of the Government concerned with the maintenance of financial stability of the country. For political reasons this department has been headed by a British official till 1946, who was chosen from the higher ranks of British Home Civil Service.

It has been pointed out by 'Shri Ashok Chanda' that 'Until 1947, the Finance department was organised in three wings *(i)* The ordinary Branch to control civil expenditure, *(ii)* The Military Finance Department to control defence expenditure and *(iii)* The Central Board of Revenue administering Income-tax, Customs and Central Excise departments. In addition there was a Financial Commission for Railways, as a part of the Railways Board, but jointly answerable to the Finance and Railway Members. The Financial Commissioner exercised the full powers of the Finance Department, had the right of direct access to the Finance Member, and would insist on a decision on a financial issue being suspended until he had obtained the directions of the Finance Member. He did not, however, form a part of the Finance Department, although he was personally responsible to the Finance Member for the economic administration of the railways.

Budget and Parliamentary Control of Finance

Budgetary Control. An important feature of the parliamentary form of government is the system of budgetary control exercised by the Finance or Treasury Department. This is made possible because—first, Parliament votes all the appropriations to the Head of the State and not to the administrative agencies individually as is done in U.S.A., and secondly, the Finance Department is the custodian of all public funds and exercises all controlling powers in matters of finance. Thus this Department is like a super-department exercising financial control over all the spending Ministries.

As soon as the annual budget is passed by the Legislature the Finance Ministry takes up the work of distributing grants to the spending agencies. For this purpose, there are Financial Codes and Rules which define the procedure and powers of each class of officers. For the purpose of money allocations, the Financial Codes provide for the appointment of 'Controlling Officers' and 'Disbursing Officers' in each Ministry and Department. Usually the Head of the Ministry, Department or Agency, is the Controlling Officer of that agency. The Finance Department allocate appropriation grants to them. These officers in turn allocate grants to the disbursing officers working under them. The basic unit of expenditure control is the sub-head (i.e., the sub-division of the minor head as we saw earlier). So the disbursing officer is allotted certain sub-heads of appropriations. He alone can withdraw money from the public accounts.

Now, the financial rules provide that no public servant can spend a paisa from the public funds unless he has satisfied himself that:

(a) the expenditure has been sanctioned by a general or special order of the authority competent to sanction such expenditure; and

(b) the expenditure to be incurred is within the limit of the appropriations granted by the Legislature for the current year.

Therefore, no expenditure can be incurred on public account unless it is provided for in the Budget and unless also it is authorised by a competent authority. But the authority also cannot go beyond the limits sanctioned by the legislature. There is, however, a practice to allow reappropriation from one minor head to another minor head. This only the controlling officer can do. The Finance department alone can allow reappropriations from one major head to another major head or to wholly a new head.

But the controlling officer's power of control does not cease with allocation of money grants. He exercises continuous control over expenditure. The disbursing officers are required to submit to controlling officers monthly detailed accounts of their expenditure under each sub-head. The controlling officers consolidate these accounts of the whole department under each sub-head for every month. This enables them to get an accurate and up-to-date picture of the financial position of their department as a while. They compare the expenditure of one office with another under the same sub-head and may thus exercise timely control over extravagance or carelessness. They also send a copy of these accounts to the Accountant-General's Office and the Finance Ministry.

Besides the internal control of the agency, the Finance Department sends to each Department, except the Defence and Railways Ministries, its own financial officers who exercise control over expenditure, through scrutiny and examination of the legality, accuracy and propriety of departmental expenditure. They also advise the departmental heads upon the financial implications of their schemes and plans and furnish to the Finance Ministry reports on the financial administration of the Ministry to which they are attached.

The Finance Department also controls the spending agencies by means of internal audit. Internal audit is an effective method of checking defalcations and embezzlements and other irregularities. External audit is, in this respect, not a very effective instrument because the Auditor-General conducts only test audits. But internal audit is thorough and continuous.

2. Parliamentary Control of Finance. The function of the Legislature does not end with the voting of grants for public expenditure. But it has also to see that the funds granted are spent faithfully and economically according to its directions. This system of legislative control over public finance first arose in England and it was more a growth than a creation. The first step that was taken in this direction during the reign of King John was towards the control of receipts and revenues rather than of expenditures. Expenditure was then considered to be a prerogative of the Crown. But the Stuart autocracy made the parliamentarians more exacting and they began to claim a share in the control of public expenditure as well. But this did not come about suddenly or according to any concerted plan or design but arose very gradually.

The various steps that were taken in this direction occurred in the following sequence:

(1) The first step was the designation by Parliament of the purpose for which moneys authorised to be raised by the Crown were to be spent.

(2) The second step was the separation of public funds from the Civil List which took place after the Restoration.

(3) The fourth step was the provision of means through which actual receipts and issues might be controlled.

(4) The next step was the establishment of the accounting and reporting system in 1787.

(5) The sixth step was the establishment of the audit system under the Exchequer and Audit Department Act of 1866.

(6) The third step was the provison that all revenues of the government should be covered in a Central Treasury and that no money should be drawn from it except on the authorisation of Parliament.

(7) The last step was the constitution of a Standing Committee of Public Accounts in the House of Commons in 1861.

Thus was built up the modern sytem of Audit and Report through which the legislature controls the finances of the State.

The Audit System. The term, audit, has been defined as "the process of ascertaining whether the administration has spent or is spending its funds in accordance with the terms of the legislative instrument which appropriated the money." It is, therefore, a means of enforcing accountability and is a part of the external control over administration maintained by the Legislature. Its main objective "is to fix the accountability of the officers of the Government, for any illegal, improper, or incorrect payments made resulting from any false, inaccurate, or misleading certifications made by them, as well as for any payment prohibited by law or which did not represent a legal obligation under the appropriation or fund involved."

Formerly, audit was conducted only in case of expenditures and that too only to ensure that money has been spent in accordance with the appropriation grants. But at present it is conducted for all financial transactions, whether for receipt or payment and extends beyond the formulae of expenditure to an examination of the "wisdom, faithfulness and economy" applied by the official. In the words of Dr. White, "To determine the validity of a disbursement, to take a single illustration, an auditor will need to have evidence of the authority of the disbursing officer, the appropriation on the basis of which the disbursement was made and the effect of any relevant statutory language in the Appropriation Act, the receipt of the money by the proper person, proof that the service for which payment was made was actually performed, proof that the charge was not excessive, and presence of the signatures of the disbursing officer, and such of his superiors as may be required. The auditor will also ascertain that funds were available in the proper appropriation head, that all the papers were in order, that the arithmetical computations were correct, and that the claim was not a duplicate." The function is such as to require a sound knowledge of law, rules and procedure, a technical knowledge of account and audit and a judicious mind to grasp situations and needs in general.

The man who is appointed as the Auditor-General is a person who is qualified to be a Judge of a Supreme Court and his salary and status as well as conditions of service also are the same as those of a Judge. The expenditure incurred upon his office is not subject to variation to his disadvantage and though appointed by the Executive, he is not removable by it.

The creation of such an office was the product of Gladstone's ingenious mind. It was he who established the mdoern system of Audit and Account when he was Chancellor of the Exchequer in the British Cabinet. He got the Exchequer and Audit Act passed through Parliament in 1866. This Act, *inter alia*, provided for the establishment of the office of the Comptroller and Auditor-General.

The chief functions of the Comptroller and Auditor-General are:

(1) Control over treasury and issues.

(2) Settlement and adjustment of claims against the government.

(3) Settlement and adjustment of claims due to the government.

(4) Serving as a general agency for the exercise of legislative control over financial administration.

(5) Control over the system of accounting and reporting and the rendering of general accounts to the Government.

Office of the Comptroller and Auditor-General of India. In India this office came into existence in 1919 when under the Montagu-Chelmsford Reforms Act, the Secretary of State for India appointed the first Auditor-General of India. He was made head of the Audit and Accounts Department. He was made responsible to the Secretary of State and held office during His Majesty's pleasure. Thus he was made independent of the Government of India whose accounts he had to audit. He was required to submit to the Secretary of State a report dealing with the total expenditure in India every year. The Government of India Act, 1935 further improved his status by giving him constitutional recognition and by requiring his appointment to be made by His Majesty. He was given the same status as Judges of the Federal Court. In the new Constitution of independent India, the position and satus of this officer have been further raised. He has been redesignated as the Comptroller and Auditor-General of India and, along with Judges of the Supreme Court, is an officer of the Constitution.

The Comptroller and Auditor-General of India is the head of the Indian Audit and Accounts Department. He is the most important officer under the Constitution, his duties being to be the guardian of the public funds and to see that not a farthing of it is spent without the authority of Parliament. In order that he may discharge these functions properly, his office should be independent of the Executive. The independence of this office has been secured by the following provisions of the Constitution (Art. 148):

(1) Though appointed by the President, he can be removed only on an address from both House of Parliament on grounds of *(a)* proved misbehaviour and *(b)* incapacity.

(2) He is disqualified for any further government office after retirement so that he may have no inducement to please the Executive.

(3) His salary and conditions of service are statutory and cannot be altered to his disadvantage during his term of office.

(4) The salaries and other administrative expenses of his office and staff are charged upon the Consolidated Fund of India and thus are non-votable. Thus his position is like that of a Judge of the Supreme Court.

Duties and Powers of the Auditor-General. Art. 149 empowers Parliament to lay down the duties and powers of the Auditor-General and further says that until that is done, the existing law will determine them. The existing law on the subject is the adaptation of the Government of India (Audit and Accounts) Order of 1939 which may be summarised as follows:

(1) The Auditor-General is responsible for the keeping of accounts of the Federation and of each State other than accounts of the Federation relating to defence and Railways.

(2) It is the duty of the Auditor-General to prepare and to submit to the President a general Financial Statement relating to the acounts of each year, showing balances and outstanding liabilities and such other information as may be required by the president.

(3) It is the duty of the Auditor-General to prepare each year accounts showing the annual receipts and disbursement for the Federation and the States and to submit the same to the respective Governments.

(4) It is the duty of the Auditor-General:

(a) To Audit and report on all expenditure from the revenues of the Federation and of the States and to ascertain whether moneys shown in the accounts as having been disbursed were legally available for, and applicable to, the purpose to which they had been applied and whether the expenditure conforms to the authority which governs it.

(b) To aduit and report all transactions of the Federation and of the States relating to debt deposits, sinking funds, advances, suspense accounts and remittance business.

(c) To give such information and assistance to the Federal Government or the Government of a State as may be required for the preparation of the Annual Financial Statements.

(d) To audit and report on all trading, manufacutring and profit and loss accounts etc., maintained by any Department of the Federation or of the State; the receipts of any Department, the accounts of stores and stock kept in any office or department.

Thus the Auditor-General is responsible for the accounts not only of the Union Government but also of the State Governments. He submits his report to the President, and Governors annually. These reports are laid before both the Houses of Parliament, and are examined by the Public Accounts Committee of the House of the People (Lok Sabha).

Thus the Auditor-General functions in India, as in Great Britain, as an agency of legislative control over public finance not only of the Union Government but also of the State Governments. This centralised feature of the Indian Audit and Accounts system has survived even after the adoption of the federal principle in our Constitution. Another feature of our financial system which distinguishes it from those of Great Britain and the U.S.A. is that Audit and Accounts have been organised under one and the same service called the Indian Audit and Accounts Department. The personnel of this Department belong to the Central Service category and being under an independent officer (i.e., Auditor-General) enjoy sufficient freedom from the Executive control.

This system has both its advantages and disadvantages. The main advantages are : uniformity of accounts throughout the country, facility in auditing the accounts and fairness and purity in public accounts, the department being outside the control of the Executive.

Legislative Committee on Public Accounts. The Auditor, although very useful in keeping a control over the financial transactions of the Government is after all an agent. His principal is the Legislature. Hence the Legislature must itself exercise this control through a Standing Committee on Public Accounts. This system was estalished in Great Britain by Gladstone, the then Chancellor of Exchequer as early as 1861. India too has adopted this system. During the British regime this Committee used to function under the Chairmanship of the Finance Member. But under the new regime this Committee is composed of members proportionately drawn from all the parties in the House of the People and its Chairman is a prominent private member of the house. The constitution and functions of the Committee are laid down in Rule 143 of the Rules of Procedure and Conduct of

Business in Parliament as amended by No. 30.C/51/130-4-51, Gazette of India, Extraordinary dated 4-5-51 which reads as follows :

Rule 143—Committee on Public Accounts. (1) There shall be a Committee on Public Accounts for the examination of the accounts showing appropriation of the sums granted by Parliament to meet the expenditure of the Government of India and such other accounts laid before Parliament as the Committee may think fit.

(2) The Committee on Public Accounts shall consist of not more than fifteen members who shall be elected by Parliament every year from amongst its members according to the principle of proportional representation by means of the single transferable vote.

(3) The term of office of the Committee shall be one year.

(4) In order to constitute a meeting of the Committee the quorum shall be four.

(5) Casual vacancies of the Committee shall be filled as soon as possible after they occur by election in the manner aforesaid and any person elected to fill such vacancy shall hold office for the period for which the person in whose place he is elected would, under the provisions of this rule, have held office.

(6) (a) The Chairman of the Committee shall be appointed by the Speaker from amongst the members of the Committee : Provided that if the Deputy Speaker is a member of the Committee he shall be appointed Chairman of the Committee.

(b) If the Chairman for any reason is unable to act, the Speaker may similarly appoint another Chairman in his place.

(c) In the case of equality of votes on any matter, the Chairman shall have a second or casting vote.

(d) If the Chairman is absent from any meeting, the Committee shall appoint any other member to act as Chairman of the meeting.

Since 1954 there has been change in the organisation of this committee. It is now a Joint Commitee of both the Houses. Fifteen members are elected by the House of the People and seven by the Council of States. Thus it now consists of 22 members.

Rule 143—Control of Committee on Public Accounts. (1) In scrutinising the appropriation accounts of the Government of India and the report of the Comptroller and Auditor-General thereon, it shall be the duty of the Committee on Public Accounts to satisfy itself:

(a) That the moneys shown in the accounts as having been disbursed were legally available, and applicable to the service or purpose to which they have been applied or charged.

(b) That every re-appropriation has been made in accordance with the provisions made in this behalf in the Appropriation Act, or udner rules framed by competent authority under the provisions of the said Act: Provided that the provision made in this Clause shall not apply to any accounts prior to the year 1950-51.

(c) That the expenditure conforms to the authority which governs it.

(2) It shall be a duty of the Committee on Public Accounts (a) to examine such trading, manufacturing and profit and loss accounts and balance sheets as the President may have required to be prepared and the Comptroller and the Auditor-General's reports thereon.

(b) To consider the report of the Comptroller and Auditor-General in cases where the President may have required him to conduct audit of any receipt or to examine the accounts of stores and stock.

These Rules are Self-explanatory. Suffice it to say that the Committee conducts a post mortem examination of the accounts, after their having been audited by the Auditor-General to detect frauds or irregularities, malpractices and misappropriations etc. There is a general feeling among the members of the Committee that by the time they examine the accounts, the issues become state and hence sufficient control cannot be exercised over expenditure. In order to overcome this difficulty it has been proposed that the Comptroller and Auditor-General may submit interim report to the Committee who will examine them and make recommendation to the Government in anticipation of the final and formal report.

In spite of this difficulty, the Committee has been serving a very useful purpose by detecting cases of misappropriation and suggesting economy. In its report for the post-partition period of the year, 1947-48 the Committee recommended that the Minsitry of Finance should frame rules and regulations to ensure that the spending Ministries exercise proper checks and show complete responsibility in the matter of budgeting and keeping control over expenditure. It pointed out certain irregularties also. In its reports for the year 1948-49 it pointed out an infructuous expenditure of Rs. 150 lakhs on the construction of the Barwadi-Sarnath Railway line in the coalfields of Bihar and West-Bengal. It also pointed out certain irregularities in the accounts of the High Commissioner of India in the United Kingdom and desired that instructions should be issued to him to deal with the audit objections expeditiously. It further recommended that the State-sponsored corporations should be regulated by Statute of Parliament and their finances subjected to audit by the Comptroller and Auditor-General and to scrutiny of the Public Accounts Committee. In its report submitted to the House of the People on August 14, 1953, the Committee suggested that a definite procedure should be laid down for writing off losses in order to safeguard the interest of the Public Exchequer and further recommended that the approval of the Cabinet might be prescribed for the writing off of losses beyond a certain limit, say rupees five lakhs.

Estimates Committee. As the Public Accounts Committee carries on only post-mortem examination of public accounts, it cannot provide sufficient checks over the excess and misappropriations and other malpractices done by the Executive.

Therefore, to check the occurrence of such malpractices the House of People adopted in 1950 the British practice of appointing a Standing Estimates Committee which is entrusted with the function of scrutinising new proposals for fresh expenditure, to sanction allotment out of the lump sum grants, and to suggest retrenchment and economy in expenditure. This Committee consists of not more than 30 members elected by the Lower House by the system of proportional representation. Its chairman is appointed by the Speaker from amongst its own members. But if the Deputy Speaker happens to be a member of the Committee, he *ipso facto* becomes the Chiarman. The Committee is renewed every year. But usually the same members are re-elected year after year. This givens them good experience in their work and thus makes the Committee more useful.

The functions of the Committee are:

(1) To report what economies, improvements in organisation, efficiency or administrative reform, consistent with the policy under lying the estimates may be effected.

(2) To examine whether the money is well-laid out within the limits of the policy implied in the estimates.

(3) To suggest alternative policies in order to bring about efficiency and economy in administration.

(4) To suggest the forms in which the estimates shall be presented to Parliament.

The Indian Estimates Committee has a much large scope of functions and responsibilities than its counterpart in the British Parliament.

The procedure which the Committee has adopted for its work is that the Committee selects the subjects concerning the estimates of the Ministry or Ministries to be examined during the year under reveiw. They ask the Ministry or Ministries concerned to furnish in a standard form, supplied by the Committee, necessary material in support of the estimates. The form is a follows:

"(a) The organisation of the Ministry and its attached and subordinate offices.

(b) The functions of the Ministry and its attached and subordinate offices.

(c) Volume of work in the Ministry covering the period of estimates and giving for the purpose of comparison, corresponding figures for the past three years.

(d) Broad details on which the estimates are based.

(e) Schemes or projects which the Ministry has undertaken. (The expenditure, period within which they are likely to be completed, yield if any, progress made to date, should be stated.)

(f) Actual expenditure incurred under each sub-head of the estimates during the preceding three years.

(g) Reasons for variations, if any, between the actuals of the past years and the current estimates.

(h) Reports, if any, issued by the Ministry on its working.

(i) Any other information that the Committee may call for, or the Ministry may think it necessary or proper to give."

The information thus secured from the Ministry concerned is circulated amongst the members of the Committee. When the Committee meets, it may frame further questions to get such information as it may desire. The Committee may divide itself into sub-committees and each sub-committee may be assigned one part of the scrutiny work. These sub-committees may undertake tours to examine the work of field establishments of the Ministry and send for further information from the Ministry or its offices. They may also summon officials of the Ministry or its officers to furnish such information as the Committee may ask for.

The Committee then draws up a report and submits it to the House of the People through its Chairman.

Since its incorporation, the Committee has so far submitted 43 reports on different Ministries. The order of submission is as follows:

1950-51	4
1951-52	1
1952-53	Nil
1953-54	6
1954-55	5
1955-56	17
1956-57	10

(upto December, 1956)

Thus the Committee has been rendering very useful service to the Indian democracy not only by checking misuse of public funds but also by putting a restraint upon the arbitrary power wielded by the all-powerful party in power and by bringing the tax-payer's point of view to the knowledge of the Civil Servants. While inaugurating this Committee on 18th April, 1950 Dr. V. Mavalankar, the then Speaker of the House of the People, had laid down four main objectives for these committees. They were :

"(1) To associate with and train as large a number of member as possible, not only in the ways in which the administration is carried out, but also to make them conversant with the various problems that Government have to meet from day to day.

(2) To exercise control on the Executive so that they do not become oppressive or arbitrary.

(3) To act as a liaison between the Government and the general public."

(4) To influence the policies of Government.

The working of these committees during these six or eight years has fully justified the hopes of the fathers of the Indian Parliament.

Parliament's Direct Control. Lastly Parliament directly exercises a control over public expenditure by examining the reports of the Committee on Public Accounts. A general discussion is held upon the Committee's and the Auditor-General's report and the Government has to reply to the charges made, if any.

Dr. Appleby's Criticism of the Indian Audit System. Dr. Paul H. Appleby, the American expert on Public Administration, severely criticised our audit system in his Second Report on the Indian Administration. Firstly, he says that the system "is in a large measure an inheritance from colonial rule. The function (of the Auditor-General) did not impede British rule; it upheld that rule and was an integral part of it. It greatly restricted the Indians who served the Government."

To this remark of Appleby, however, Mr. A.K. Chanda Auditor-General of India, replied very appropriately : "I do not know the historical basis for such an observation. I do not know of any colonial system which had, or has any analogous post, independent of the Executive with freedom to criticise administrative lapses. The conception of such a post runs counter to that of a colonial or autocratic system." "Any student of constitutional history," continuing he said, "would be aware that this post was an essential one in a democratic form of government as its functions were so defined as to secure public accountability of the administration."

Secondly, Appleby observes that the Parliament and the public in India give too much importance to the Auditor's report. The result is that in "so doing, Parliament increases the timidity of public servants at all levels, making them unwilling to take responsibility for decisions, forcing decisions to be made by a slow and cumbersome process of reference and conference in which everybody finally shares dimly in the making of every decision, not enough get done and what gets done is done too slowly." "The Comptroller and

Auditor-General's function is really a very important one. Auditors don't kwon, and can't be expected to know, very much about good administration : Their prestige is highest with others who don't know much about administration."

On this remark. Mr. Chanda commented as follows "Dr. Appleby seems allergic to audit which he describes as 'a highly pedestrian function with a narrow perspective and very limited usefulness.' This attitude of mind has obviously coloured his observations on the Indian Audit Organisation." Emphasising the importance of the Auditor-General's office, Mr. Chanda showed how the system was extending its scope in every democratic country. He said, "In the U.S.A., the Comptroller General's audit covered banking institution and other corporations in which the Government had any financial interest, even when it was not a majority. The U.S. Comptroller-General had also been given the power to issue surchanges against corporation and individual officers to effect recovery of expenditure which, in his opinion, was illegal." "The powers of the Comptroller and Auditor-General in U.K.," he said, "as defined in the Exchequer and the Audit Act, were not also different from the present powers of his counterpart in India, except that they were more comprehensively defined. The audit of the U.K. Comptroller and Auditor-General extended beyond the formulae of expenditure to an examination of its 'wisdom, faithfulness and economy'." "In the Continental democracies," Mr Chanda added, "there was a constituted court of accounts which a president who fulfilled analogous functions as the Comptroller and Auditor-General. It is only against this background that the validity or usefulness of Dr. Appleby's recommendations should be assessed.

Thirdly, Dr. Appleby maintained that the function of Auditor-General is stricIty negative and agrressive and hence does not suit the needs of a Welfare Administration. He, therefore recommended that "auditing in each enterprise must be done in a fashion as to fit the nature of its operations. This means that for this purpose auditing should be done at the direcion of the board of directiors according to principles and methods set forth from time to time by the board." He further recommended that "Auditing can be done in ways to satisfy both requirements in the case of industrial and commercial enterprises operated by the government or by private auditing firms."

But, according to Mr. Chanda, this suggestion "ignores the basic differences between the structure of public and private enterprises." "While, in the case of a private enterprise, those in control have a significant financial stake in the concern and are also vitally interested in its financial operations, there is no such incentive in the case of State undertakings. These are managed by officials without any direct financial interest..." There is a basic difference between the functions of the Auditor-General and a professional auditor. Mr. Chanda said, "A public auditor responsible for the audit of commercial enterprises is primarily concerned with the certification of the profit and loss account and the balance sheet. So long as any expenditure is concerned by a sanction of the appropriate authority and it does not contravene the provision of the Company Law, he is precluded from commenting on the properity of such sanctions or on the manner of exercise of discretion by the authorities concerned." "But the audit by the organisation of the Comptroller and Auditor-General," he said, "is much more comprehensive in its scope. Its functions are not merely to ensure that the appropriations made by Parliament have not been exceeded without a supplementary vote or that the expenditure conforms to rules, but also to be satisfied as to its 'wisdom, faithfulness and economy'." These words are comprehensive in their scope and have led to a broarder and newer approach, with greater attention to efficiency and to development of a discretionary audit directed towards discovering waste and matters beyond accounting, which though *intra vires*, are apparently unwise or extravagant." According to him, the Auditor-General's office is "one of the essential ingredients of a parliamentary democracy," whose rule is to "uphold the Constitution, and the laws in the field of financial adminstration." He has not only to disallow any expenditure which, in his opinion, either violates the Constitution or infringes the laws but also "to challenge any improper exercise of discretion and also comment on the propriety of the sanction and expenditure." "His role is to maintain the dignity, independence, detachement of outlook and fearlessness necessary for a fair, impartial and dispassionate assessment of the Executive in the financial field."

While Mr. Chanda is critical of any suggestion for the curtailment of any of the powers of the Auditor-General, he too feels the need of reorientation in our audit service so as to meet the requirements of the social ideology and objectives of the national government. "In the past, audit and administration," he says, "have functioned in watertight compartments. There has been little inclination to get together to understand each other's points of view and what is more important to clarify issues and take remedial measures. Objections are raised, technical in character, even in respect of schemes and projects which have been executed with competence and expedition.

The Issue of Decentralisation of Financial Control

The demand of decentralised control over finance had often been raised before the Government of India. The question of decentralising financial control was raised again in the context of 'a speedy and effective implementation of the Third Five Year Plan.' In 1961, another scheme of delegation was prepared and included in a paper on "Measures for strengthening of Administration" laid by the Prime Minister on the table of the Lok Sabha. It was mentioned in it : "Responsibility for financial management should be devolved in greater measure than before both on the Ministries and executive agencies. The scheme now approved includes: *(a)* formulation of programmes for intensive pre-budget scrutiny between the Ministry of Finance and administrative Ministry necessitating the preparation of budget estimates earlier than usual; *(b)* further liberalisation of financial powers to the Ministries in order to avoid references to Finance Ministry in the post-budget period except in vital matters; and *(c)* the exercise of control of important financial aspects by the Finance Ministry through adequate reporting system and test checks."

This scheme was introduced in September 1961, and under if the delegation of powers introudced in 1958 was further widened in important aspects. This was confined in the beginning to four administrative Ministries; *(1)* These were Ministry of Commerce and Industry *(2)* Ministry of Community Development *(3)* Panchayat Raj and Cooperation *(4)* Ministry of Information and Broadcasting; and also Department of Food in the Ministry of Food and Agriculture.' This scheme provided a ground for the exercise of control by the Ministry of Finance by way of pre-budget scrutiny and through random checks and work studies.

The Main Features of the Revised Scheme

According to the Adiminstrative Reforms Commission, the main features of the revised scheme are:

(1) A proper scrutiny of the schemes, etc., submitted by the administrative Ministries for incorportion in the budget should be carried out by the Ministry of Finance before including such proposals in the budget. It has, therefore, been decided that budget proposals should be prepared by Ministries in greater detail and with as much precision as possible and referred to Finance Ministry a few months earlier than usual, say from the beginning of July each year.

(2) Arrangements have been made with the Accountants General for the regular and timely supply of accounting data to the administrative Minstries to enable the latter to study the expenditures against the appropriations.

(3) This scheme of delegation of powers also provides that any amounts, without specified limits, may be sanctioned by the administrative Ministries if the projects for which such amounts are sanctioned have been earlier scruitnized and accepted by the Ministry of Finance. It may be that under the power delegated in 1958, the administrative Ministriers were authorised to sanction expenditure upto Rs. 50 lakhs only.

(4) Lump provision can be made for urgent schemes not yet ready in detail. But sanction against such provision can be issued only after the scheme had been accepted by the Ministry of Finance.

(5) The administrative Ministries have been delegated power to incur expenditure on all items irrespective of the fact whether these are new items or otherwise, so long as such new items form part of an approved project.

(6) The administrative Ministries have also been delegated full powers for reappropriation between the primary units. To facilitate the exercise of these powers, it has been provided that the primary units consisting of schemes be formed into groups and such groupings be got approved by the Ministry of Finance.

(7) Powers have been delegated to the administrative Ministries to sanction excess expenditure over the original estimates upto the limit of 10 per cent or Rs. one crore, whichever is less, in cases where the administrative Ministry is satisfied about the special circumstances justifying the excess.

(8) The administrative Ministries have been authorised to create posts upto a pay scale of Rs. 3000 p.m.

(9) It has been made an integral part of the scheme of 1962 that each Ministry should set up, internally, a competent work study unit which would assist the Ministry in laying down norms for particular types of work and would also examine such poposals for staff reorganisation or creation of posts (both in the Department and in offices under it) as are referred to it.

Later in October 1962 in wake to the emergency arising out of Chinese Aggression the scope of the delegation of financial powers was modified in certain important aspects, such as "*(a)* posts (other than those required for security and Plan purposes) could be created only with the concurrence of the Ministry of Home Affairs and the Ministry of Finance, and *(b)* proposals for new construction could be sanctioned only with the concurrence of the Ministry of Finance, even though covered by the existing budgetary allotments." This Scheme was reviewed, in 1965, and 'revived in March, 1966 with emphasis on some aspects but without much alteration in its essential features.' Under the March, 1966 scheme the Ministries were given full authority to spend within their budget provision however in consultation with the Internal Financial Advisers, but without the sanction of the Finance Ministry. In addition the administrative Ministries have been empowered to sanction expenditure 'on the various constituent schemes included in a project irrespective of the magnitude of the expenditure involved, provided that the project as a whole has been scrutinised and accepted by the Ministry of Finance.'

The order issued by the government, in very clear terms, reaffirm the duties and responsibilites of the administrative Ministries : "Within the limits of the budget provisons and subject to observance of financial principles, standards and procedure prescribed under the various rules and standing orders, the administrative Ministries are free to incur expenditure in the exercise of the powers delegated to them and no reference to the Finance Ministry is necessary. The Secretaries of the administrative Ministries can also overrule the advice given by their Internal Financial Adviser (including officials of the Finance Ministry where they are consulted in respect of the delegated powers). The Secretaries thus have complete discretion in sanctioning expenditure within the delegated field. It also follows from this that each secretary must assume full responsibility for decision taken in the exercise of delegated powers and for watching expenditure so that the budgetary provisions are in no case exceeded."

The Administrative Finance Commission, observed that, "the Secretary of the administrative Ministry is, under the latest scheme of delegation, fully competent to take a decision after obtaining the advice of the Financial Adviser in such case as he may deem necessary. Moreover, the procedure for consultation with the Financial Adviser has to be laid down by the Ministry itself in its own discretion. Thus, the Ministries are not under any obligation to consult their Internal Financial Adviser in all financial matters and it is open to them to prescribe the cases or types of cases in which they would consult the Financial Adviser. Further, it is not even obligatory for a Ministry to have an Internal Financial Adviser. In Ministries, where Internal Financial Advisers are not considered necessary, officers of the concerned Expenditure Division of the Finance Ministry will continue to be available for consultation and the Secretary of the administrative Ministry will have the power to overrule such officers of the Finance Ministry also in the delegated field." The most important feature of the present system of delegation is has been pointed out that 'the scrutiny by the Ministry of Finance is prmarily pre-budget. Once such pre-budget scrutiny is completed and the schemes projects are included in the budget, the administrative Ministries have large powers to incur expenditure, enter into contracts, and generally proceed with the execution.'

"The devolution of greater responsibility for financial management and of financial powers to the Ministries", according to the Administrative Reforms Commission, "would-involve the acceptance of certain obligations and restraints by the Ministeries. First, the Administrative Ministries would have to work in financial matters within the general standard/norms laid down by the Finance Ministry and secondly; the responsibility of expenditure for each department would squarely be on the shoulders of the Secretary of the administrative Ministry who is held accountable for all expenditure. The role and functions of the Financial Adviser, who will under the new shceme be 'internal' and not 'external' to the Ministry as before, assume great importanec."

Role of Financial Adviser

The Financial Advisers are of two distinct categories *viz: (1)* the External Financial Adviser (who is mainly responsible for exercising some of the powers of the Finance Ministry and advice on its behalf; and *(2)* the Internal Financial Adviser, (who is responsible to assist in the exercise of powers delegated to the administrative Ministry.)

Points of Difference

These the followings:

(1) The External Financial Adviser, is responsible to the Ministry of Finance, put while discharging various functions on behalf of the Ministry of Finance, he can also be asked to advise on the deleagted financial powers as well. In one way this implies a combination of the roles of 'External and Internal Financial Adviser.'

(2) An Internal Financial Adviser, is concerned with only 'the financial matters finally disposed of by the administrative Ministry but also with those which being outside the delegated powers necessitate a refrence to the Ministry of Finance.'

(3) The Internal Financial Adviser's advice may be overruled by the Ministry itself. At present there are some matters where an administative machinery may overrule the advice of the internal financial adviser.

In the opinion of Administrative Reforms Commission:

The role and functions of the Financial Adviser, who is now 'internal' and not 'external' to the administrative Ministry occupies a significant importance. "It should be obligatory, in our view, for each Department or Ministry to have a whole-time Internal Financial Adviser of adequate seniority and rank and it should not be left to the discretion of the individual Department or Ministry to decide whether it should have an Internal Financial Adviser. The Internal Financial Adviser should be placed incharge of Finance and Budget Cells of the Ministry and should be responsible for the financial management and control in all matters within the Ministry's field of responsibility and for maintaining requisite liaison with the Finance Ministry."

The Administrative Reforms Commission further stated that,"the Internal Financial Adviser should be reponsible to and under the administrative control of the Secretary of the Ministry. The Finance Ministry should, however, be required to concur in the appointment of this officer and should have overall and coordinating interest in the development of careers of Financial Advisers. The annual assessment of his work should be made by the Secretary of the Expenditure Department, who should obtain the views and comments of the Secretary of the administrative Ministry under whom the Financial Adviser may, for the time being be working. While it will be open to the Secretary of the administrative Ministry to overrule him without being required to report the fact to any other authority, the relationship between him and the administrative Secretary should, as envisaged by the Study Team on Financial Administration be that of senior partners in a common enterprise."

Thus under the present rules the adminstrative Ministry, has the discretion in respect of the delegated financial powers to lay down, the procedure for consultation with the Financial Adviser. "In view of the increased delegation to the administrative Ministries and of the dimensions of expenditure controlled by one Ministry, it is necessary that a set of model rules should be framed for the guidance of administrative Ministries in these matters."

❐

6

The Execution of Budget

Preparation of the budget involves, in India, the following operations which follow in the order given below:

(1) Preparation of the preliminary estimates by the disbursing officers (*i.e.*, heads of offices).

(2) Scrutiny and review of the revised estimates by the Accountant-General and the Administrative Department.

(3) Scrutiny and review of these revised estimates by the Finance Ministry.

(4) The scrutiny and review of these estimates by the Controlling Officers.

(5) The final consideration of the consolidated estimates by the Cabinet.

(1) Preparation by the Disbursing Officers. In the month of July or August, the Accountant-General sends prescribed forms for estimates of revenue and expenditure separately to the various departments which send them to their disbursing officers (*i.e.*, the heads of offices, for example, Deputy Commissioners in Districts). These disbursing officers prepare the estimates on the prescribed form. Each form contains columns for—*(i)* Actuals of the previous years; *(ii)* Sanctioned estimates for the current year. *(iii)* Revised estimates for the current year; *(iv)* Budget estimates for the next year. Separate columns are provided for the revised estimates of the Head of the Department and there is also a column for explanation for increase or decrease proposed in the estimates.

We give below a specimen copy of the estimate form:

Budget Estimate for the Year

Minor head and Sub-head of appropria-tion	Actuals for the last year	Budget estimates as sanction-ed for the current year	Revised estimates for the current year		Budget estimates for the next year		Explanation of increase or decrease
			Disbursing officers	Head of Deptt.	Disbursing officers	Head of the Deptt.	

These preliminary estimates are prepared by the heads of offices, *i.e.*, the disbursing officers. The task of filling in the columns of budget estimates is a very difficult one, as it requires a lot of judgment and experience. In India, it is all the more difficult due to two factors, namely, first, these estimates are prepared some eighteen months earlier, and secondly, in India the whole economy depends upon the monsoon and yet these estimates are prepared much before the advent of monsoons. Hence there sometimes remains much difference between the budget estimates and the actual amount spent or required to be spent. (That is one of the reasons for having Contingency Fund provided by the Constitution for the Union as well as State Governments). There are rules, provided for, which the heads of offices have to follow while preparing these estimates. In fact, the heads of offices have to give estimates not only of the next year but also of the current year as these estimates are submitted in August/September while the financial year goes upto 31st of March following.

These estimates are prepared by the Heads of Offices in three parts, namely Part I, Part IIA and Part IIB. Part I relates to revenue and to standing charges like permanent establishment, travelling allowances etc. Part IIA relates to such existing items as are liable to fluctuate materially from year to year and, therefore, require to be scrutinized by the government before going into the budget.

Part IIB relates entirely to new objects of expenditure for which previous sanction of the Finance Committee is to be taken or has been taken.

(2) Scrutiny by Heads of Departments. These forms go to the respective heads of departments or the Controlling Officer for scrutiny and review. This scrutiny is purely of an administrative type and not of a financial nature. There is a column provided for him in the form and he has to fill it in by either repeating his subordinates' estimates or modifying them by his own judgment. By the beginning of October, these forms go into the hands of the Budget Officers.

(3) Preliminary scrutiny of the estimates by the Accountant-General and General Administrative Department:

About the beginning of October, the estimates leave the desks of the Controlling Officers. Part I is submitted to the Accountant-General and the General Administration Department. If the Department wants to make any reduction in the estimates, that has to be communicated to the Accountant-General. If, however, it wants to increase the estimates that is to be submitted to the Budget Department and if that Department agrees, then the Accountant-General is to note the change.

The Heads of Departments prepare estimates of revenue and expenditure only. But besides revenue and expenditure, there are other estimates under debt, deposit and remittance heads. These are prepared by the Accountant-General's Office.

After completing his scrutiny the Accountant-General has to submit Part I to the Administrative Department. Then, if the Department wants to suggest any change, that is to be communicated to the Finance Department.

By the middle of November, these estimates go to the Budget Department of the Finance Ministry.

Part II Section A, is submitted to the Administrative Department alone by the beginning of October. The Department Scrutinizes it and summarizes its recommendations in a tabular statement which is to be submitted to the Finance Department in the beginning of November.

Scrutiny of Section B is more than a departmental affair. Heads of offices have to submit proposals for new expenditure as soon as the necessity arises. They have, however, to submit them to the department in a consolidated form. The Administrative Department consolidates all these items and submits them to the Finance Department for sanction. By December the Estimates Committee of Parliament considers these items and those which are approved are communicated to the Finance Department for incorporation in the Budget.

(4) Forecast of the Budget and its Consolidation. By December, thus, the preliminary stages of budget formulation is over. In the end of December the Budget Department prepares a budget forecast and consolidates all heads of expenditure and income in the form having following columns.

(a) Actuals for the major heads for the first 3 and 9 months and the last 4 or 3 months respectively and then totals of the preceding 5 years.

(b) Budget estimates for the rest of the current year for the major heads.

(c) Revised estimate for current year for major heads.

(d) Actuals for the major heads of the first 8 or 9 months of the current year.

(e) Budget estimates of the next year for major heads.

(f) The details of minor heads of:

(i) Actuals of the last 5 years.

(ii) Budget estimates of the current year.

(iii) Revised estimates of the current year.

(iv) Budget estimates of the next year.

In December, the first edition of the budget is ready. As another month comes to an end, further notes are prepared by the Accountant-General and on their basis he prepares the second edition of the Budget. The first edition is on the basis of eight-monthly figures while the second edition is on nine-monthly figures.

(5) Some time in January, the Finance Minister examines the budget estimates and in consultation with the Prime Minister prepares his financial policy with regard to taxation, etc. This, however, is kept a very close secret. After that has been done, the budget is submitted to the Cabinet for joint consideration.

When it has been finally approved by the Cabinet the budget is ready for submission to Parliament. The Budget Session of Parliament commences in the last week of February.

The Form and Content of the Budget. (1) The 'Annual Financial Statement' is composed of two parts:

(a) Budget speech of the Finance Minister, and

(b) Budget estimates.

The Statement includes Estimates of the coming year, the revised estimates for the current year (roughly on the basis of the accounts of the first ten months) and actual accounts for the past year.

In his budget speech the Finance Minister gives the following information:

(a) General economic condition of the country.

(b) Financial policy of his government.

(c) Explanation for the differences which occur between the budget estimates and the revised estimates of the current year.

Explanatory memoranda, which explain the reasons for variations from the current year's original estimates and for new demands and other data of the character of economic statistics are also attached to the budget estimates.

The budget speech of the Finance Minister is an event of very great importance in the annual activities of the nation and is very eagerly awaited by not only the business community but by all sections of the people, official as well as non-official. The budget speech lays down not only the financial policy of the country but the administrative programme also depends upon it.

(2) Budget Estimates. The Indian Constitution enjoins upon the President the presentation of the Budget Statement showing separate estimates for expenditures charged on the Consolidated Fund of India and for expenditures charged on "Public Accounts" of India. By Art. 112, the expenditure charged upon the Consolidated Fund of India comprises:

"(a) The emolument and allowances of the President and other expenditure relating to his office.

(b) Salaries and allowances of the Chairman and the Deputy Chairman of the Council of States and the Speaker and the Deputy Speaker of the House of the People.

(c) Debt charges for which the Government of India is liable, including interest, sinking fund charges and redemption charges and other expenditure relating to the raising of loans and the service and redemption of debt.

(d) (i) The salaries, allowances and pensions payable to, or in respect of, Judges of the Supreme Court.

(ii) The pensions payable to, or in respect of, Judges of the Federal Court.

(iii) The pensions payable to, or in respect of, Judges of any High Court which exercises jurisdiction in relation to any area included in the territory of India or which at any time before the commencement of this Constitution exercised jurisdiction in relation to any area included in a Province corresponding to a State specified in Part A of the First Schedule.

(e) Salary, allowances and pension payable to, or in respect of the Comptroller and Auditor-General of India.

(f) Any sums required to satisfy any judgment, decree or award of any Court or arbitral tribunal.

(g) Any other expenditure declared by this Constitution or by Parliament by Law to be so charged."

These items are non-votable. But all other expenditures which are paid from the Consolidated Fund are voted by the appropriate Legislature.

The Consolidated Fund of India is composed of all the revenues raised by the Government of India, subject, of course, to provisions regarding the Contingency Fund and the assignment of the whole or part of the net proceeds of certain taxes and duties to States, all loans raised by the Government of India loans or ways and means advances and all money received by the Government of India in repayment of loans.

All other moneys received by the Government of India are to be accredited to the Public Account of India. It includes money like receipts from commercial operations of the Government like the Post and Telegraph Department and from the exercise of the sovereign rights of the State like escheat. It also includes moneys received by or deposited with, public officers in their public capacity and by the Courts.

(3) Classification of Estimates. An important question with regard to the contents of the Budget is: Under which heads will the grants of Fund be prepared? They may be prepared either from the organisational point of view, or from the activities' point of view, or from the character of the grants' point of view or from the objects' point of view. So far as accounting and reporting are concerned, information regarding expenditure is to be given from all these points of view. But it is not possible to classify estimates from all these points of view in the Budget Statement to be placed before Parliament. Therefore, the estimates are prepared only from the stand-point of organisation units.

This system has a number of advantages:

(1) It places financial responsibility upon those who hold administrative responsibility, that is, upon heads of the divisions and sub-divisions rather than upon persons-in-charge of the different services carried on by the departmental unit.

(2) It makes the preparation of budget an easy affair. The local heads prepare the preliminary estimates which are first revised by the departmental heads and are then submitted to the Budget Department. The former will examine them from the broad administrative points of view while the latter from financial points of view.

(3) Then, by keeping accounts according to organisation units, it is possible to determine the efficiency with which the individual services are being run. Only when the heads of units know that their services are going to be considered on the basis of work for which they are individually responsible will there exist a real incentive to efficiency and economy.

Now, while organisation units will be the primary basis for classifying the estimates of expenditure, Parliament would also like to see how much funds are proposed to be spent upon what services.

(4) Supplementary Budget. In certain countries there is a practice of having Supplementary Budgets for the last six or four months of a current year. This practice causes more harm than good and hence must be discouraged. The only point that can be stated in its favour is that under Supplementary Budgets more facts are brought before Parliament and thereby it can exercise more control over public finances. But the defects in the system overweigh its advantages. The defects are:

(i) It produces a feeling of general insecurity in administration. No government can follow one uniform policy for a long period when it has to go to the legislature for grants of fund after every six months or so.

(ii) The government would feel less responsibility in calculating her need more accurately.

(iii) It will increase extravagance in administration,

(iv) It will increase the work of the government in preparing both budgets in a year.

But this system may be beneficially made use of in periods of emergency such as outbreak of war or economic depression. The Indian Government made use of this in 1947 after partition. But our government makes use of this system very sparingly. It is employed in certain States of U.S.A.

(5) Supplementary Grants. These are different from Supplementary Budget. In America they are called "deficiency bills". Article 115 of our Constitution authorises the President to cause to be laid before both Houses of Parliament another statement if the amount authorised by the Appropriation Act of the year is found to be insufficient for the purposes of that year or when a need had arisen during the current financial year for supplementary or additional expenditure upon some new service not contemplated in the annual Financial Statement of that year or if any money has been spent on any service during a financial year in excess of the amount granted for that service and for that year.

Thus if the Government contemplates to spend more in a service or the Government has already spent more from the

Contingency Fund, it may approach Parliament for supplementary grants. This power, however, must be exercised with restraint and with the sole object of public service and better economy.

(6) Extraordinary Budgets. These are generally used in order to finance war, war preparations or large capital programmes such as Railways. Usually the term 'extraordinary expenditure' is confined to new capital expenditure which is met from loans, and therefore the cost of amelioration is shifted to future years. Such is the practice in Continental countries like Germany, France and Belgium. In Great Britain and India, however, no such distinction is made between extraordinary budget and ordinary budget; and it practically means a supplementary budget whose need might have been felt due to the occurrence of an extraordinary happening, as occurred in 1947 after Independence and Partition of the country.

This practice of Extraordinary Budget is subject to the same objections which have already been pointed out with regard to Supplementary Budgets. Besides those, other objections are:

(1) It leads to the practice of charging regular expenditure to Extraordinary Budgets—a practice that does away with the main advantages of a single budget system. The Cour des Comtes of France pointed out this defect a number of times and France had abolished this practice in 1922. But the rule is not being strictly followed there.

(2) "It leads the general public to think that the Government can meet such expenditure by the proceeds of loans instead of from taxation."

(3) Another objection to Extraordinary Budgets is that "they open the way to subterfuge and offer temptation to abuse." The government is tempted to balance the budget by trick devices and thus give an erroneous idea of the country's state of financial affairs to the public.

Advantages of the Single Annual Budget System. The practice of a single annual budget has the following advantages:

(a) It will ensure unity of purpose and unity of action. Administrative policy itself very much depends upon the financial policy of the government. Therefore, the government should formulate both these policies at the same time and seek the approval of Parliament to both.

(b) It will create certainty and trust in the minds of the business communities particularly and of the public generally with regard to the government's financial policy.

(c) It ensures more responsibility on the part of the government which means more efficiency and economy in administration.

(d) It avoids the malpractices of window-dressing of the Budgets and thereby enabling the government to place before the legislature and the public the correct financial condition of the country.

PRINCIPLES AND IMPORTANCE OF BUDGET

In the past usually there was no system of preparing budgets. Whatsoever the treasury received was the property of the monarch who spent that in the manner he liked. The whole system was thus discretionary. But as the time passed and the public awakened and with that exerted itself it was stressed that there should be proper system of taxation and spending. There was a desire that wasteful expenditure should be avoided and there should be some minimum earmarked amount for each state activity. It was this desire of the masses which gave rise to regular budgeting system. Budget literally means leather bag, but today it means a statement of income and expenditure. It can be that of a family department, organisation state or nation. It can also be monthly, quarterly, half-yearly and yearly. A comprehensive budget reflects national sources of income and expenditure and also the surplus and deficit in the period under review. It has come to stay as effective tool of administration. For Taylor a budget is financial plan of the government for a definite period. For Wilne it is or comparative chart of revenue and expenditure.

Willoughby says that "it is or should be the document through which the chief executive....comes before the fund raising and fund granting authority and makes full report regarding the manner, in which, he and his subordinates, have administered affairs, during the last completed year...." Dimock says, "A budget is a financial plan summarising the financial experience of the past, stating a current plan and projecting it over a specified period of time in future." Prof. Munro has defined budget by saying that, "Budget is a plan of financing for the incoming fiscal year.

Principles of Budget. Of a good budget it is expected that it should receive wide publicity so that the masses are prepared to bear the taxes and at the same time they are also given an opportunity to express their view point. Not only this, but the budget should be very clear and quite understandable by the masses. It should not be confusing. It should be very detailed and comprehensive. It should give a complete picture of all the heads of income and expenditure. It should not leave any aspect untouched. The whole budget should be consolidated into one and the whole amount should be appropriated for a very specified period. It should be very convincing, scientific and rational. In addition to this, it should be accurate to the extent possible and should neither over nor underestimate either one or the other side of the problem.

It is also said that as far as possible a good budget should be balanced one. It is felt that such a system enables the country to remain within its resources. Then another principle is that a good budget must take into consideration both the recurring as well as non-recurring expenditures and a clear distinction must be maintained between the two. Then it is said that budgeting should be not gross but net. From gross budget we mean that all transactions should be shown in the budget and not merely resultant net position. As far as possible in good budgeting close estimates should be achieved and extreme variations should be avoided. In order to facilitate subsequent auditing and checking it is essential that form of the budget should be the same as that of the account. About a good budget it is also said that it must follow the rule of lapse. It implies that if the amount earmarked for a specified project is not spent in a specified period, it should lapse and not be automatically carried over to the next year. Lastly, it is said that though the budget should be divided into various heads and sub-heads, yet care should be taken to see that there is sufficient flexibility in the budget so that amounts can be appropriated from one head of account to the other without much difficulty.

Importance of the Budget

From the foregoing it is clear that the budgeting is a very complex and lengthy process. It is not easy to prepare a budget for a country. But today the importance of 'budgeting is not only being realised but appreciated as well. It is through budget that economic inequalities, which are the root cause of many of our present day social and economic problems, are removed. It is through a proper budgeting policy that the state can tax those who are in a position to pay and can benefit the poor and the down trodden. Through proper budgeting alone the state can mould the trade channel and create or check inflation in the country. Through budget the state can also help in promoting social welfare activities and reduce the disparities between the 'haves' and 'have nots'. Such serious problems as those of the employment and economic deficiencies can also be removed through budgeting alone. Such financial advantages as, *e.g.*, providing free medical facilities, education and similar other facilities and amenities can be provided through proper budgeting alone. In a word, it can be said that a good and sound budgeting system is most useful both socially, economically and politically. That precisely is the reason that it is said that budget is the instrument of social control in the country.

BUDGETARY SYSTEM

Budget is an annual feature in India. Since India is a federation, therefore, each state prepares its own budget. The central government prepares budget for the approval of the Parliament, which is presented to it on the last days of February each year.

Budget System in India. Budget in India is called 'Annual Financial Statement'. 'This financial statement is prepared separately for the railways and other than railways or that is called general budget. It is felt that income and expenditure of railways are subject to fluctuation and the combination of the two will result in the fluctuation of national budget. Moreover, in India, railways are being run on commercial basis, therefore, a separate budget gives an idea of the profit and loss which the railways incur.

Then another significant feature of the budget in India is that it is divided into two categories namely 'Non Voteable' and voteable budget, the former includes the salaries and allowances of such high dignitaries as the President of India, Chairman and Members of UPSC or Chief Justice of India and other Judges etc.

Passage of Budget in India. Heads of the offices in India are required to prepare preliminary estimates giving the development plans of their departments and the approximate income and expenditure under each head. In case the department is interested in including any new item, it will have to give a detailed explanatory note for the purpose. The budget proposals thus prepared are then scrutinised by the controlling officers and finally passed on to the Finance Ministry. The Finance Ministry is empowered to cut down any proposal forwarded by the department. The main idea of loading the Ministry of Finance with this responsibility is that it is not a spending ministry and secondly that being the overall incharge of all the proposals made by different departments it has a very comprehensive picture of the situation and financial limitations. In case a department feels that its proposals have unreasonably been turned down, the matter can be referred to the cabinet which is the final authority. All the budget estimates are prepared under three heads:

Part (i) indicates establishment charges,

Part (ii) deals with such items of expenditure in which there is considerable fluctuation and Part (iib) deals with such expenditure which is more or less of none fluctuating nature.

Part (iii) deals with new items of expenditure and on which sanction of the government is yet to be taken. It must however, be remembered that in India a budget is prepared only for the financial year. This financial year varies from country to country. In India it starts from 1st April and ends on 31st March of the succeeding year whereas in U.S.A. it starts from first July and ends on 30th June of the succeeding year.

Budget is divided into heads and sub-heads and also into major and minor heads. It also indicates the figures of the last year and also the amount required for the current financial year. Variations if any, are also supported by explanatory notes. The budget is also prepared on the basis of standing charges, continuing schemes and new schemes. Those items which are approved by the Ministry of Finance are incorporated in the budget. All the schemes of income and expenditure are consolidated into a statement by December of each year. It is at this stage that Accountant General comes in. He examines the whole budget technically.

Planning Commission and Budget. India has decided to have planned economy and as such the views of the Planning Commission are invariably ascertained before any item is included in the budget. All projects which have been cleared by the Planning Commission are included in the budget and get over-riding priority over non-approved items. The Commission, of course, approves a project after taking into consideration financial resources of the country.

Should Ministry of Finance Scrutinise Budget Proposals? Some of the critics have however, not appreciated the idea of scrutiny of budget proposals, as approved by the controlling officer, by the Ministry of Finance. According to them the Ministry of Finance is usually conservative and normally averse to all new schemes. It is also said that since the Ministry of Finance is not as much aware of the proposals and their importance, as are known to the departmental head, the ministry should not be given a right to sit on judgment over the decision of the controlling officers. It has also been said that usually the Ministry of Finance is over-burdened with work and it even cannot scrutinise all budget proposals submitted to it.

Pre-Budget Exercise. Before the budget is prepared and any item included in that each ministry is expected to give information about what its present allocation, actual expenditure incurred till October of the year, estimated expenditure for the existing projects, proposed expenditure on the new projects and whether during the last year there were any surrenders. Each ministry is also required to provide information about targets fixed and achieved during the last year.

Introduction of Budget in the Legislature. As already pointed out all the items of income and expenditure are properly classified under the heads:

(a) Names of the Scheme,

(b) Pay and allowances of the officers and staff required for the execution of the scheme and

(c) other details.

These are compiled into an annual financial statement. On the appointed day which is last working day of February in India, the Finance Minister will present his budget before the Parliament/ Legislature. In his budget speech the minister will review economic conditions of the country and also the financial policy of the government for the ensuing year. He will also explain the reasons, if any, about extraordinary variations on items of income or expenditure over those of last year budget and will indicate about the new schemes being introduced in the current financial year.

Presentation of Budget. It is constitutional obligation of the government to get the budget approved from the Parliament/ Legislature. The budget is divided into *(a)* Consolidated Fund of India and *(b)* Public Accounts. The items charged on the consolidated fund include salary and aliowances of President. Vice President, Comptroller and Auditor General, Chairman and Members of U.P.S.C. and Election Commission, Judges of Supreme Court and Auditor General. These are not to be discussed in the House. This is done with a view to not bringing their conduct before the House and securing their impartiality. All other items are to be discussed by the House and every member is give an opportunity to express his/her view point on the working of the department.

The budget in India can be broadly divided into three categories namely the standing charges, continuing schemes and new schemes. The expenses on standing charges are directly dealt by budget section of the Department of Economic Affairs. The proposed expenditure on two other heads is dealt with by the Department of Expenditure. About the new scheme Ministry of Finance usually wants to know as to why the expenditure should be incurred and how should that be met and what additional gains will the nation have by accepting the new scheme.

The System of Budgeting. Before we discuss further passage of the Bill it is essential to mention here that in India we have annual budget as against the system of supplementary budget. From annual budget we mean that the budget is prepared and passed for the whole financial year. Those who believe in the system of supplementary budgeting believe that the government can give better estimated budget and can have realistic approach because instead of seeing the things for full year, the events are seen only for the half year. But on the other hand, it is believed that such a system creates uncertainty in the minds of administrators who may take the budget lightly. Moreover, they do not attach much significance to budgeting which is quite a common process. The system will be comparatively costly and increase the work of the government as well. On the other hand, annual budget means unity of action and purpose and creates a sense of security and trust. It also helps in avoiding malpractices and makes the government more responsible. We however, in India, follow the system of demanding supplementary grants only when the budget provision in respect of a particular item, as provided in the general budget, has been exhausted and there is need and necessity of continuing the project. In some cases supplementary budgets are also presented. Such budgets are presented only when certain extraordinary situations have arisen *e.g.*, outbreak of war, famine, and fire etc. or when the government has to inçur expenditure on unexpected items or due to sudden rise or inflation.

Introduction Stage. As already said after making his budget speech the Minister for Finance introduces the budget. The budget is introduced first in the Lok Sabha which has wider financial powers than the Rajya Sabha. A separate budget is presented by the Railway Minister for the Railways; few days in advance of the general budget. There is then general discussion on the budget in which important members of each House are given an opportunity to give their reaction to the budget proposals.

Voting of Demands. After the discussions over Appropriation Bill indicating expenditure side is taken into consideration. It is at this stage that the members are provided opportunity to discuss the working of each department before passing the money for the ensuing year. A time is fixed for the discussion of each item and also for the department as a whole. The members are also authorised to make suggestions for the improvement of working of the department. They also propose cuts in the amounts proposed by the government for expenditure. The minister concerned is given an opportunity to reply to the points of criticism about his department raised by the members during the course of discussions. It is of course, for the minister to accept or not to accept proposed cuts. Usually 26 days are allotted for the discussion of the whole budget.

Then comes the other side of the Bill which proposes to levy taxes on the people. It proposes reduction of old taxes and also abolition of existing taxes for meeting the expenditure already voted by the House. All such taxation proposals are also embodied, in the form of a Bill called Finance Bill which when passed, the budget is supposed to have been passed by the House in which it originated *i.e.* the Lok Sabha in case of India. After the budget has been approved by the Lok Sabha, after passing through different stages it is sent to Rajya Sabha for approval. Rajya Sabha, as we know, is the Upper House of our Parliament and does not enjoy co-equal financial powers with the Lok Sabha. The Rajya Sabha is required to approve, reject or amend the budget within 14 days and if it fails to do so it will be presumed that "the Bill has been passed by that House. In case, however, if any amendments are made, the budget is sent back to the Lok Sabha, which, if it does not agree and passes the budget in the same manner in which it was originally passed by it, need not be sent to the Rajya Sabha but is sent direct to the President for his approval. After the budget has been passed by the Parliament it is sent to the President for his final approval and after he has signed the government is authorised to levy taxes and draw money. A reference may also be made about the 'Votes on Grant'. This is comparatively a recent device under which estimates are approved by the Parliament for a month or so to enable the government to carry on day-to-day administration, till such time as the general budget is approved.

Budget and the House. Budget time is rather very tiring one for the government. The members propose cut motions and taken cuts in order to get an opportunity to discuss the demands and also to embarrass the government. The members can also refuse grant of the demands presented by the government and in case such a motion rejecting the government proposal is carried out, the government is forced to resign and as such no budget proposal should be rejected by the House unless the government so desires.

Estimates Committee. Before we close our discussion of the budgetary process let us have few words about Estimates Committee. It is one of the parliamentary committees which is presided over by the Deputy Speaker and suggests measures for economy. The committee also suggests ways and means for promoting efficiency and administrative reforms consistent with the budgetary policy. It is to see whether the money made available was spent within the basic frame work approved. It can also make special reports on urgent matters, as and when necessary. The committee consists of 30 members belonging to all political parties in the Lok Sabha and some independent members. It was established in 1950. The members are elected on the basis of proportional representation, single transferable vote system.

Public Accounts Committee. It is an other committee of Parliament which is concerned with the budget. It has 15 members of Lok Sabha and 7 of the Rajya Sabha as its members. The committee is to see that the expenditure does not exceed the approved expenditure and money has been spent for the purpose for which it was approved. It is also to see that money has been spent by the competent authority. The committee also goes into the wisdom of expenditure incurred and makes suggestions about improvement.

Budget as Instrument of Social Control. No one can deny that in India budget has proved an instrument of social control. It is through budget that the government can bring about much needed and much cried economic equality and end economic inequality. In India, the government is trying to tax those at higher rates who have capacity to pay the taxes. Plan targets for achieving social control are set forth in the budget proposals by providing finances for executing plan projects. It is through budgets that more houses education, health and medical facilities have been provided to the poor.

EXECUTION OF THE BUDGET IN INDIA

Legislation of the Budget. The next step in the completion of the Budget as a control instrument of financial administration is its enactment or legalisation. This operation lies with the legislature mainly and is, therefore, part of the constitutional law of the country. As such, the parliamentary procedure as regards finances differ from country to country. But in spite of this diversity, it is quite possible to indicate the main features of the system.

The main steps in this procedure are:

(1) Initiation of Money Bills,

(2) Financial procedure in the legislature,

(3) Committee system,

(4) Re-appropriation, or power of virement, granted by the legislature,

(5) Power of the two Chambers, and

(6) Veto power and power of restoration of certain grants rejected by Parliament.

Initiation of Money Bills. The most fundamental principle of financial administration is the distinction between ordinary bill and money bill. The parliamentary procedure with regard to the former type of bill is called as general legislation, while with regard to the latter as Appropriation Acts. The distinction is of a fundamental type and can in no case be ignored. The former lays down certain work programme for the Government while the latter provides money for the carrying out of that programme.

Therefore, general legislation and appropriation acts differ from each other in their aims, objects and scope and hence they should be separately and differently dealt with by the legislature. It would be a wrong and harmful practice to join the act of appropriation with the act of authorisation, although from the practical point of view, it is quite possible for the legislature to lay down in the same bill the work programme and to grant money for its performance. Such a practice will suffer from the following dangers:

(a) It will make the financial system very rigid on the one hand; no discretion will be left with the Executives to allot funds to more needy services. On the other hand, there would be no scope left for economy and efficiency.

(b) Financial policies cannot be laid down for long time, as this system presumes.

(c) Such a system fails to take into consideration the changing needs of the government departments with the change in time. A department may need more money one year and less in another year.

Coming to the question of initiation of money bills, it is now a universal practice that the Chief Executive, as the general manager of administration, initiates all money bills. Even America, whose Constitution is based upon the theory of separation of powers, follows this practice.

An important question in this connection is whether the legislature can grant more money than asked for, or levy more taxes than proposed by the Chief Executive. On this point there are two systems—one, the British and other American or to be more accurate, one, the system of Parliamentary Government and the other, the system of Presidential Government. In Parliamentary Constitutions, it is a well-established principle that the legislature may refuse or reduce but may not originate or increase supplies or taxation. Bage hot well puts this principle in his book on English Constitution. He says, "On common subjects any member can propose anything but not on money—the ministers only can propose to tax the people." In India too, this principle came to be established with the advent of responsible government in the country. As early as 1921 the President of the Indian Council of States gave his ruling on this matter in these words: "I think it will be quite clear to the House members if they refer to Sec. 67A(2) of the Government of India Act, 1919 that the framers of the Act have therein given statutory expression to the English constitutional rule that demands for supply must proceed from the Crown. In other words, the Legislature can reduce, but it cannot increase expenditure." But the system in America is otherwise. There the Congress may decrease as well as increase expenditure and taxation. And this is in strict conformity with the constitutional principle of America, that is, the separation of powers. All legislative functions there, which include not only ordinary laws, but also money bills, are put in the charge of the Legislature.

The American system suffers from the following defects:

(a) The Chief Executive being the actual expending authority is the better judge of how much money is required for a particular purpose.

(b) To give the Executive more than what it needs is a wastage in administration rather than expansion in the service.

(c) It would be difficult to enforce responsibility upon the Executive for the money which it did not need.

(d) This system is not an integral part of the Presidential form of government while its counterpart is so, that is, of the Budgetary System which America has already adopted.

Financial Procedure. Different countries follow different procedures. Still we can deduce some common features of these systems.

(a) Financial procedure is simpler as a rule than that followed in general legislation.

(b) Sufficient time is to be given to the Lower House for consideration of each item.

(c) Items are to be closely reviewed by the Estimates Committee of the House.

(d) There is distinction made between grants of supplies and the Appropriation Acts.

In India the Budget is placed before both the Houses of Parliament on the opening of the Budget Session which usually falls in the third week of February. As the authority with regard to money bills lies mainly with the Lower House, it is, therefore, the House of the People which first proceeds with the bill. Unlike Great Britain, there is no introduction of the Budget. The Finance Minister only presents the Annual Financial Statement (*i.e.*, Budget) to the House of the People. The presentation of the Budget is followed by a general discussion of the Statement as a whole in both the Houses separately. It is to be noted that no item of expenditure is exempted from this general discussion. This discussion is to be only of a general character relating to policy and involving a review and criticism of the administration of the Department concerned, and a ventilation of the grievances of the people. The procedure is strictly in accordance with the British practice, that voting of supplies must be preceded by ventilation of grievances. About a week is allotted for this discussion.

Voting of Supplies. The next stage is the voting of supplies which is solely the business of the House of the People. Hence the practice wholly differs from that of Great Britain. There the House first goes into a Committee of Supply and then into that of Ways and Means and only afterwards the House, having heard the report of these Committees, votes the supplies.

That a sum not exceeding Rs.... be granted to the President (or the Governor) to defray the charge which will come in the course of payment during the year ending March 19.. in respect of.... (subject of the Demand *e.g.*, Home Department). In making the demands the minister reviews the good work done by his Department or Ministry and states the policy of the current year. The speech is political as well as financial.

In the House of the People, after the general discussion is over, the estimates are submitted in the form of demands for grants on the particular heads. The Rules of procedure are as follows:

"**R.130.** There shall be no discussion of the Budget on the day on which it is presented to Parliament.

R. 131. *(1)* A separate demand shall ordinarily be made in respect of the grant proposed for each Ministry, provided that the Finance Minister may include in one demand grants proposed for two or more Ministries or Departments or make a demand in respect of expenditure which cannot readily be classed under particular Ministries. *(2)* Each demand shall contain, first, a statement of the total grant proposed, and then a statement of the detailed estimate under each grant divided into items. *(3)* Subject to these rules, the Budget shall be presented to Parliament in such form as the Finance Minister may, after considering the suggestions, if any, of the Estimates Committee, settle.

R. 132. *(1)* On a day to be appointed by the Speaker subsequent to the day on which the Budget is presented and for such time as the Speaker may allot for the purpose, Parliament shall be at liberty to discus the Budget as a whole or any question of principle involved therein, but at this stage no motion shall be moved nor shall the budget be submitted to the vote of Parliament. *(2)* The Finance Minister shall have a right of reply at the end of the discussion. *(3)* The Speaker may, if he thinks fit, prescribe time limit for speeches.

R. 133. (1) The Speaker, in consultation with the Leader of the House, shall allot so many days as may be compatible with the public interest for the discussion and voting of demands for grants. (2) On the last day of the allotted days, at 5 o'clock, the Speaker shall forthwith put every question, necessary to dispose of, all outstanding matters in connection with the demands for grants. *(3)* Motions may be moved to reduce any grant. *(4)* No amendment to motions to increase any grant shall be permissible.

Estimates Committee. These Rules are self-explanatory. But it may be added here that at this stage much of the spade work is done by the Estimates Committee. This Committee was created after the inauguration of the Constitution in place of the old standing Finance Committee. The Deputy Speaker is the chairman of this Committee and it is composed wholly of private members of the House of the People. It functions as a continuing Economic Committee. It scrutinises the demands for estimates and recommends how far economy can be effected in the carrying out of policies approved by Parliament. Under the new Rules of Procedure framed in October 1956, the powers of the Committee have been increased. Under the old rules, the Committee was to report, "What, if any, economies consistent with the policy underlying the estimates may be effected therein." Under the new rules, the Committee will "report what economies, improvement in organisation, efficiency or administrative reform consistent with the policy underlying the estimates, may be effected, suggest alternative policies in order to bring about efficiency and economy in administration and examine whether the money is well laid out within the limits of the policy implied in the estimates." Further, in accordance with the practice of the House of Commons, the Committee may in future make a special report on any matter that comes to light in the course of its work even if it does not fall within its terms of reference.

The procedure which is usually followed by the Committee is to study thoroughly the affairs of a couple of Ministries every year, summon witnesses and call for documents and, on that basis, make recommendations to the Government for economy.

Appropriation Act. Voting of grants, however, does not empower the Government to withdraw money from the public fund because the Constitution [Art 110(1)(d)] lays down that no money shall be appropriated out of the Consolidated Fund "Except in accordance with law..." The Appropriation Act provides such a law.

Hence, the next stage in the enactment of the budget is the passage of the Appropriation Bill. This Bill includes all the grants for the year whether votable or non-votable. Although this Bill is in the nature of a formal legislation to authorize the Government to withdraw money from the Consolidated Fund, yet it offers scope to a general debate on matters of public importance and administrative policy and questions affecting economy accounts.

They are: *(i)* No amendments may be proposed which will have the effect of varying the amount or altering the destination of any grant, and *(ii)* no amendment shall be proposed varying the amount of any expenditure charged on the Consolidated Fund.

Finance Bill. So far as the enactment of the grant of fund is concerned, the work of legislation is complete. But the legislation of the Budget is, by no means, complete as no provision has so far been made for collecting the required money from the people. For this purpose, a Finance Bill is placed before the House. This bill embodies the taxation or revenue proposals for the financial year, that is, it includes all the existing taxation schemes with modifications or without modification.

This practice is quite in consonance with the well-known principle of democracy that "no tax shall be levied or collected except by authority of law," as embodied in Art. 265 of our Constitution. So, while the passage of the Appropriation Bill authorizes the Government to appropriate money from the Consolidated Fund, the passage of the Finance Bill authorizes it to collect taxes.

Powers of the Second Chamber. After the passage of the budget in the lower House, the Budget goes in the Upper House. The practice followed in the Upper House is in accordance with the principle that the direct representatives of the people will hold sole control over the finance of the government. So, in India, also the

Council of States has neither the power of amending nor rejecting the Budget. It can only make recommendations to the popular House and that too within a period of fourteen days. If the recommendations are not communicated to the Lower House within the specified period, the House shall not consider them. But if submitted in time, then the House will have to consider them and after consideration may reject them or include them in the Budget.

Veto of the Executive Head. When the Budget has been passed or is deemed to have been passed by Parliament, it goes for the assent of the Head of the State. Here the question arises whether the Head will have a right of veto over the money bills. Veto may be of two types—absolute and suspensive. In no modern democratic constitution is there a right of absolute veto given to the Head of the State. But in most constitutions, the Head is given a right to send the Bill back to the Lower House with his recommendations. For this he is given a period of five to ten days. In India, the President may return the bill for reconsideration within a period of 10 days of the date of its submission to him. If he neither returns it nor signs it within that date limit it automatically becomes law. But if he returns it to the Lower House with his recommendations the House has to consider the recommendations but is not bound to accept them. The President cannot withhold his assent in time.

But this is only in theory. So far as practice goes it is a well-established convention of parliamentary form of government that the nominal Head of the Executive takes no responsibility for the acts of the government and hence has no say in financial matters which is the sole concern of the Cabinet.

The Execution of the Budget. After the enactment of the Budget, the next step in financial administration is its execution. Execution of the Budget must be based upon two principles, namely:

(a) That it must conform to the terms of the Appropriation Act, and

(b) That its machinery must work with a very high degree of integrity and efficiency.

If it does not conform with these two principles, then the whole work of preparation and legislation will be negatived.

Execution of the Budget involves a number of operations which are:

(1) Collection. (2) Custody, (3) Disbursement, (4) Accounts (5) Audit and Report.

(1) Collection. Collection of revenue is the first step towards execution of the Budget. Collection involves two kinds of operations. First is the assessment of the revenue and second is its collection. Assessment means act of determining how much amount is to be collected from different individuals or bodies in accordance with the authority given by the Legislature, while collection is the act of actually collecting the amount as assessed.

The distinction between assessment and collection is of great importance from the administrative standpoint. They are not only two steps in the collection of Public Fund operation but they are different in character. Assessment requires a high sense of judgment and wide use of discretion, while collection needs a high degree of integrity and accuracy.

So the question is whether these two acts should lie in one and the same service or with different services. The advantages of the first system are:

(a) It will ensure greater control over collection of moneys due to the Government.

(b) It will facilitate the work of audit because when the same service has the duty of determining the amount due and of collecting it, it would become easy to check one of these operations against the other.

Disadvantages of the system are:

(a) It throws heavy burden upon the service. Both the operations are in themselves quite extensive and hence need different services.

(b) The two activities are different in nature and hence need different forms of organisation. One requires sufficient sense of judgment and hence needs the board system or organisation while the other needs full concentration of responsibility in one hand.

The main objections to having two independent services are:

(a) That such a system entails mere expense through the necessity of maintaining separate organisations, duplication of records and the interchange of communications between the two services; and

(b) That it may effect enforcement of responsibility as the two acts are complementary to each other and hence need the centering of responsibility in one person.

Perhaps the best method will be the concentration of both the functions in a single service but to so organise the service as to entrust the two operations to two subdivisions of the service. It is this system which is followed in India. There is, in the Centre as well as in the States, a Revenue Department. The Finance or the Revenue Minister is incharge of this department. Under the Minister there is a Board of Revenue which carries on the functions of assessment, supervision of collection and adjudication of revenue disputes.

In the Central Government the Revenue Department forms part of the Finance Ministry. This Department is headed by the Central Board of Revenue which comprises of:

(a) A chairman, who has the status of a Secretary to the Government, and

(b) Four members who have the status of Joint Secretaries to the Government. There are a number of Deputy Secretaries and Under Secretaries to assist the Board. There are three Directors of Inspection under the Board—two for income tax (one for inspection and the other for investigation) and the third for Customs and Union Excise.

This Division is divided into the following sections, each headed by a Superintendent:

(1) Income tax, Excess Profit Tax and Business Profits Tax.

(2) Customs (including land and air customs),

(3) Central Excise.

(4) Opium.

(5) Stamps.

The above comprise the Central Secretariat. Besides the Secretariat, the Department has a very large number of Field Establishments. Every Section has its own field stations with station officers and inspectors. For example, the Income Tax Section has an Income Tax Commissioner at every State capital who has under him Assistant Commissioners, one at each group of districts and Income Tax Officers, one for each group of districts and Income Tax Offices at district headquarters.

Collection of Revenue in States. In the State Governments, collection of revenue is vested in the Revenue Department. The Department is headed by a Secretary who is usually assisted by an Additional Secretary, or some Joint Secretaries and Assistant Secretaries. The Department is divided into sections, each dealing with a separate head of revenue, such as, land revenue, excise, sales tax, agricultural income tax, entertainment tax, forests etc. The major income of the State Government is from land revenue. Moreover, the question of land revenue is intimately connected with the overall question of the agrarian policy of the Government.

Actual collection of the revenue is made by the field staff of each section separately. The land revenue is collected in each district by the Collector with the assistance of Tehsildars and other subordinate staff. Similarly, for the collection of other taxes there are Tax Commissioners, Assistant Commissioners and other officers.

With regard to collection, the question arises whether there should be one service or different services for the purpose. An answer to this question will be better given if we first make the distinction between different classes of revenue. Revenues maybe of three classes:

(a) Tax, *e.g.*, Income Tax, Excise Tax.

(b) Revenue producing enterprise receipts, *e.g.*, postage, railway fare.

(c) Miscellaneous, *e.g.*, fines, fees, royalties etc.

So far as the last are concerned, they occur in connection with the current work of operating services and hence may best be collected by those services themselves.

With regard to the second class, we have already dealt with the question that revenue producing enterprises need financial and administrative autonomy and hence they must have full control over assessment and collection of their revenue.

With regard to taxes, it is in the interest of simplicity of organisation and efficiency and economy of work that there should be a single collection service.

2. Custody of Funds. After collection comes the question of custody of the Funds. This operation is to be organised on two main considerations, namely:

(a) To avoid all possibilities of embezzlement and misappropriation.

(b) To ensure convenience and promptness in money transactions.

The Financial Administration of any country, from the custody point of view, depends upon its history, its area, and the banking facilities. Before the development of the banking system, the Government used to keep their own Treasuries at different places and there used to be elaborate systems of its custody and accounts. But now in India need for the Government to keep Treasuries for the custody of its funds is fast disappearing. Banking facilities exist now in almost every town, big or small. Moreover, through the use of the banking system it is no longer necessary to carry on all the financial transactions through cash money as most of the work may now be done through cheques, drafts, hundies, and bank bills.

But in a country like India such a centralised system is not possible due to the vastness of its area and more due to the lack of proper banking facilities. That is why India still has about 300 district treasuries and 1200 sub-treasuries. But the Reserve Bank of India and where there is no branch or agency of the Reserve Bank, the State Bank of India, conducts the Treasury business of the Government. When a payment has to be made to Government, the payer pays in the money with a challan (in duplicate, one part serving as a receipt and the other for record signed by the Treasurer) to the Bank. When any one has to receive a payment from the Government, he presents a receipted bill or cheques issued in his favour by a competent officer in the Government treasury and obtains payment from the Bank.

In the U.S.A., it is only recently that State Banks have begun to come into existence. The Central Government still has no bank of its own. Therefore, most of the public receipts and payments are made through private banks. Formerly, it was left to the Heads of Departments to decide as to in which bank the public funds would be deposited. But this caused corruption and loss of public money. Hence, now statutory rules have been laid down and bank accounts are opened through tenders.

To the question as to which system is the better one there can be no single reply. Both the systems have their advantages as well as disadvantages. Treasury management includes not only the custody and safe keeping of public funds but also the depositing of substantial portion of money in Banks, safe investments of surplus money, the turning over of interest on public money to the public treasury, the disbursement of funds on the authority of the Comptroller and the maintenance of adequate cash reserves to meet daily requirements. And, therefore, the question whether public funds should be deposited in private banks must be solved on these considerations. This has a number of advantages:

(1) Public money will be safe.

(2) All the advantages of banking will be secured for public money.

(3) This will help in establishing the financial stability of the country.

(4) This will avoid all the dangers of corruption and malpractices which have been noticed in the U.S.A.

3. Disbursement of Funds. After collection and custody of public funds, there comes the question of their disbursement. After all, funds are collected not to be kept reserved, but they are meant to be spent. In fact the work of disbursement begins immediately after the passing of the Budget by the Legislature.

Different countries have different systems of disbursement.

Disbursement system in India is based upon the British system. The procedure is like this:

The work of communicating grants to the disbursing and controlling officers is taken up immediately after the enactment of the Budget. Expenditure against appropriation is watched by dividing grants into primary units of appropriations, for example, the pay of officers, establishment, contingencies etc. These appropriations are sometimes further divided for purposes of financial control. Before any expenditure can be incurred, both Budget provision and administrative sanctions are required, because in India, unlike the U.S.A., grants are made to the Government as a unit and not to the spending services individually. In engineering works, besides Budget provision and administrative sanction, technical sanction also has to be secured before money can be drawn.

Thus a heavy duty lies on the disbursing officer who withdraws the money from the treasury and disburses it. The function of the treasurer is only of a technical character, that is, he has only to see whether the challan or cheque is signed by a competent authority or not and further he has to keep a record of all receipts and payments. But the work of the disbursing officer is heavier. He has:

(a) to examine the claims from the point of view of the Budget provisions;

(b) to examine the claims from the point of view of administration and in case of engineering work also of technical sanction;

(c) to examine whether payment of claims is just;

(d) to keep accounts and rendition of reports showing these transactions.

Today money transactions are mostly carried on by means of cheques or bills. Hence the procedure of actual disbursement is no longer so complicated as it used to be in olden days.

4. Public Accounts. (1) The next step in the execution of Budget is that of accounting. Francis Oakey defines the term thus: "Accounting is the science of producing promptly and presenting clearly the facts relating to financial conditions and operations that are required as a basis of management." Accounting has a dual function to perform:

(a) First is the determination of the fidelity of all officers who handle the fund.

(b) Second is the furnishing of information needed regarding financial condition and operation for policy determining and administrative purposes. In the words of Dr. White, "The primary functions of a system of accounts are to make a financial record, to protect those handling funds, to reveal the financial condition of the organisation in all its branches or purposes at any time to facilitate necessary adjustments in rate of expenditure, to give information to those in responsible positions on the basis of which plans for future financial and operating programmes can rest, and to aid in the making of an audit."

(2) Types of Accounting System. In recent years both Government as well as private business enterprises have given considerable attention to the science of accounting. The result has been the growth of new systems of accounting, the most important being double-entry book-keeping, cost accounting, accrual and cash accounting system.

Double-entry Book-keeping. It is the system of accounting in which every item of expenditure is entered at two places. One entry remains with the operating service while another is sent to the Accounts Officer if there is a separate department of the Government or to the controlling officer of the same service. The advantage of this system is that every entry is controlled by a similar entry elsewhere and therefore,if an error is to be deliberately made, it will have to be made at two places which is a difficult task.

Cost Accounting. It is the determination of inclusive costs per unit. It may be applied in production, *e.g.*, the unit cost of commodity manufactured in a government factory,or even in service, *e.g.*, unit cost of holding examinations of different types. This system is mostly made use of in the Public Works Department because this Department had a reputation for extravagance in most countries.

The chief uses of this system are two-fold. Costs may be compared in a single institution or single operation over successive periods of time and the comparative costs of similar operations in different agencies or in different jurisdictions may be determined. Of course, variations in operating conditions from place to place will have to be taken into consideration.

Accrual Accounting System. It is that system of accounting by which the right to a receipt, or the obligation to make a payment, is established or as is technically called, accrues. Under this system appropriate entry is made in the account books of all actions having for their result an undertaking with the right to an asset or placing it under an obligation to pay.

Cash Accounting System. It is that system of accounting by which the right to a receipt, or the obligation to make a payment, is realised upon, or as the technical term goes, is liquidated. This system disregards all operations of the actual type and seeks to record only those operations in which an actual transfer of cash has taken place. It gives us no information regarding the accrual of assets and liabilities but gives data regarding liquidation alone.

Governments mostly make use of the cash accounting system because it is simple. Moreover, governments, unlike private business concerns, do not have to evaluate all their assets and liabilities every year. Their main aim of keeping accounts is merely to render correct information regarding the income and expenditure to the Legislature and the people and to make use of this information in formulating future policy of action.

The main advantage of the accrual system is that it gives detailed information regarding every transaction of the Government. For example, the tax assessed is a more accurate information regarding the assets of the government rather than actual cash collected by way of taxes and deposited in the Bank. More often the cash in the treasury of a government represents merely the government's working bank balance. And hence the cash accounting system "furnishes no information regarding the financial condition of the government than does a man's bank balance regarding how much he is worth."

(3) Forms of Government Accounts. There are different parties which are interested in the financial operations of a government. They are the public or the tax-payer, the legislature or the policy-determining body and the directing officers. The interest of the tax-payers is to enforce accountability upon the Government; of the Legislature, partly to enforce accountability and partly to seek information for formulating future policy, and of the officers, supervision and control.

Therefore, a government has to maintain accounts keeping in view these varying interests of the different parties. The main forms of government accounts are:

(a) Control Accounts.

(b) Proprietory Accounts.

(c) Supplementary Detailed Accounts.

Control Accounts. These accounts have for their main purpose the ensuring of fidelity on the part of officers having the duties of collection, custody, disbursement and the ensuring of rigid adherence to all directions and limitations to levy and collect income and make expenditure. With this end in view, every government maintains its Revenue Accounts, Appropriation Accounts, and Fund Accounts Revenue Accounts are accounts for each head of income; similarly Appropriation Accounts are accounts for each major and minor head of expenditure; and Fund Accounts are accounts of different funds which government maintains. The main kinds of Funds which governments usually maintain are:

(1) General Fund,

(2) Special Revenue and Expenditure Funds,

(3) Revolving Funds,

(4) Loan Funds,

(5) Sinking Fund,

(6) Endowment Funds,

(7) Public Trust Funds,

(8) Private Trust Funds,

(9) Suspension Funds.

Proprietory Accounts. The above forms of accounts are kept mainly from the point of view of the convenience of internal administration. They do not serve the purpose of the external interested parties, namely the legislature and the public. For this, Supplementary Accounts are maintained. These accounts are called "Proprietory Accounts".

Supplementary Detailed Accounts. Besides the above, detailed accounts, regarding the assets and liabilities, receipts and expenditure of the government received from different view points, may be maintained and published after one or two years for the information of the public.

5. The Accounting System of India. Accounting is an executive function and is usually vested in the spending agencies of the Government. But in India, accounting has been separated from the control of the Executive and is vested in the Audit and Accounts Department of India. This Department is headed by the Comptroller and Auditor General of India who is an independent officer of the Constitution. The Comptroller and Auditor-General discharges his audit and accounting functions wish the help of Accountants General. There is an Accountant-General for the Central Civil Departments, except for the Railway Ministry which has its own Accounting Officer, and one each in the State Governments. These Accountants-General are responsible for keeping all the Government accounts in their own spheres.

6. Maintenance of Accounts. There are four stages in the building up of accounts, namely:

(1) The initial entry in the treasury or the administrative office where the financial transaction originates.

(2) Classification of the transaction according to heads of account to which it relates.

(3) Monthly compilation of accounts by the Accounts Officers.

(4) Yearly compilation of accounts by the Auditor-General of India.

Functions and Powers of the Comptroller and Auditor-General of India

The power of accounting and audit is vested in the Indian Audit and Accounts Department which is headed by the Comptroller and Auditor-General of India. The office of the Comptroller and Auditor-General of India came into being in 1919, when the first Auditor-General of India was appointed by the Secretary of State under the Mountague—Chelmsford Reforms Act. We have borrowed this office from England where it was established under the designation of Comptroller General of Receipts and Issue of His Majesty's

Exchequer and Auditor-General of the public accounts, in 1834 and the incumbent of that office was charged with the duty of seeing that no money was issued from the Exchequer except in accordance with the Appropriation Act passed by the Legislature. The Auditor—General in India was then made responsible to the Secretary of State and held office during His Majesty's pleasure. He was thus made independent of the Government of India whose accounts he had to audit. The Government of India Act 1935 gave him a constitutional recognition. Our new Constitution also, under Article 141, makes provisions for such officer re-designated as the Comptroller and Auditor-General of India.

Comptroller and Auditor General of India. The Comptroller and Auditor General is the head of the Indian Audit-Accounts Department. He is the guardian of public finance and he is to see that not even a naya Paise of it is spent without the authority of the Parliament. In order that he may perform his functions properly, it is necessary that he should be independent of the Executive. He has accordingly been given a status equal to that of the Judge of Supreme Court.

He is appointed by the warrant under the hand of the President of India. He holds office for a period of six years without any age restrictions, draws the same pay as a judge of the Supreme Court and is entitled to a special rate of pension. Though appointed by the President, he can be removed by him on grounds of misbehaviour and incapacity only when an address is presented to him by each House of Parliament supported by a majority of not less than two thirds members of that House present and voting. His salary and emoluments have been made a charge on the Consolidated Fund of India and are non-votable, Further the conditions of service cannot be altered to his disadvantage during his term of office. To the same end, he has been made ineligible for any further office of profit under the Union or State Governments after retirement.

It may be mentioned here that an exception has, however, been made to the last condition in case of Mr. A.K. Chanda, former Comptroller and Auditor General of India by appointing him as chairman of the Third Finance Commission. The propriety of this appointment has been questioned on the floor of the Lok Sabha. It has been contended that the office of the chairman of the Finance Commission amounted to a Government appointment and miliated against the spirit of the Constitution which envisaged that high officials like the Supreme Court Judge and Auditor-General should be free from the allurements of the Executive after retirement. On the other hand the Government is of the view that the chairmanship of the Finance Commission is neither an office of profit nor a further office the holding of which has been prohibited by the Constitution, as it did not carry any salary except tour allowance nor was the incumbent of the office entitled to any free house or electricity. It was an independent office and the Finance Commission was not within the control of Government of India. There was, therefore, no question of his being lured by the offer and the Government had not infringed any discretion. No doubt, Mr. Chanda is one of the fittest persons to hold this position.

Peculiar Features of our Account and Audit System

(1) Combination of Accounting and Auditing Functions. Though the office of the Comptroller and Auditor-General of India is organised on the British model, yet there is one substantial difference between the two. In England the Comptroller and Auditor General is not concerned with the accounts but deals only with the Audit. But in India, audit and accounts have been organised under one and the same service called Indian Audit and Accounts Service and therefore, the personnel of this department are concerned with accounts as well as audit.

(2) Centralisation of Audit and Accounts Services. Indian audit and accounts system has also a centralised feature which means that there are no separate Audit and Accounts Services for the Union Government and the State Governments as they are generally in a country with a federal constitution. In Indian federation there is one single agency in form of Auditor-General both for the Union Government and the State Governments. The Auditor-General as the Head of the Audit and Accounts administration exercises control over public finance not only of the Union Government but also of the State Governments. He is, however, assisted in his functions by Accountants General in the States. This system of centralization has both its advantages and disadvantages. The uniformity of accounts throughout the country, consequential facility in auditing, fairness and purity in public accounts and the fact that the personnel of this Department belong to a central service and they, being under independent Auditor-General, enjoy sufficient freedom from the control of the Executive, are some of its advantages.

Duties and Powers of Auditor General. The duties and powers of the Comptroller and Auditor General of India are laid down in the Audit and Accounts Orders of 1936, as adopted by the India (Provisional Constitution) Order 1947. Article 149 of our Constitution provides that the Parliament shall lay down through an Act defining the duties and powers of the Comptroller and Auditor General of India but it has not been done so far and, therefore, he derives his powers from the above mentioned Orders.

Audit is a Central subject and is provided in the Union List. The Comptroller and Auditor-General has, therefore, statutory duties and powers over both the audit and accounting of all the financial transactions of the Union and the States. He performs the work of audit and accounts of local bodies also in regard to all States except Madras, U.P. and Punjab who have made their own arrangements for the performance of this work.

Accounting Functions

(1) Maintenance of Accounts. In his capacity as the head of the accounts administration, he with the help of his Accountant-General at the Centre and Accountants-General in the States keeps the accounts of the Government of India and those of the State Governments. No payment out of the Consolidated Fund can be made except in accordance with the grants made by the Parliament through the passing of an Appropriation Act. As the demands come from the various departments, he checks each of them against budgetary provisions. He orders payment only if he finds the demand covered by the grants. Without his authorisation no payment can be made. Likewise, the Accountants-General of the States keep accounts of their respective States and order payment when they are satisfied that an amount is covered by provision in the budget. Thus the Comptroller and Auditor-General is responsible for the keeping of accounts of the Central Government and of each State.

(2) Preparing Each Year's Accounts. He has also the duty of preparing each year's accounts showing the annual receipts and disbursements for the Federation and the States and to submit the same to the respective governments.

(3) Prescribing Methods and forms of Keeping Accounts. Further he is empowered to prescribe the form in which the accounts of the State are to be kept, which also includes the power to give any direction with regard to methods and principles in accordance with which any accounts are to be maintained.

(4) Submitting Annual Financial Statement to the President. His duty also extends to prepare and to submit to the President a general financial statement relating to the accounts of each year showing balances and outstanding liabilities and such other information as may be required by him.

Audit Functions. In his capacity as Auditor-General, the Comptroller and Auditor-General is responsible for auditing the accounts of Government of India and these of the States. He is to ascertain whether money as shown in the accounts as having been disbursed was legally available for and applicable to the purpose to which it had been applied and whether the expenditure confirmed to the conditions which governed it. It is also his duty to audit all transactions of the Federation and of the States relating to debts, deposits, remittance etc., all trading, manufacturing and profit and loss accounts etc., maintained by any department of the Federation or of the States. He is also to give such information and assistance to the Federal Government or the governments of States as may be required for the preparation of annual financial statements. Lastly, he is to prepare an annual report for each of the governments whose accounts are audited. The audit report contains the comments of Audit-authority on the correctness or otherwise of the expenditure and other financial transactions. The report particularly points out the more important financial irregularities like cases of budgetary grants being exceeded, failure to obtain the necessary sanction of expenditure, non-compliance with rules and regulations, cases of improper and wasteful expenditure and of misappropriation and embezzlement. He submits this report in the case of the Centre to the President and in the case of States, to the Governors who are required by the Constitution to cause them to be laid before their respective legislatures.

One point need be made clear. The Comptroller and Auditor-General does not exercise any powers under the title 'comptroller'. Unlike his counterpart in Great Britain, he does not control the issue from the treasuries. When the title of his office from 'Auditor-General' was changed to 'Comptroller and Auditor-General' a few years back, the object was to power him to control the issue of currency from the treasuries but since this has not been made possible due to certain unavoidable reasons, the title 'comptroller' stands just an appendage to his official designation.

❐

7

Union and State Budget

The word 'budget' is derived from a French word, Bougette, meaning a leather bag or wallet. The term was used for the first time in 1733 in a satire entitled 'Opened the Budget' pointed against Walpole's financial plan for that year. The Chancellor of the Exchequer used to carry a leather bag containing papers on the financial plans for the country to the House of Commons. So when he set off to place his financial plans before the House, he used to open his 'budget', that is, the bag, and it is because of this association of the financial plan with the 'bougette' that the financial statement of a country has come to be known as budget. The term budget, in modern times, therefore, denotes that document which contains estimates of revenue and expenditure of a country, usually for the fixed period of one year. Some of the definitions of the word 'budget' are the following:

(i) "A budget is a financial plan summarizing the financial experience of the past stating a current plan and projecting it over a specified period of time in future"—Dimock.

(ii) "A budget is a financial statement prepared in advance of the opening of a fiscal year, of the estimated revenues and proposed expenditures of the given organization for the ensuing fiscal year"—Harlod R. Bruce.

(iii) "Budget is a plan of financing for the incoming fiscal year. This involves an itemized estimate of all revenues on the one hand and all expenditures on the other"—Munro.

(iv) "Budget is a detail of estimated revenues and expenditures—a comparative chart of revenues and expenditures—and over and above this it is an authority and direction of the competent authority given for the collection of revenues and expenditure of public money"—Wilne.

(v) "Budget is a document containing a preliminary approved Plan of Public Revenue and Expenditure"—Rene Stown.

(vi) "The budget in a modern state is a forecast and an estimate of all public receipts and expenses and for certain expenses and receipts an authorisation to incur them and collect them"—Rene Gaze.

(vii) "Budget is a financial plan of government for a definite period"—Tayler.

From the above definitions of budget we conclude that the following are the elements of budget:

(i) It is a statement of expected revenue and proposed expenditure;

(ii) It requires some authority to sanction it;

(iii) It is for a limited period, generally it is annual;

(iv) It also sets forth the procedure and manner in which the collection of revenue and the administration of expenditures is to be executed.

The budget is the nucleus round which the financial activities of the state oscillate. It is both the scale and the limit of all the financial operations.

However, it may be noted that the meaning of budget is no longer confined to a mere statement of the estimated revenue and expenditure. It is now given a wider meaning.

With the gradual development of financial management, it has come to include not only a plan of public revenue and expenditure but also "the entire condition of material finances as disclosed in the ministerial statement placed before the legislature and the orderly administration of the financial affairs of the Government". It "not only gives an account of the year's 'house-keeping' and of the year to come, so far as the State is concerned, but it is the basis of control of the financial affairs of the State regarded as a house-hold.

According to Prof. Willoughby, "It is or should be, at once a report, an estimate and a proposal. It is, or should be a document through which the Chief Executive...comes before the fund-raising and fund-granting authority and makes full report regarding the manner in which he or his subordinates have administered affairs during the last completed year, in which he exhibits the present condition of the public treasury, and on the basis of such information, sets forth his programme of work for the year to come and the manner in which he proposes that such work shall be financed".

Thus, budget "is a proposed work programme, with estimates of the funds necessary to execute it". It is a plan of action.

Types of Budgets

The budgets can be classified on the basis of the following principles:

(i) The period covered.

(ii) Number of budgets introduced in the legislature.

(iii) The overall financial position depicted in the budget.

(iv) The principle adopted in taking the items of income and expenditure in the budget.

(v) The classification of the receipts and expenditure in the budget.

On the basis of these principles the budgets can be either:

(1) Annual or Long-term Budgets. Generally, the Government budgets are Annual, *i.e.*, they are prepared for one year. In India, England and most of the other commonwealth countries the financial year begins on 18th April and ends on the 31st March but in the

U.S.A., Australia, Sweden and Italy the dates are 1st July and 30th June. In France these dates are 1st January and 31st December. Some countries have adopted the policy of planned economy and to meet the needs of long-term planning, they have resorted to long-term budgeting, *i.e.* preparing the budget for three or more years. Such budgets are in fact long-term planning rather than long-term budgets because what is provided for is financial planning over a period of years to finance the plan. These countries spread the estimated plan expenditure over a number of years. The legislature approves the plan along with its estimated expenditure but that does not amount to actual voting of appropriations for the entire period.

(2) Single or Plural Budget. When the estimates of all the Government undertakings find place in one budget, it is known as single budget. The advantage of single budget is that it reveals the overall financial position of the Government, as a whole. But if there are separate department-wise budgets which are passed separately by the legislature, it is called plural budgeting. In India we have two budgets—one for the railways and the other for all the other remaining departments. The practice of having a separate railway budget started in 1921.

(3) Surplus, deficit or Balanced Budget. A budget is surplus if the estimated revenues are in excess of the estimated expenditure. But if the anticipated revenues fall short of the anticipated expenditure, it is a deficit budget. According to the economists, a deficit budget is a sign of the country's making progress. A balanced budget is one wherein the anticipated revenues equal the anticipated expenditure. The budgets are generally deficit budgets.

(4) Cash or Revenue Budget. A cash budget is one wherein the estimates of the various items of income and expenditure include the amounts actually to be received or spent in one year. In revenue budget the revenue and expenditure, accruing in one financial year, are budgeted in that financial year irrespective of the fact whether the revenues are realized or the expenditure is incurred in that financial year. In India, Britain and U.S.A., there is cash budgeting, in France and other continental countries there is revenue budgeting.

(5) Departmental or Performance Budget. The present practice is to have departmental budgets, *i.e.*, the revenues and expenditure of one department are grouped under it. It does not give any information as to the activity or performance for which money is budgeted. The performance budget is one where the total expenditure of a particular project is grouped under the head of the particular programme. It is prepared in terms of functions, programmes, activities and projects, for example, in the case of Education (a function), it will be divided into programmes like those of Primary, Secondary and Higher Education. Each programme will be divided into activities, for example, training of teachers is an activity. Project is the last unit of functional classification. It signifies such an activity as is of a capital nature, such as, construction of a school building.

Budget as a Tool of Administration

Budget today has become one of the primary tools of financial administration. It is "the master financial plan of the Government. It brings together estimates of anticipated revenues and proposed expenditures implying the schedule of activities to be undertaken and the means of financing these activities." Budget is the very core of democratic government and in the words of Harold Smith, "The objectives of the Budget should be to implement democracy and provide a tool which will be helpful in the efficient execution of the functions and services of government... The budget is a device for consolidating the various interests, objectives, desires, and needs of our citizens into a programme whereby they may jointly provide for their safety, convenience and comfort. It is the most important single current document relating to the social and economic affairs of the people". It lays emphasis on the need for state programmes to be executed as efficiently as possible so that maximum results are obtained for the money spent on them.

Budget as an instrument of Social and Economic Policy

Apart from budget being a "tool of administration" and the basis of an orderly finance, it has now become a very powerful instrument of social and economic policy. The modern states are welfare states and as such budget is used as a means for the promotion of welfare objectives. This aspect of the budget has assumed all the more importance with the adoption of socialistic pattern of society by our Government. Besides realising the plans for higher production in various sectors, the Government aims at correcting the inequalities in the distribution of wealth by higher taxation for the rich and proportionately lower taxation and sometimes even exemption for the poorer sections of community through the instrumentality of budget. In the days of laissez-faire, budget was a simple statement of estimated income and expenditure, but now in the modern social welfare states it has become an instrument of promoting the social and economic welfare of the people. The budget is awaited anxiously by the people. It has wide ramification. It plays a vital role in the economy of a state. Every citizen is interested in it. From the budget the citizens can know what benefits they are going to derive and how much tax they will have to pay. The taxation policy of the Government in the Budget may lead to narrowing down of the class distinctions and inequalities. The production policy as reflected in the Budget may help in removing poverty, unemployment and maldistribution of wealth. It can check inflation and enable the citizens to lead their life in safety and with comfort and happiness. To cut short, budget has tremendous social and economic implications in modern states.

Lloyd-George in his People's Budget of 1909 utilised for the first time the potentialities of the fiscal instrument for social welfare. In his Budget speech, he said: "Four specters haunt the poor: old age, accident, sickness and unemployment. We are going to exercise them. We are going to drive hunger from the hearth. We mean to banish the workhouse from the horizon of every man in the land". By taxing the rich on a progressive scale and utilising the proceeds in providing social amenities, such as better housing, educational and medical facilities, etc., for the poorer classes has come to be accepted as one of the most important objectives of budget.

Budgeting and Planning

Mr. Sachin Chaudhuri, while presenting the Budget proposals for 1966-67 to the Lok Sabha on February 28, 1966, said: "The

Budget of the Government of India is a major instrument for implementing our Plans and policies. It has to be framed, therefore, in response to current economic trends as well as the long-term requirements of the economy". Budgeting is, therefore, an instrument for short-term as well as long-term planning. "In restricted sense, budgeting is planning. The primary concern of both the agencies is to facilitate the formulation and selection of policies and programmes which are most likely to achieve the goals of government. But they differ from one another in some important respects. For instance, planning in terms of whole range of government policy requires a perspective of time and a broad perception of the inter-relationships between policies. On the other hand, budgeting is simply a matter of providing most economically for already agreed upon programmes.

The relation between planning and budgeting is very close. In the words of Thavaraj: "The marriage of 'planning' and 'budgeting' must begin at the 'grass roots' level in the respective departments and agencies." The programming, planning and budgeting staff in the various government agencies must work as a team to exercise continuing surveillance of the respective programmes. The programmes must be reviewed and evaluated at the Departmental level in relation to the objectives of the department, not only in terms of the needs of today or next fiscal year, but also in terms of the overall departmental goals at least for several years ahead. Programmes established many years ago must be re-evaluated in the light of conditions of today and the years ahead.

Budgetary Principles

Budget, as we have seen above, is an effective instrument of economic and social changes. It is the basis without which there can be no lasting social progress. It is desirable that it should conform to certain budgetary principles. The more important principles of budget-making are the following:

(1) Budget should be a Balanced One. Budget should be a balanced one, *i.e.*, the estimated expenditure should not exceed the revenue or income. When the amounts of the expenditure and revenue in a budget are equal or nearly so, it is called a 'Balanced Budget'. If the expenditure is less than the anticipated revenue it is a 'Surplus Budget' and if the expenditure is more than the anticipated revenue, it is called a 'Deficit Budget'. "The balancing of the Budget", says, Mr. P.K. Wattal, "is the first requisite of financial stability, and occupies the same place in the financial administration as the maintenance of law and order in the Executive administration. On the other hand, unbalanced budgets are bound sooner or later to weaken the faith of investors and lead to monetary inflation, which if uncontrolled will terminate in national disaster". An occasional deficit budget, however, need not cause worry. The newer trends of economic thought consider deficit budget in certain circumstances not only excusable, but also necessary. According to them a deficit budget can cure the ills from which the modern capitalist economy suffers. Deficit budget has now become a common phenomenon of the developing countries. It is resorted to meet the huge costs of development plans.

(2) Budget Formulation is the Responsibility of the Executive. As the Chief Executive is responsible for running the administration, he is in the best position to say what funds are required for it. It should, therefore, be the duty of the Chief Executive to formulate the Budget. But the Budget framing is a stupendous task and he must, therefore, be aided and advised by a body of specialists. In India, the Ministry of Finance, in England the Treasury and in U.S.A. the Bureau of the Budget, help their respective Chief Executives in the Budget-planning. In Parliamentary government there exists the well accepted principle "that no demands for grants can be made except on the recommendation of the Executive, The principle also makes it clear that it is the function of the Executive alone to prepare the budget. The Parliament can decrease or refuse the demands presented to it by the Executive but it cannot increase them. This principle is of great merit because the Chief Executive being the actual expending authority is the better judge of how much money is required for a particular purpose and if more is given to the Executive than what it needs, it cannot be made responsible for money it did not need. That would, obviously lead to wastage and extravagance. This last principle is not strictly followed in the U.S.A. as there is a separation of powers and all legislative functions including those of money bills are that of the Congress which is accordingly competent to decrease as well as increase expenditure and taxation.

(3) Estimates should be on a Cash Basis. The principle of the cash basis of the Budget means that it should be prepared on the basis of actual receipts and expenditure expected during the year and not on the basis of receipts which are to be realised in some other years or the expenditure which is ordered in that year but is likely to be incurred in the next financial year, *e.g.*, if certain sums on account of arrears of tax relating to the year 1971-72 are realised in the year 1972-73 they should be shown in the receipts estimates of the latter year and not of the former. Similarly, if the liability for any payments was incurred in the former year but was actually met in the latter year, it should be shown in the expenditure of the latter year only.

(4) Budgeting should be Done on the Basis of Gross and not net Income. Budget should present a clear-cut picture of the gross and not the net income of the country. Both the receipts and expenditure should be fully shown in the Budget and not merely the resultant net position. For example, if there is a department with an estimated expenditure of Rs. 45 lakhs and receipts of Rs. 35 lakhs it should show in the Budget both the expenditure and receipts and not merely Rs. 10 lakhs only. If the department prepares the estimates on the net basis, it would mean that it would approach the legislature for grant of Rs. 10 lakhs only and hence deprive the legislature of its control over the expenditure of Rs. 45 lakhs, which it met out of its receipts. Gross budgeting is, therefore, essential to ensure complete financial control of the Legislature.

There are exceptions to this general rule of gross-budgeting in India some of which are only apparent but some are real. The main exception to this rule is the estimating (and accounting) of land revenue collections. The lambardar from time immemorial, is paid, in lieu of his services for the collection of land revenue, five per cent on the revenue he collects. This is known as 'pachotra' which he

(iii) It will be more expensive and it shall involve unnecessary duplication of records, etc.

The best method will, therefore, be that both the functions should be concentrated in a single service, but there may be two sections in the organisation to deal with the two phases of the problem. In India this system is followed. There is in the Centre as well as in the States a Revenue Department under the charge of the Finance Minister.

(2) Custody of Funds. All revenue that is collected has to be placed in safe custody. This involves two main considerations, namely:

(i) There should be no possibility of embezzlement and misappropriation.

(ii) There should be ensured convenience and promptness of payment.

In former days huge stocks of Public money were maintained in the Treasury in specially constructed strong boxes. But with the development of the Banking system, how there is little need for the Government to keep treasury for the custody of its funds. Moreover, it is not necessary to carry on all the financial transactions through cash money as most of the work may now be done through cheques as payment by cheque minimises the chances of foul play and embezzlement. In most of the countries, therefore, the Central Bank carries all the money transactions on behalf of the Government as does the Bank of England in London. But in a country like India where the banking facilities are not sufficient, it is not possible to have such a centralised system for receiving money and for making payments on behalf of the Government. The Reserve Bank of India and where there is no branch or agency of the Reserve Bank, the State Bank of India, however, conduct the Treasury business of the Government of India.

(3) Disbursement of Funds. Disbursement is the process of withdrawal of money from the Treasury for payments of various liabilities. Every care should be taken in the work of disbursement against illegal and inaccurate withdrawals or payments. Particular control is, therefore, exercised by the Ministry of Finance over expenditure. The legislature makes the grants to the Government as a whole, technically to the President and not to individual departments. The Ministry of Finance designates the Head of each administrative department as a controlling officer in respect of the expenditure occurring in his department. These officers in turn allocate grants to the disbursing officers-heads of offices working under them. The work of communicating grants to the controlling and disbursing officers is taken up immediately after the enactment of the budget. Expenditure against appropriation is controlled by dividing grants into primary units of appropriation, for example, the pay of officers, establishments, contingencies, etc. These appropriations are sometimes further divided for purposes of financial control.

A great responsibility falls on the disbursing officer. He has to satisfy himself before withdrawing the money:

(i) that the expenditure has been sanctioned by a general or special order of the authority competent to sanction such expenditure;

(ii) that the expenditure to be incurred is within the limits of the appropriation granted by the legislature; and

(iii) that payment of the claims is just.

He has also to keep the accounts of the various transactions and to make a report about them to the Head of the department and to the Accountant-General. The treasurer, *i.e.* the officer in charge of the Treasury is also to be equally vigilant while making the payments. He has to see whether the warrants of payment the challan cr a cheque is signed by a competent authority or not and further he has to keep a record of all receipts and payments.

The power of control of expenditure of the Head of the department is not finished with allocation of money grants to the disbursing officers. He exercises continuous control over the expenditure in his department. The disbursing officers are required to submit monthly accounts to the controlling officer of their departments. The controlling officer gets these accounts classified and consolidated under the various sub-heads and can thus get an accurate and up-to-date picture of the financial position of his department as a whole. He also sends a copy of these accounts to the Accountant General's office and the Finance Ministry. The departmental accounts are reconciled with those of Accountant General on the basis of fortnightly accounts received by him from the treasuries.

It may be noted that the controlling officers are sometimes authorised by the Finance Department to allow re-appropriations from one minor head to another minor head. But the Finance Department can allow re-appropriation from one major head to another major head or to a wholly new head only with the approval of the legislature which has to be taken by way of Supplementary grants.

(4) Accounting. Accounting means keeping a systematic record of financial transactions. A good accounting system is indispensable for adequate budgetary control. It is only through systematic accounts supported by vouchers and receipts that the legality and honesty of the transactions as also the fidelity of the officers handling the funds can be determined. Secondly, it is through accounts only that it can be ascertained whether provisions of the budget as voted by the legislature have been properly implemented or not, *i.e.*, how much has been spent and for what purpose and whether within the budgetary limits or not. Thirdly accounts furnish the valuable information needed regarding financial conditions and operations for policy determining and programme making. Francis Oakey in his book titled 'Principles of Government—Accounting and Reporting', rightly defines the term accounting "as the science of producing promptly and presenting clearly the facts relating to financial conditions and operations that are required as a basis of management." In the words of Dr. L.D. White, "The primary functions of a system of accounts are to make a financial record, to protect those handling funds, to reveal the financial condition of the organisation in all its branches to facilitate necessary adjustments in rates of expenditure, to give information to those in responsible position on the basis of which plans for future financial and operating programmes can rest and to aid in the making of an audit."

(5) Audit. The last stage in the execution of the budget is audit. The term, audit, has been defined as "the process of ascertaining whether the administration has spent or is spending its funds in accordance with the terms of the legislative instrument which appropriated the money. It is a means of enforcing accountability. The Audit Department is headed by the Comptroller and Auditor-General. His functions are not merely to ensure that the appropriations made by Parliament have not been exceeded by the executive without a supplementary vote or that the expenditure conforms to rules but also to satisfy himself on behalf of Parliament as to its 'wisdom, faithfulness and economy. The Comptroller and Auditor-General acts as an agent of the Parliament. The Parliament itself, too, exercises control over expenditure through its three important financial committees—The Public Accounts Committee, the Estimates Committee, the Committee on Public Undertakings.

TYPES OF EXECUTIVE CONTROL

To keep the expenditure within the budgetary limits and prevent it from being improper, extravagant or wasteful, the executive has to apply various types of control. The more important of them are control to prevent over-expenditure, control to prevent illegal expenditure, control to prevent misappropriation, and embezzlement of funds, and control to prevent extravagant and wasteful expenditure.

There is no greater financial sin which the executive can commit than to allow the expenditure to exceed the budgetary provision. To prevent such excess is, therefore, the primary object of financial control. For this purpose control is exercised through the techniques of allotment, apportionment, and special regulation on certain special blocks of expenditure.

Allotment means the division of the funds voted by the legislature into various categories for different purposes. The estimates of expenditure as sanctioned by the legislature are divided into separate votes, heads, sub-heads, etc., in the budget. The first subdivision of the budget is into votes or grants. Usually the entire expenditure of a department is the subject-matter of a separate vote or grant. In India the vote or grant is further sub-divided into major heads, minor heads, sub-heads, and detailed sub-heads. We may illustrate these sub-divisions of the budget with reference to say, education, as follows:

Education vote or Grant

Major Head	–	Education
Minor-Head	–	Schools and Colleges
Sub-head	–	Allowances and Honoraria
Detailed Sub-head	–	Travelling allowance

These sub-divisions of the budget, except the last, are called units of appropriation, and control is exercised through them. The vote or grant is the highest unit of appropriation, and the subhead, the lowest. The note or grant must not be exceeded without fresh authorization by the legislature, and so the ultimate concern of the executive control is to keep expenditure within its limits but to provide an additional margin of safety and avoid the risk of the vote being unwittingly exceeded, executive control being with the lowest unit of appropriation, the sub-head. The controlling officers can transfer savings under one detailed sub-head to another within the same sub-head, but diversion of funds from one sub-head to another is not allowed except by formal reappropriation. Even within the same sub-head there is no complete freedom to divert funds and spend them. All new services, all increases in establishment and salaries, and all additional works require the sanction of the Finance Ministry.

The usual sub-heads of the grant in the Indian budgets are ten, namely:

1. Pay of officers.
2. Pay of Establishments.
3. Allowances and Honoraria
4. Works
5. Assignments and compensations
6. Charges payable to other Governments, Departments, etc.
7. Other charges
8. Grants-in-aid, contributions, etc.
9. Deduct charges recoverable from other Governments, Department, etc.
10. Suspense.

We have said that transfer of funds, from one sub-head to another requires reappropriation. Reappropriation requires formal sanction by competent authority, which may be the Finance Ministry or heads of departments to which the necessary power may have been delegated. The financial rules of the Government lay down the scope and limits of such delegation to the various officers. Reappropriation is thus an executive act and not legislative. It is permissible, only within the same vote or grant and is subject to the following restrictions:

(1) Reappropriation is not permissible to meet any expenditure which has not been sanctioned by the legislature or other competent authority.

(2) It is not permissible as between voted and charged items.

(3) It is not permissible as between different grants voted by the legislature.

(4) It is not permissible between the revenue and the capital parts of the budget.

(5) It is not permissible to meet any expenditure (other than contingent expenditure) which may involve outlay in a future financial year.

(6) It is not permissible to meet the expenditure on a new service not provided for in the budget.

Another technique of preventing excess over grants is the apportionment method. This consists in dividing total amount of the annual grant for the department or agency into four quarterly on 12 monthly parts, not necessarily equal, but corresponding to the expected rate of expenditure. Then the expenditure is watched quarter by quarter or month by month in the light of the apportionment fixed, and if it exceeds the apportionment in any quarter or month, a corresponding reduction is imposed in the following quarter or month. Thus a continuous pressure to prevent excess is maintained. A third technique to avoid excess is to require each department to set up a reserve of estimated savings under each head as a margin of safety and not to allow it to be spent except by special authorization of the Head of the department. Still another device is to impose an all round cut, say of 10 or 20 per cent on the sanctioned estimates of expenditure, and ask the spending agencies to keep within the remaining percentage of their grants.

Besides these checks on the routine expenditure, certain big blocks of expenditure are subject to special procedures of control. Examples of these are expenditure over personnel and salaries, contracts, purchase of supplies, etc. New posts cannot be created without the sanction of special authorities, and salaries are subject to the classification of posts and the scales prescribed. For contracts, a special procedure requiring inviting of competitive tenders, obtaining proper sanction and executing them in specified form is prescribed.

To prevent improper, wasteful, or extravagant expenditure the techniques used are, a system of sanctions for expenditure, enforcement of the rules of internal check, pre-audit, and observance of the canons of financial propriety. A hierarchical system of sanctioning authorities authorized to sanction varying kinds and amounts of expenditure exists in every well managed organization. It defines the financial competence of the officers of various ranks, *i.e.* lays down the limits within which they can incur expenditure. For expenditure beyond these limits, the sanction of the higher financial officer has to be taken. Before sanctioning an expenditure, the sanctioning officer must satisfy himself regarding its propriety, legality, reasonableness, etc. Sanctions are thus a check on improper expenditure. The rules of internal check are intended to prevent misappropriation and embezzlement of public funds. A few examples of these rules are that receiving of cash and accounting should be in the hands of separate persons, that cash collected shall be deposited in the treasury daily, that payments except the petty ones, shall be made by cheques, etc.

Pre-audit is a scrutiny of orders for goods or services by the accounting officers before they are placed and obligation in respect of them is incurred. The accountant or auditor examines the legality of the proposed expenditure and sees whether budget provision exists for it or not. If he is not satisfied on these points, he objects to the proposed expenditure, and it cannot then, be incurred. Thus pre-audit, if properly applied, effectively prevents illegal expenditure or expenditure in excess of budgetary provision. Pre-audit is an executive responsibility and would not be confused with post-audit which is conducted by the external audit authorities after the expenditure has been incurred.

Finally, every spending officer is expected to observe the canons of financial propriety in the expenditure of the public funds. The details of these canons are given later in connection with audit. Their substance is to require that in spending public funds, the officers should exercise the same care and economy as an ordinarily prudent person would in spending his own money, so that there may be no extravagant or wasteful expenditure.

Collection Custody and Disbursement of Funds

Annual and Permanent Taxes

Democratic theory requires that no tax should be imposed or collected except under the authority of law. For the effectiveness of legislative control over the executive, it is necessary that most of the taxes should be annually authorised. All the taxes are not, however, annual in their duration. In India, for example, several of the State taxes like the land revenue, excise, stamps, water rate, registration, etc., are governed by permanent Acts. Some of these, *e.g.*, irrigation rates, excise, registration rates, etc., in the states and protective tariff duties at the centre can also be varied by executive action. The bulk of the taxation at the centre and goodly part of it in the states has, however, to be annually voted by the legislature.

The tax proposals embodied in the Finance Bill take some time to be enacted. Meanwhile, to prevent speculation and loss to the exchequer, it is essential that the taxes like customs and excise duties should be collected at the proposed new rates from the very date of the introduction of the Finance Bill. This is done by giving effect to the new rates immediately under the provision of the Provisional Collection of Taxes Act, 1931 which empowers the Government of India to collect taxes and duties for a temporary period, in anticipation of the passing of the Finance bill.

Tax Administration and Collection

The administration and collection of Taxes is a duty of the executive and it involves at least five steps, *viz.*

(1) The creation of the machinery and determination of procedure of tax administration,

(2) Collection,

(3) Following up and realization of arrears.

(4) Assessment of the tax,

(5) Provision for hearing of objections and appeals.

As regards (1) the legislature often confines itself to authorizing a tax payable by certain classes of persons or in respect of certain things at certain rates, and leaves the whole problem of creating a suitable machinery and rules of procedure to the executive. The tax may require for its administration the creation of a new department with its complement of officials, or it may be entrusted to one of the existing agencies. In any case, the devising of suitable machinery procedure for the administration of a tax is a mighty problem requiring much experience and skill for its solution. Different taxes require different techniques of administration.

Assessment involves the preparation of a list of persons liable to pay the tax, and determining how much each has to pay according to the prescribed rate. Preparation of a list of assessees in advance is possible only in case of certain taxes like those on income, property, etc. when liability in respect of them is foreknown. In other cases, *e.g.*, of custom duties, a person bringing goods is assessed and asked to pay on the spot. The great problem of assessment is to prevent evasion. Through the ignorance or carelessness of the assessing authorities, a person liable to pay a tax may escape unnoticed, or there may be under-assessment as a result of the concealment by him of a part of his liability. Various kinds of steps are taken to prevent evasion, *e.g.*, employing a preventive staff, calling of information from employers and holding of investigations into concealed income as in case of income tax. Determination of the amount of assessment also is a complicated problem in case of some taxes like the income tax.

An assessee may not consider the assessment of his liability to a tax to be correctly or fairly made. In such a case, he is entitled to make objections within a prescribed period, usually before the assessing officer himself. If he is not satisfied with the decisions on his objections, he is usually entitled to appeal to some higher officer or tribunal. In the income tax department, *e.g.*, there are in each jurisdiction some assistant commissioners who deal with appeals.

After assessment comes collection, *i.e.*, realization of the amount due from the several assessces. The mode of collection varies according to the nature of the tax. In certain cases *e.g.*, of customs, payment has to be made on demand on the spot. In other, bills may be sent to the assessee and he may be asked to pay the amount in the nearest treasury. In certain cases again, *e.g.*, of income tax from salaried employees, deduction of the tax may be made at the source.

Finally, in some cases, *e.g.*, of land revenue, the agents or officials of the Government may approach the tax payer directly and demand payment from him, depositing their collections later in the treasury. Not all tax payers pay readily. There are always some defaulters who refuse payment, or whose payments are delayed and fall into arrears. A sound tax administration must follow up these arrears and make all possible effort to realize them. The methods of dealing with arrears vary from a penal increase in the amount due, to restraint and sale of the defaulter's movable goods, imprisoning him, or realizing the dues by a suit filed in a court of law. Arrears, which are absolutely irrecoverable, have to be written off.

The Custody and Disbursement of Public Funds

For receiving money on account of the Government dues, and for making payments, there are in India some 300 treasuries, one in each district. Under each district treasury, there are one or more sub-treasuries, one in each sub-division of the district. These treasuries are the units of fiscal system of the country, and the points at which public accounts start. Receipts and disbursements of moneys take place daily in these treasuries and sub-treasuries in respect of the financial transactions of both the Union Government and the Government of the State in which they are situated. Separate initial accounts of receipts and payments are kept for the Union and the State Government. The sub-treasuries render daily accounts to the head or the district treasury which after classifying them and its own accounts, forwards them to the Accountant-General fortnightly, with the supporting vouchers.

Normally, a treasury keeps the cash received by it, for payments which it has to make, but occasionally receipt may be less than what is needs for making payments or conversely, large amounts may accumulate which are not locally required. In such cases it may ask for funds which may be sent to it from other treasuries which have a surplus, or it itself may be required to send cash to other treasuries which may be in want. If such regional adjustments are not possible, the Reserve Bank of India has to come to the rescue of the treasuries.

The Reserve Bank of India was established under an Act of the Indian legislature in 1934. Among other things this Act provides that the Governments of India and of States shall deposit, free of interest, all their cash balances in the Reserve Bank. In return for this the Bank under an agreement with the Government, has undertaken to keep it supplied with the required amount of cash whenever it may be required. In case the balance of Government deposits with the Bank runs low, advances repayable within three months may be made. The Reserve Bank functions through its own branches and the agency of the State Bank of India. Where there is no branch or agency of the Reserve Bank, government may carry on their own transactions and hold such balances as they may require.

Today the position is that a great part of the Treasury balances is deposited with the Reserve Bank of India which uses the State Bank of India as its agent. The Sub-treasuries, however, still continue, because branches of Reserve and State Bank do not yet exist at sub-divisional headquarters, and to consolidate and supervise the work and accounts of Sub-treasuries, District treasuries also continue.

The Consolidated Fund of India

All revenues received for the Government of India from whatever source and all loans raised including moneys received, in repayment of loans are credited to a single fund known as the Consolidated Fund of India and all the legally authorized payments on behalf of the Government of India are made out of it. No payments from the Consolidated Fund can be made except under the authority of an appropriation law duly passed by the Parliament.

Similarly each of the State also has a Consolidated Fund of its own into which its receipts go and from wnich its payments are made.

The Contingency Fund of India

There is also a Contingency Fund of India. This Fund is in the nature of a permanent advance or imprest to the President who can make advances from it to the Government to meet unforeseen expenditure, pending its authorization by the Parliament. This fund was established by the Contingency Fund Act 1950 with an amount of 15 crores of rupees. The President is the operating authority in respect of it. Similar Contingency Funds at the disposal of the Governors have been created in the State also.

The Public Account of India

While the proceeds of revenue and loans are credited to the Consolidated Fund, all other public moneys received by or on behalf of Government of Ii dia are credited to the Public Account of India. The other public moneys consist of such items as deposits (*e.g.*, Savings Bank deposits, provident fund deposits, departmental and judicial deposits), and remittances, *e.g.*, from one treasury to another between England and India, etc. The receipts and payments involved in these items are only apparent. The deposits, for example, have to be paid back, and remittances sent by one agency are received by another.

Borrowing

Borrowing is the recognized method of financing large-scale capital expenditure on projects of improvement or development. It is not possible to raise the big amounts needed for these purposes by taxation without causing great hardship to the tax-payers, nor would it be fair to the present generation to lay on it the entire burden of the cost of works whose benefits will be enjoyed by successive generations for a long time. Since borrowing is one of the methods of raising funds for the needs of the states, it should be subject to the financial control of the legislature in the same way as levying of taxation. In Britain and the U.S.A. that is the case. In these countries, not only the raising of each loan, but its amount, purpose, term, etc., also are subject to authorization and approval of the legislature.

In India however, largely as a result of the legacy of the past, borrowing power is vested in the executive. The constitution says that the executive power of the Union extends to borrowing upon the security of the Consolidated Fund of India within such limits, if any, as may from time to time be fixed by Parliament by law, and to the giving of guarantees within such limits, if any, as may be fixed. The Union Government may make loans to the States or guarantee state loans within limits fixed by parliament. It may borrow within India or outside. The States also are empowered to borrow on the security of their Consolidated Funds and guarantee loans within limits laid down by the law of their own legislature. The States cannot, however, borrow outside India, and in cash they are indebted to the Government of India or have debts outstanding which have been guaranteed by the Government of India further borrowing by them is subjected to the consent of the Government of India.

Thus borrowing in India is largely an executive affair. So far Parliament has laid down no limits within which it should be done. It is not called upon to approve the purpose and terms of the loan. Of course, it controls the expenditure out of the loan moneys, but it has no control over raising of the loans as such. This is curious lacuna in our financial system. An ex-Accountant-General has suggested that the receipt portion of the Capital budget also should, by convention, be submitted to Parliament through the introduction and passage in it, of an Annual Development Loans Bills.

Government requires long-term as well as short-term borrowing—the latter to bridge the gap between the revenue receipts and expenditure, *e.g.*, in the earlier part of the financial year. Short-term borrowing by the Government of India takes two forms—Ways and Means Advances and Treasury Bills. Ways and Means advances are sought from the Reserve Bank of India and paid back to it with interest as soon as revenue begins to come in.

Budget Prepared in the Government of India

(1) Preparation of Preliminary Estimates by the Local Officers. The work of the preparation of the Budget starts in the months of July or August when the Ministry of Finance sends out to the various departments "skeleton forms" for preparing estimates of revenue and expenditure. The Heads of Departments send those forms to the disbursing officers, heads of the local offices, who prepare the preliminary estimates. The task of preparing the estimates is perhaps the most important one. In the words of Mr. P.K. Wattal, "It is not a simple arithmetical exercise in striking out averages of previous years and putting in a safe figure which would not look exactly like repetition of the last year's performance. Behind figures lie the insistent realities of administration. The circumstances of no one year are exactly similar to those of the previous year and yet they are not quite dissimilar. One has therefore, to use one's judgment in estimating the similarities and dissimilarities and making due allowance for each. Every care should, therefore, be taken in the preparation of the estimates. While preparing the estimates the local officers are to fill in four columns of the prescribed form;

(i) Actuals of the previous year,

(ii) Sanctioned estimates for the current year,

(iii) Revised estimates for the current year and

(iv) Budget estimates for the next year.

According to Mr. Ashok Chanda, "The preparation of the estimates on new projects at the time of their inclusion in the Budget proves in most cases to be difficult. The estimates given have often to be based on mere expectations and no nothing more concrete and positive. Nevertheless, unless a figure is communicated to the Finance Ministry for inclusion in the budget estimates the scheme cannot be taken in hands when it matures.

(2) Scrutiny of the Estimates by Heads of Departments. The departmental officials complete their work connected with the preparation of the budget estimates for the coming financial year by October of the current year and send one copy of the estimate to their administrative Ministry and another to the representative of the Comptroller and Auditor-General.

(3) Pruning by the Finance Ministry. The Administrative Ministry prunes the demands, of its subordinate offices and forwards them after consolidation to the Finance Ministry by about the middle of November. The Finance Ministry as the agency responsible for managing the finances of the Government, passes the demands of the other Ministries, calls for justification of expenditure, if necessary and arrives at a net figure for each ministry. Normally the decisions of the Finance Ministry and binding on the administrative ministries but if the matter is of such an importance that a Minister is prepared to appeal to the cabinet, then matters are different.

The Finance Ministry's criticism of the budget estimates is not confined to the period between its receipt from the departments and its presentation of Parliament. Throughout the year as important questions of finance arise, the finance ministry sits in judgement on proposals which affect the expenditure of the following year. It goes on continuously sanctioning schemes, approving increase in staff and estimates regarding most of the decision which have already been taken. It watches expenditure very closely all proposals which impose a new or increased charge on the Government.

(4) Scrutiny by Accountant-General. As it has been mentioned above one copy of departmental estimates has to be sent to the Accountant-General concerned. He does not scrutinise the needs of the department but checks the estimates from an accountant's angle to see that all sanctioned charges are present in the estimates and that unsanctioned charges have not been included therein. Accounting classification of various items is also checked. The scrutiny of the Accountant-General is of the type which is applied in a good business house by a competent accountant.

Again as an accountant, the Accountant-General is in the higher position to frame the estimates of the government relating to the interest on debts, pensions and other similar charges for which he alone has complete information. He furnishes these to the Finance Ministry by about December and they are accepted without question, since the Government has already assumed liability for these charges.

When the comments of the Accountant-General arrive the Finance Ministry is in possession of both the viewpoint of the administrative department and the technical accounting viewpoint.

The Accountant-General has now to work on the rough estimates finalised by the Finance Ministry, and putting together the estimates figures in the position required for presentation to Parliament. They record the estimates sent by the Finance Ministry in two ways: one by major heads of accounts for formulating Annual Financial statement and the other by "demand" for presenting the Demands for grants. This work is completed in the Accountant General's office sometime in January. Both documents are sent to the Finance Ministry by the Accountant-Generals and the Ministry then adds up all the figures to produce the Annual Financial statement and the demands for Grants.

In the meantime, feverish activity goes on in the administrative departments and in the Finance Ministry to include last minute projects in the budget. The Finance Ministry communicates the acceptance of fresh schemes of expenditure to the Accountant-General by means of orders on budget notes and the Accountant-General immediately has to send back figures after recasting them as before.

By the middle of February, each Accountant-General has taken the last step which makes the estimates of expenditures and receipts of the Government each month. On the basis of the latest available expenditure and revenue figures, he notices trends and decides if variations of more than a lakh of rupees should be made in the estimates. Minor variations are disregarded. He telegraphs his findings to the Finance Ministry and brings the estimates of expenditure for the year under forecast to close.

(5) Estimating the Revenue. The work of estimating the revenue is also the responsibility of the Finance Ministry. Depending on whether expenditure has increased or decreased, compared with the previous year, the Finance Ministry varies the rate of taxes. Proposals for variations are placed as Bill, before Parliament, and have to be kept secret till the day of presentation, so as not to affect adversely the public revenues.

Budget Passed in Parliament?

Ans. Article 265 of our Constitution provides "No tax shall be levied or collected except by authority of Law" and Article 266 provides that "no moneys out of the Consolidated Fund of India or the Consolidated Fund of State shall be appointed except in accordance with Law and for the purpose and in the manner as passed by the Legislature." The sanction and approval of the Parliament or the State Legislature concerned is thus necessary to be obtained before money can be spent or raised. In other words, The Parliament or the State Legislature are in actual practice authorised to raise revenue and expend money. The budget passes through the following stages of Enactment:

(1) Introduction in the Legislature. The budget is to be introduced in the Parliament or the Legislature of the State concerned much in advance of the commencement of the financial year *i.e.*, 1st of April, so that the Legislature should have ample time to study and discuss it and pass it by that date. The Finance Minister of the Government of India introduces it usually in the first week of February in the name of the President of India and the Finance Minister of the state concerned does so in the name of the Governor of the state. The Budget is placed before both the Houses of Parliament or State Legislature concerned. The Rajya Sabha in the Union Parliament and the Legislative Council in the State Legislature can only discuss it as the power over grants is vested in the lok Sabha and the State Legislative Assemblies respectively. The Budget is composed of two parts—Budget speech of the coming year, the revised estimates for the current and the actual accounts for the past year. The speech of the Finance Minister is always of very great importance and is eagerly awaited by the business and finance circle as it contains information about general economic conditions of the country and reveals what new taxes are to be imposed and which of the existing taxes are to be increased or reduced or remitted.

(2) General Discussion. According to Rule 130 of the rules of Conduct of Business of Parliament, "No discussion of the Budget shall take place on the day on which it is presented to Parliament. The speaker, therefore, fixes a date on which general discussion on the Budget is to take place. Such a date is generally fixed one week after the presentation of the Budget and about four days are allotted for the purpose. Discussion is confined to the general principles or policy underlying the budget, and involves review and criticism of the administration and ventilation of the grievances of the people. At this stage no motion is moved nor is the Budget submitted to the vote of Parliament.

(3) Voting of Demands. After the general discussion on the budget is over, the demands for grants are taken up which is solely the business of the Lok Sabha or the State Legislative assemblies. The total number of days allotted for the voting of demands is 20 as in Britain. The speaker in consultation with the Leader of the House fixes a time limit for particular demands or groups of demands and for the entire expenditure part of the Budget. As soon as the time for any demand is reached, it is immediately, put to vote whether the discussion on it is complete or not. Similarly on the last day allotted for the voting of the demands, at 5 P.M. the speaker puts all the demands which remain outstanding to vote and disposes them irrespective of the fact whether they have been discussed or not. Any way this gives the opposition an opportunity to criticise the Government or any Department of Minister. The Minister concerned has to defend administration against all criticism that is levelled against it by the opposition. At the end of the discussion of each demand, the demand is put to the vote of the House in the following form "That a sum not exceeding Rs...be granted to the President (or the Governor) to defray the charges, which will come in the course of payment during the yea ending March 19...in respect of....(subject of the Demand)."

(4) Introduction and Legislation of the Appropriation Bill in the House of People (Lok Sabha). Voting of the grants however does not empower the Government to withdraw money from the Public fund. Article 144(1) of the Constitution provides that after the grants have been made by the House of People a Bill to provide for the appropriation of Consolidated Fund of India money shall be introduced in the House to meet the grants made by the House of People and the expenditure charged on the Consolidated Fund of India. The appropriation bill is accordingly introduced in the House. This bill includes all the grants for the year votable or non-votable. The bill follows the same procedure in the House as any other money bill except in this that no amendment to the grants as voted by the House previously or to the Consolidated Fund charges can be proposed in either House.

Procedure in the Rajya Sabha. The Rajya Sabha or the Legislative Council or Vidhan Parishad in the States has neither the power of amending nor rejecting a money bill; it can only discuss and make recommendations within 14 days to the Lok Sabha or the Legislative Assembly in Vidhan Sabha in the States which may or may not accept them. Even if the Lower House rejects the suggestion of the Rajya Sabha the bill will be considered as passed by both the Houses in the form it was passed by the Lower House. In case the Upper House does not make recommendations within the above specified period, even then the bill will be deemed as passed by the Upper House also.

President's Assent. When the Budget has been passed or is deemed to have been passed by the Parliament it goes for the assent of the Head of the State. The President or the Governor cannot return a money bill for consideration and his assent to it follows as a matter of course.

(5) Passage of the Finance Act. Appropriation Act authorises the Government to appropriate money from the Consolidated Fund but it has not so far been provided wherefrom the money for expenditure would come. Provision is, therefore, to be made for collecting the required money by way of taxation. For this purpose a finance bill is placed before the House. This bill embodies the taxation or revenue proposals for the ensuing financial year. The finance bill follows the same procedure as any other bill and when it is passed by the Parliament, the Government is authorised to collect the taxes.

❐

8

Zero Base Budgeting

ZBB is a cost-benefit approach whereby it is assumed that the cost allowance for an item is zero, and will remain so until the manager responsible justifies the existence of the cost item and the benefits the expenditure brings. In this way a questioning attitude is developed whereby each cost item and its level has to be justified in relation to the way it helps to meet objectives and how the expenditure benefits the organisation. This is a forward looking approach as opposed to the all too common method of extrapolating past activities and costs, which is a feature of the incremental budgeting approach.

ZBB is formally defined by the CIMA thus; A method of budgeting whereby all activities are re-evaluated each time a budget is formulated. Each functional budget starts with the assumption that the function does not exist and is at zero cost. Increments of cost are compared with increments of benefit, culminating in the planning maximum benefit for a given budgeted cost.

ZBB can be applied in both profit seeking and non-profit seeking organisations. The technique gained wide publicity when the then President Carter directed that all US government departments adopt zero base budget.

In a manufacturing firm. It is best applied to service and support expenditure including, administration, marketing, personnel, information and computer services, research and development, finance and accounting, production planning and so on. These activities are less easily quantifiable by conventional methods and are more discretionary in nature. Manufacturing costs such as direct materials and labour and production overheads can be more easily controlled by well established methods which compare production outputs with resource inputs rather than using ZBB. Budgeting and controlling manufacturing expenditure uses techniques such as work study and standard costing which are described later in the manual.

Zero base budget can successfully be applied to service industries and to a wide range of non-profit seeking organisations. For example local and central government departments, educational establishments, hospitals and so on. It could be applied in any organisation where alternative levels of provision for each activity are possible and the costs and benefits can be separately identified. It is concerned with alternatives and means that established activities have to be compared with alternative uses of the same resources. It takes away the implied right of existing activities to continue to receive resources, unless it can be shown that this is the best use of those resources.

There are several formal stages involved in implementing this type of budget but of greater importance is the development of an appropriate questioning attitude by all concerned. There must be a 'value for money' approach which challenges existing practices and expenditures and searching questions must be asked at each stage; typical of which are the following:

(a) Is the activity essential or one of the frills?

(b) How much should the activity cost? Is this expenditure worth the benefits achieved?

(c) What is the best way to provide the function? Have all alternative possibilities been considered?

(d) What is the correct level of provision? Has too much or too little been provided in the past?

(e) How does the activity—existing or proposed—contribute to the organisation's objectives?

(f) Does the activity need to be carried out at all? What would be the effects, if any, if it ceased?

and so on.

The overall process of implementing this type of budget can be sub-divided into three stages thus:

I. Definition of Decision Packages

A decision package is a comprehensive description of a facet of the organisation's activities or functions which can be individually evaluated. The decision package is specified by the managers concerned and must show details of the anticipated costs and results expected expressed in terms of tasks accomplished and benefits achieved.

Two types of decision package are possible:

(a) Mutually-Exclusive Decision Packages. These are alternative forms of activity, tasks and expenditure to carry out the same job. The best option among the mutually exclusive packages is selected by comparing costs and benefits, and the other packages are then discarded. Naturally, mutually-exclusive packages would only be prepared when there are quite clearly different approaches for dealing with the same function. As an example, an organisation with a distribution problem might consider two alternative decision packages: Package I might be an in house fleet of lorries, whereas Package 2 could involve contracts with independent hauliers.

(b) Incremental Decision Packages. These packages reflect different levels of effort in dealing with a particular activity. There will be what is known as the base package, which represents the minimum feasible level of activity, and other packages which describe higher activity levels at given costs and resulting benefits. As an example, a base package for a Personnel department might provide for staff engagement and termination procedures and payroll administration. Incremental packages might include; education and training, welfare and social activities, pension administration, trade union liaison and negotiations etc. Each package would have its costs and benefits clearly tabulated.

II. Packages are Evaluated and Ranked

When the decision packages have been prepared, management will then rank all the packages on the basis of their benefits to the organisation. This is a process of allocating scarce resources between different activities, some of which already exist and other that are new.

Minimum requirements which are essential to get the job done and activities necessary to meet legal or safety obligations will naturally receive high priority. It will be found that the ranking process focuses management's attention on discretionary or optional activities.

Because of the large number of packages prepared through out the organisation the ranking process can become onerous and time consuming for senior management. One way of reducing this problem is for lower level managers to rank the packages for their own budget centre and for these rankings to be consolidated, with others, at the next level up the hierarchy. Alternatively, there could be a cut-off limit for expenditure so that packages for a lower amount, say less than £2,000, could be ranked within the department and need not be referred higher.

III. Resources are Allocated

When the overall budgeted expenditure level is decided upon the packages would be accepted in the ranked priority sequence up to the agreed expenditure level.

Where the ranking of lower cost packages has been delegated to departments the proportion of the expenditure budget remaining after the more expensive packages have been ranked would be allocated to individual departments. The departments would then rank their own small packages up to their allocated expenditure level.

Advantages of Zero Base Budget

(a) It is a systematic way of challenging the status quo and obliges the organisation to examine alternative activities and existing cost behaviour patterns and expenditure levels.

(b) This leads to greater staff and management knowledge of the operations and activities of the organisations and can increase motivation.

(c) It develops a questioning attitude and makes it easier to identify inefficient, obsolete or less cost-effective operations.

(d) If focuses attention on value for money and makes explicit the relationship between the input of resources and the output of benefits.

(e) Properly carried out, it should result in a more efficient allocation of resources to activities and departments.

Disadvantages of Zero Base Budget

(a) It may emphasise short term benefits to the detriment of longer term ones which in the end may be more important.

(b) there are considerable problems in ranking packages and there are inevitable many subjective judgements. Political pressures within organisations also contribute to the problem of ranking different types of activity, especially where there are qualitative rather than quantitative benefits.

(c) ZBB is not always acceptable to staff or management or trade unions who may prefer the cosy status quo and who see the detailed examination of alternatives, costs and benefits as a threat not a challenge.

(d) It may encourage the wrong impression that all decisions have to be made in the budget. Circumstances change and new opportunities and threats can arise at any time and organisations must be flexible enough to deal rapidly with these circumstances when they occur.

(e) There is considerable management skill required in both drawing up decision packages and for the ranking process. These skills may not exist in the organisation.

(f) It is a time consuming process which can generate volumes of paper work especially for the decision packages.

Problems of ZBB

Guy Peters mentions two problems which limit the political acceptability of ZBB. First, organisations, for obvious reasons, do not like to allow outsiders to know on how little they could survive. Second, if there is an assumption that the survival level of funding for an organisation is open to challenges every year political conflicts are perpetuated and old disputes opened annually. This may threaten such social programmes as do not have strong public support. Moreover, the major problem is the threat that many bureaucrats feel towards a process which evaluates the effectiveness of their programmes. It would be dangerous to regard ZBB as a sure remedy for financial laxity. The success of ZBB in American industry is largely due to profit motive and organisational residency, both of these factors do not operate in the governmental setting. Moreover, the bureaucratic temperament is conditioned by the growth impulse which clamours for larger budgets rather than for more challenging assignments. Also, the powerful impact of political pressures on financial decision-making makes the prospects of ZBB very uncertain.

Advantages of ZBB

The Zero-Base Budgeting is said to have several advantages. Its advocates regard it as a pragmatic approach which offers an extremely flexible management tool. It can lead to substantial savings. Dr. Burns while admitting that ZBB approach may be difficult to achieve, asserts that substantial savings could undoubtedly be realized if it were required that every department make a case for its entire appropriation request each year, just as its programme or programmes, were entirely new. Pyhrr considers the following four reasons that make the ZBB approach, worthwhile: Law priority programmes can be eliminated or reduced,

(2) Programme effectiveness can be dramatically improved, although it may or may not have a budgetary impact,

(3) High impact programmes can obtain increased financial allocation by shifting resources within an agency,

(4) Tax increases can be checked. The first three benefits can substantially reduce the necessity for increased taxes by allowing agencies to do a more effective job with existing revenues.

In the end it, may be said that the strategy of implementing the ZBB approach must be developed for each organisation, depending on its specific needs and capabilities. It should be considered a management and budgetary improvement effort that may require several years to reach full utilization and effectiveness.

BUDGETING & BUDGETARY CONTROL

A budget is a blue print of the projected plan of action expressed in quantitative terms for a specified period of time and the process of preparing a budget is called budgeting. Budgetary control refers to the principles, procedures and practices of achieving given objectives through budgets.

The difference between budget, budgeting, and budgetary control has been stated thus: "Budgets are the individual objectives of a department, etc. whereas budgeting may be said to be the act of building budgets. Budgetary control embraces all this and in addition includes the science of planning the budgets themselves and the utilisation of such budgets to effect an overall management tool for the business planning and control."

A budget is defined as a "comprehensive and coordinated plan, expressed in financial terms, for the operations and resources of an enterprise for some specified period in the future." According to this definition, the following are the essential elements of a budget:

(1) Plan. The first ingredient of a budget is its plan. The term "plan" with reference to budgeting has a specific connotation. It includes two aspects which have a bearing on the operations of an enterprise. One set of factors which determine a firm's future operations are wholly external and beyond its control. Included in this category of factors are general business conditions, government policy and size and composition of population. The second set of factors affecting future activities are within the firm's control and discretion, *i.e.*, they are internal. Promotional programmes, manufacturing processes are illustration of these factors. Budgeting, as a plan, covers both these aspects. In other words, budgeting not only suggests what will happen but should also make things happen.

In brief, a budget (plan) is an expression partly of what the management expects to happen and partly of what the management intends to happen.

(2) Specified Future Period. A Budget relates to a specified period of time, usually one year. If it is not related to a time horizon, it will be meaningless. Planning merely for a given amount of say, sales/profit will not constitute a budget unless a time dimension is added, *i.e.*, the budgeted sales/profit is planned to be achieved in a pre-determined time framework.

(3) Comprehensiveness. A budget is comprehensive. The term "comprehensive" here means that all the activities and operations of an organisation are included in it. It covers the organisation as a whole and not only some segments. The modus operandi is that budgets are prepared for each segment/facet/activity/division of an organisation and these are integrated into an overall budget for the entire organisation. The overall budget is referred to as the master budget.

(4) Coordination. Budgets are prepared for the different components/segments/ divisions/facets/activities of an organisation so as to take care of the situations and problems of each component. The budgets for each of the components are prepared in harmony with each another. This is called coordination.

(5) Operations and Resources. A budget is a mechanism to plan for the firm's operations and resources. The operations are reflected in revenues and expenses. This means that a budget should quantify the revenues to be realised from products/services and the expenses to be incurred on goods/services used in generating revenues.

The plan also covers the resources of the firm. The planning of resources means the planning of the various assets and the sources of capital to finance these assets. The assets could be fixed assets as well as current assets.

(6) Financial Terms. Budgets are prepared in financial terms, *i.e.*, in-terms of monetary value such as the rupee, dollar, and so on.

The reason is that the monetary unit is a common denominator. The various activities and operations are pressed in different units, *e.g.*, material in terms of weight, labour in terms of number/man-hours, sales in terms of territories, advertisement in terms of magazine space, and so on. If they have to be integrated in a plan, they must be expressed in comparable units of measurement. Monetary units provide such a measure.

The essentials of a budget are

(i) It is prepared in advance and is based on a future plan of actions;

(ii) It relates to a future period and is based on objectives to be attained;

(iii) It is a statement expressed in monetary and/or physical units prepared for the implementation of policy formulated by the management.

Budget is a financial plan, budgeting is the art of planning and budgeting control is the art of adhering to the plan. Whatever programmes and policies are chalked out by the management, budgets put them in a concrete form. The follow up action to see that the plans are adhered to completes the system of budgetary control. Adherence to plan means that effort is made to contain the actual costs within targeted limits. Thus a system of budgetary control secures control over costs and performances in different segments of business.

Most human endeavour is more fruitful if directed by a well-advised and intelligently conceived programme. The conduct of business is no exception. Sometimes no sustained and continuous effort is made to chart a future course which would seem, all circumstances considered, to point the surest way towards the ultimate part of business success. If management carefully studies and gives proper attention to planning its activities in advance, operations would be more efficiently conducted and profits would be higher. The fundamental purpose of budgeting is to find the most profitable course through which the efforts of the business may be directed in meeting its primary service objective. The purpose of budgetary control system is to assist management in holding the business as early as possible on that charted course. Thus, the emphasis of budgeting is on the necessity for advance decision on future course of action to be followed. However, budgeting control system points out the result which would accrue by following that course of action.

According to the Institute of Cost and Management Accountants, England, budgetary control consists of "the establishment of budgets relating the responsibilities of executives to the requirements of a policy and the continuous comparison of actual with budgetary results either to secure by individual action the objective of that policy or to provide a basis for its revision."

Thus, budgetary control involves:

(a) Revision of budgets in the light of changed circumstances;

(b) Placing the responsibility for failure to achieve the budget figures;

(c) Continuous comparison of actuals with budgets for achievement of targets;

(d) Establishment of budgets.

In the words of J. Batty, budgeting control is "a system which uses budgets as a means of planning and controlling all aspects of producing and/or selling commodities or services."

Budgetary control system operates through different budgets, prepared for various departments and activities. According to the Institute of Cost and Management Accountants, England, a budget is a "financial and/or quantitative statement, prepared prior to a defined period of time, of the policy to be pursued during that period for the purpose of attaining a given objective."

Difference Between A Forecast and Budget

Forecats and budgets both refer to the anticipated actions and events in a specified future period but there is a wide difference between the two. The points of difference have been explained hereunder:

Forecast	Budget
(i) Forecasts can be made in those spheres also where budgets cann't interfere.	(i) Budgets can be made of phenomenon non-capable of being expressed quantitatively.
(ii) Forecasting is a preliminary step for budgeting. It ends with the forecast of likely events.	(ii) It begins when forecasting ends. Forecasts are converted into budgets.
(iii) Forecasts, being statements of future events, do not connote any sense of control.	(iii) A budget is a tool of control since it represents actions which can be shaped according to will so that it can be suited to the conditions which may or may not happen.
(iv) Forecast is a mere estimate of what is likely to happen. It is a statement of probable events which are likely to happen under anticipated conditions during a specified period of time.	(iv) Budget shows the policy and programme to be followed in a future period under planned conditions.

Budget Terminology

Budget Manual. It is defined by the terminology as: "A document which sets out standing instructions governing the responsibilities of persons and the procedures, forms and records relating to the preparation and use of budgets." It is a booklet containing standing instructions regarding the procedures to be followed and the time schedules to be observed. The following are some of the important matters dealt with in the budget manual:

(i) the matters, included in budgets, on which action may be taken only with the approval of top management.

(ii) the manner in which budgets, after acceptance and issuance, are to be revised or amended;

(iii) the reporting of the remedial action;

(iv) the form in which the various reports are to be made out, their periodicity and dates, the persons to whom these and their copies are to be sent;

(v) the finalisation of the functional budgets and their compilation into the master budget;

(vi) the manner of scrutiny and the personnel to carry it out;

(vii) the matter which must be settled only with the consent of the managing director, departmental manager, etc.;

(viii) the categorisation of expenses, *e.g.*, variable and fixed, and the manner in which each category is to be estimated and dealt with;

(ix) the important factors that must be considered for each forecast or plan;

(x) the dates by which preliminary forecasts and plans are to be submitted.

The main idea behind the budget manual is to inform line executives beforehand about procedures to be followed rather than issuing frequent instructions from the controller's office regarding procedures and forms to be used. Such frequent instructions can be a source of friction between the line and staff management.

Budget Controller

To link up the various functions, to bring them together and to coordinate their efforts in the matter of preparation of target figures, there should be a person usually designated as the Budget Controller, who can provide ready data relating to all the functions. He is more or less the secretary to the budget committee. The Budget Controller does not control; he is a 'staffman'; he advises but does not issue instructions. His duties will comprise chiefly:

(a) compiling information about actual performance on a continuous basis comparing it against the budget figures, ascertaining causes of deviation and preparing reports based thereon and sending them to the appropriate executive;

(b) helping in preparation of the various budgets and their coordination and compilation into the master budget;

(c) bringing to the notice of the management the need for revision of budgets and assisting them in the task; and

(d) compiling information of all types for the purpose of efficient preparation of budgets and proper reporting.

Budget Key Factor

A budget key factor or principal budget factor is described by the Terminology as: "The factor which at a particular time or over a period will limit the activities of an undertaking. The limiting factor is usually the level of demand for the products or services of the undertaking but it could be a shortage or one of the productive resources, *e.g.*, skilled labour, raw material or machine capacity. In order to ensure that the functional budgets are reasonably capable of fulfillment the extent of the influence of this factor must be assessed". As noted already, all the functions in all organisations are interlinked. The target of one has influence on that of the other. If the sales department could sell only 50,000 units, it is no use producing 1,00,000 units. If the production department has the capacity for 50,000 units, a sales potential of 1,00,000 units is not of much consequence. Deliberations in the budget committee would lead to a decision regarding steps to get over a limiting factor. If one limiting factor is got over, another may crop up. Thus, there is a possibility of varying limiting factors under different circumstances. Decision will have to be taken resulting in optimum production keeping in view the different limiting factors. The basic issues is an enquiry into the future. All probabilities under different circumstances are to be worked out to fix the target at the optimum level. This may sometimes involve lengthy mathematical calculations.

The following is a list of principal budget factors which will influence the targets: *(i)* customer demand, *(ii)* plant capacity, *(iii)* availability of raw materials, skilled labour and capital, *(iv)* availability of accommodation for plant, raw materials and finished goods, and *(v)* governmental restrictions.

If a limiting factor cannot be got over by any means, then the whole budget involving all functions will have to be built around that factor. For instance, if the production capacity is 50,000 units and if it cannot be increased in the short run, all budgets, say, the sales budget and raw materials purchase budget, will have to be based on the production of 50,000 units. To achieve maximum profitability, a key factor must be overcome, if not, at least efforts should be made to minimise its adverse effect.

(4) Forecast. A forecast is the statement of events likely to occur. It is defined by the Institute of Cost and Management Accountants, London, as "a statement of probable event." It connotes a degree of looseness so that it is usually the practice to judge the accuracy of forecasts on the basis of actual performance, taking the latter to be correct. The forecast of a function need not necessarily be well coordinated. The desired coordination could be obtained before the budget is finalised. A forecast forms the basis for the budget. A budget indicates "a target". It is a statement of planned events, generally evolved form the forecast. It is defined by the terminology as: "A financial and/or quantitative statement, prepared and approved prior to a defined period of time, of the policy to be pursued during that period for the purpose of attaining a given objective. It may include income, expenditure and the employment of capital."

(5) Budget Committee. The budget committee is a group of representatives of various functions in an organisation. As all functions are interrelated and as any change in one's target will have its impact on that of the others, it is necessary to discuss the targets so that a mutually agreed programme is determined. This is really the coordination in budget making. "It is a powerful force in knitting together the various activities of the business and enforcing real control over operations." The budget manual should specify the responsibilities and duties of the budget committee, which should include the following:

(i) Make recommendations for the budget manual.

(ii) Consider recommendations for changes in budget policies and procedures.

(iii) Consider and make recommendations for revision of the budget when conditions warrant.

(iv) Receive, study and analyse periodic reports comparing the budget with actual performance. Consider policies with respect to follow-up procedures.

(v) Recommend changes and approval of the revised budget.

(vi) Recommend decisions on budget matters where there may be conflict between departments or divisions.

(vii) Receive and review budget estimates from the respective divisions or departments and make recommendations.

(6) Budget period. It refers to the period of time covered by a budget. In the broad classification in this regard has already been stated as "Long-term budget" and "short-term budget".

The short-term budget itself could be bifurcated into yearly and quarterly budgets. Long-term budgets provide the perspective, since one would be able to have a view of what is likely to be achieved and what the chief problems are likely to be, such as, competition from new products. However, these are necessarily rather vague. Short-term budgets, say for a year, are quite exact and those for a quarter even more so. These are particularly suitable for control purposes. A short-term budget need not necessarily be for one year. It is generally long enough to cover one season or business year.

In determining the length of the budget period the following factors should be considered; *(a)* The budget period should be long enough to complete production of the various products, *(b)* For the business of a seasonal nature the budget period should cover at least one entire seasonal cycle, *(c)* Major operations and drastic changes in plant lay-out or manufacturing methods must be planned far in advance to determine financial requirements, *(d)* The budget period should coincide with the financial accounting period to compare actual results with budgeted estimates. *(e)* The budget period should be long enough to allow for the financing of production well in advance of actual needs.

A budget period should be distinguished from "control period". The latter indicates the periodicity with which reports are sent to the various levels of management. It need not be the same as the budget period. Reports are sent usually at shorter intervals so that corrective action may be taken within the budget period. This would ensure that the overall variation between budget and actual is minimised. The periodicity of the reports is also dependent upon the urgency and significance of the matter under report.

ADVANTAGES OF BUDGETING

1. Correlation of Human Effort with in Business Structure. If in some divisions of business, there is uncertainty of programmes, full steam cannot be applied in other divisions. To secure full power of untied action, it is essential to properly time and co-ordinate the effort of all divisions. Budgeting helps in achieving co-ordination of human effort within the organisation.

2. Relation of Business Activities to General Economic Trend. The plans of the business must reflect courage or caution depending upon the expected general trend of business or economic conditions. Budgeting assists the management to co-ordinate the activities of the business to the signals of high and low economic trends. Particularly, the danger signals which act as forewarners to the business are reflected in budgeting which cautions the entire organisation well in advance.

3. Optimum use of Available Facilities. Budgeting entails in itself the most effective use of physical equipment and other facilities. It helps in checking waste related to their uneconomical use.

4. Fixation of Objectives. When the objectives are not the product of hope but rather the logical sequence of carefully laid plans, the executives can command the cooperation and loyalty of their associates. This leads to successful execution of the programmes.

5. Employment Stability. The days have gone when workers could be shunted out at will when not required like flasks or patterns in the foundry. Intelligent budgeting offers the greatest hope for providing stability of employment.

6. Elimination of Uncertainty. The organisation should be schooled in basic policies, which are the real guide to a business. The budget procedure provides a vehicle through which basic policies are periodically re-examined, restated and set forth as guiding principles for the organisation at large.

7. Combined Judgment of Entire Organisation. The budgeting process takes the assistance of the entire organisation in determining the most profitable course, thus the bias or prejudice is eliminate and the final plans are expressive of the combined judgment of entire organisation.

8. Early Study of Problems. Most of us prefer to postpone difficult decisions until necessity compels. In the business also, people are normally opportunists, they wait till a decision is forced. Intensive study, which is to many a distasteful exercise, is not taken up beforehand and when the troubles crop up abruptly, easiest immediate escape is resorted to. Budgeting instills into the organisation the habit of thorough study before decision is put to action.

9. Prevention of Waste. A searching inquiry into every contemplated expenditure and the reason therefore an analytical approach extending to every function and every department of the business-will constitute an effective prevention of waste.

10. Control of Specific Operations. The budget provides a valuable tool of control over certain business operations, *e.g.* investment in plant, quantity to be produced, quantum of expenditure to be incurred for sales promotion etc. Expenditures are limited and directed into the channels which offered most promise. Certain activities can be controlled if sales and production performance does not meet the expectations.

11. Most Profitable Channelisation of Capital and Effort. Budgeting leads to a balanced and unified programme and through it the capital and effort are directed into the most profitable channels. Where planning and decision-making is made on a day to day basis, the programme frequently becomes unconsciously warped. Careful advance planning results in balancing of factors and a proportionate emphasis on sales, finance, production, inventories etc. This leads to attainment of goals laid down.

12. Curtain-raiser Over Weaknesses. Budgeting reveals the weaknesses in the organisation, since the responsibility for the execution of budgets is delegated. The responsibility, however, will be acceptable to executives only when lines of authority are so delineated that they remain unhampered in the execution of their tasks.

Thus, budgeting serves as a communication device which permits a full and free interplay of ideas with the objectives of selecting the best plan. This is the role of budgeting as a management tool for planning. The most feasible plan is put to action and budgeting is used as a control mechanism by the management through assigning responsibilities for execution of the plans. In an effective environment, the necessary co-ordination is achieved in both planning and control aspect of budgeting. To summarise, budgetary control acts as a friend, philosophy and guide to the management.

Limitations of Budgeting

Budgetary control can be a powerful technique in the hands of management to achieve the objectives, but it rests on the quality of management and the attention given to motivating staff to react favourably to the discipline the technique imposes.

Budgetary control can be used as a motivator by allowing those responsible for budget achievement to be involved in the budgeting process and by supplying them with monitoring information to facilitate control. In order to be fully effective, the budgetary control should have participative type of budgeting rather than merely serving as authorisation procedures.

1. Regarded as a Pressure Instrument. The technique is regarded by staff as a pressure instrument rather than a procedure to assist the executive to do a better job. Thus, there is opposition against the very spirit of budgeting.

2. Danger of Rigidity. As budgets are prepared by quantifying all relevant data, there is tendency to attach some sort of finality to budget figures but, as they are meant to deal with business conditions which are constantly changing, they would lose much of their usefulness if they acquire rigidity. Therefore, it is essential that budgetary programme must be continuously adapted to changing conditions in and off a business unit.

3. Misplacement of Motivation. Managers may be satisfied with budget performance when better performance is possible and could reasonably be attained if a low level of attainment had not been in the budget.

4. Thinking too Ahead. If forecasting is practised too for into the future, the budgetary control technique may not be that fruitful. Appropriate techniques must be developed before the purpose.

5. Manager's Discretion in Submitting Budget Estimates may be Fatal. If it is left entirely in the hands of managers to submit budget estimates and the same are accepted as such the performance may not improve since the estimates may not be too demanding on their performance.

6. Prohibited Cost. It is quite common to find that the structure of the budgetary system becomes top heavy and costly so much so that small concerns cannot afford to adopt it. However, it is essential that there must be some correlation between the most of the system and the benefits obtained from it. No cast iron rules can be laid down for this as much depends on the size and nature of the activities of individual business.

7. Ineffective Accounting System. If the accounting system, which is the bedrock of successful budgeting is not effective, the control technique would not work.

8. Weak Organisation Structure. The entire organisational structure should be very solid and sound. Wherever there are inherent weaknesses in the organisational structure, no control system would prove to be effective. Delegation of authority and responsibility should be very specific.

9. No Action or Delayed Action. If even after knowing that particular person or department is responsible for off-budget performance, no action is taken or the action is delayed, the technique of budgetary control could be blamed unnecessarily for unsatisfactory achievements of targets in future also.

10. Change in Conditions. If the conditions that are anticipated are changed, the budgetary targets cannot be achieved. The budget may be revised for the future, but still in these days of uncertainty, even the revised estimates may go wrong. The utility of the technique lies in correctly estimating as far as possible the influence of future contingencies.

11. Gestation Period not Allowed. The system, itself, demands some time to be developed fully within the organisation. The required experience, if not there, can lead to a failure of the system in its initial stages.

12. Impersonal Approach. sometimes it is managed that the introduction of the budget system is alone sufficient to ensure its success and to guarantee future profits. After the preparation of the budget, it is necessary that the energies and efforts of the entire organization are harnessed for the realization of budgetary goals. In this connection, it must always be kept in view that budgeting can never be more than a perfect way of observing results, to indicate more closely and quickly than any other system as to how far more rationalization is necessary; it is not rationalization it itself. Thus, it constitutes only an impersonal approach to the conduct of business activity and has to be supplemented with proper management and administration.

13. Budget Plan is Based on Estimates. Absolute accuracy is not possible in forecasting and budgeting though a high standard is always aimed at. The adequacy or otherwise of a budgetary programme depends to a very large extent on the accuracy with which estimates are made. If the budgeted figures are removed from reality, very little purpose would be served by them. The fact of the budget being based on estimates must be kept in view in interpreting the results thereof.

ENACTMENT OF THE BUDGET

In India, the budget goes through five stages in the course of its passage in the Parliament namely,

(1) introduction in the legislature,

(2) the general discussion,

(3) the voting of the demands for grants,

(4) the consideration and passing of the appropriation bill, and

(5) the consideration and passing of the taxation proposals, *i.e.*, the Finance bill.

The Introduction. As already stated, it has become customary in our country to frame, introduce, and pass the budget in two parts the railway budget, and the general budget. The former consists of the estimates of only the railway receipt and expenditure, and its introduction usually precedes that of the general budget. The general budget deals with the estimates of the departments excluding railways. The budget or the annual financial statement as our constitution calls it, is introduced in the House of People by the Finance Minister with a speech called the budget speech. This speech is eagerly awaited by the business and the financial circles as it gives them the first intimation of the taxation proposals, the tariff trends protection to the industries, and the general economic and financial policy of the Government for the ensuing financial year. The budget speech is a lengthy document and printed copies of it, of the budget estimates, and explanatory memoranda are circulated among members.

The annual financial statement is laid before the council of states also, though this chamber can only discuss it and has no power over grants at all.

The General Discussion

The general discussion of the annual financial statement begins a few days after its presentation. Two to three days are allotted for it. It is confined to the general principles or policy underlying the budget. No discussion of details or cut motions are in order at this stage. The general discussion takes place in each of the Houses.

The general discussion of the budget is a hang-over from the past when the Indian legislature had no power to vote the budget, but could only discuss it. It is retained under the present constitution because it enables the members to discuss the revenue estimates, and the ways and means programme of the government as a whole at an early stage and also the charged expenditure which does not come up for voting.

The Voting of Demands

After the general discussion is over, the House of People proceeds to the voting of demands, *i.e.*, to the voting of the expenditure part of the budget. It should be carefully noted that the power of voting money for expenditure belongs exclusively to the House of People and the council of states has no say in it. While voting the budget, the House of People sits as the House and not as the committee of the whole House as is the practice of the House of Commons.

The total number of days allotted for the voting of demands is 26 days as in Britain. Expenditure to the tune of hundreds of crores of rupees has to be voted within this short-time. This, of course, means that many of the demands are voted without any discussion at all. What happens is that in consultation with the Leader of the House, the speaker fixes a time limit for particular demands or groups of demands and for the entire expenditure part of the budget. As soon as the time limit for any demand is reached, it is immediately put to vote whether the discussion on it is complete or not. Same way, on the last day allotted for the voting of demands, at 5 p.m. all the demands which remain outstanding, are put to vote and disposed of, whether they have been, discussed or not. The cardinal rule governing the voting of supplies is that no demand for a grant can be made except on the recommendations of the President. This means that the members of the House cannot make any addition to, or increase in, any item of expenditure proposed in the budget which, technically speaking, comes before the House on the President's recommendation. They can only reject or reduce the items of expenditure proposed. In practice, the House is precluded from doing even that, unless a cut motion in respect of any head or item is accepted by the cabinet. The reduction of any item of the budget in opposition to the wishes of the cabinet amounts to a vote of no-confidence in it. What, therefore, happens in the House during the voting of supplies is not a discussion of the heads of items of the budget from the financial point of view, but a general airing of grievances, against the administration of particular departments. As each head of expenditure comes up for discussion, some member rises and moves a cut of one rupee or a hundred rupees in its estimates and then proceeds to criticize the administration of the department to which it relates. At the end of the discussion, the Minister in charge of the department replies rebutting the points of criticism made, or giving assurance for the removal of the grievance pointed out, and the mover withdraws his cut motion. If he did not withdraw it, it would be voted down by the majority behind the cabinet. Members know this, and so, every cut proposed is merely a token cut. Its object is not to secure economy but simply to raise a discussion.

Altogether, there are 109 demands in the general budget 103 for civil and 6 for defence expenditure. The railway budget is divided into 23 demands. Each demand is the subject of a vote, *i.e.*, voted separately by the House of People. Its form is 'that a sum not exceeding Rs.... be granted to the President, (or the Governor in case of the States) to defray the charge which will come in course of payment during the year ending 31st March in respect of (the subject of demand) A demand, when voted duly, becomes a 'grant'.

The Consolidated Fund Charges

There is one part of the estimates of expenditure which is not submitted to the vote of the House at all though it can be discussed by it. This part is known as the Consolidated Fund Charges. The Consolidated Fund Charges include the salaries and emoluments of the President of the Republic, of the judges of the Supreme Court, of the Chairman and the Speaker (and their deputies) of the two Houses, and of the Comptroller and Auditor-General of India, charges in respect of public debt of India (such as interest, sinking funds, etc.) certain pensions; sums required to satisfy any judgment of decree of a court or arbitral tribunal; and any other expenditure declared by law or Parliament to be a part thereof. The reason for excluding these items from the vote of the House is that they are of a fixed or inevitable nature and admit of no reduction or variation. The rest of the estimates of expenditure are voted by the House.

The Appropriation Bill

When the House of People has voted all the demands, they, together with the consolidated fund charges are incorporated into a bill called the Appropriation Bill. It follows the same procedure in the House of People as any other bill except in this that no amendment to the grants as voted by the House previously or to the Consolidated Fund Charges can be proposed in either House. After being passed by the House of People, it is certified by the speaker as money bill and sent to the Council of States. this House has no power to reject or amend it. It can only discuss it and make recommendations within 14 days to the House of People which may accept or reject them just as it pleases. In any case, it can be presented to the President for his assent after 14 days of its passage in the House of People. The President cannot return a money bill for reconsideration and his assent to it follows as a matter of course.

The Voting of the Taxes

The Finance Bill. With the passing of the appropriation act, the disposal of the expenditure part of the budget is complete. Money for the expenditure, however, must come from some where and for that resort has to be had to taxation. All the taxes do not have to be authorized annually. Some of them are permanent and their rates can be varied from time to time by the executive Government, under the provisions of the law governing them. The rates of others, however, have to be annually fixed by the legislature as for example, the income tax, customs etc.

All the taxation proposals of the Government for the ensuing Financial year are embodied into a single bill known as the finance Bill. All the conditions governing the passage of a money bill apply to it. This procedure has-been described in the previous para in connection with the appropriations bill, but a few differences deserve notice. To the appropriations bill no amendments can be moved at all, in either House. To the Finance Bill, amendments seeking to reject or reduce a tax can be moved, and what is more, are even accepted by the Government sometimes.

With this difference, the Finance Bill follows the same procedure as the appropriation bill or any other money bill. It is usually referred to a select committee also.

The budget contains the ordinary annual estimates which constitute the bulk of the annual receipts and charges. To meet special circumstances, there are four other kinds of grants which the House of People may be asked to make, *viz.*,

(1) Votes on Account,

(2) Votes on credit,

(3) Special grants, and

(4) Supplementary grants.

We discuss these now.

Votes on Account

Under the financial procedure of the pre-republican days, the budget had to be passed by the legislature before the new financial year began on April 1. Unless this were done, the new year would begin without any financial provision for it. Now the House of People is no longer confined to this time. It can take its own time over the budget, continuing its consideration even in the new financial year for some time. This has been made possible for the device of the votes on account'. Votes on account are advance grants made by the House of People in respect of the estimated expenditure for a part of the ensuing financial year, pending the regular passage of the budget.

Votes on Credit and Special Grants

The House of People can also grant votes on credit to meet an expenditure whose amount or details can not be precisely stated in the budget on account of the indefinite character of the service to be financed. such grants are necessary to provide for matters like an impending war. It may also make special grants which form no part of the current service of any financial year. When unforeseen expenditure not provided for in any of these ways, suddenly arises, it can be met from advances made by the President out of the Contingencies Fund of India.

Supplementary Grants

If the budget grants for any service are later found to be insufficient, or if expenditure on some new service becomes necessary or if expenditure incurred on any service exceeds the amount provided for in the budget, a supplementary financial statement has to be laid before the House.

Authorization of Charges Involved in Ordinary Legislation

There is a possibility that, ordinary legislation may in an express or implied way, impose certain charges on the public exchequer. To safeguard against this, it is the practice both in Britain and India to require that no bill involving such charges can go beyond the second reading, unless the charge is authorized by a financial resolution of the House of Commons or the House of the People. A financial resolution can be moved only by a minister in conformity with the rule that all demands must come from the President.

Voting of Demands in Britain and the U.S.A.

Broadly speaking, the British procedure for the enactment of the budget is the same as in India but certain differences of detail deserve notice. In the first place, in Britain only one budget for all the receipts and expenditure is prepared and passed. No separate budget for railways or any other service exists. Secondly, the British budget is not introduced or discussed in the House of Lords. After 30 days of its passage in the House of Commons it is sready for presentation to the queen for her signature. In India, however, the budget is laid before and discussed by the Council of States also though the power voting the demands lies solely in the House of People. Thirdly, in Britain, the voting of demands and of taxes is done in the Committees of the whole known as the Committee of Supply (for expenditure part) and the Committee of ways and Means (revenue part) respectively, while in India, the House of People itself takes up and passes the budget at all its stages, the procedure by committees of the whole House being entirely unknown. Lastly, the timing of the budget speech in the two countries differs. In India, the speech is made in the very beginning of the introduction of the budget, but in England, the budget speech of the Chancellor of Exchequer is made, not at the time of the presentation of estimates of expenditure in the Committee of Supply, but at a later stage when the revenue part of the budget is introduced in the Committee on Ways and Means.

For the rest, the budgetary procedure in Britain has the same features as in India. As a matter of fact the former is the model on which the latter is based. There is the same executive leadership in budgetary matters, the same political kind of discussion of demands in the House of Commons, the same prohibition on the members of the House of Commons to propose in or addition to the demands as they come from the executive, and the same practice of voting the demands as they originally figure in the budget without any real attempt at reduction. A unified and well-co-ordinated budget prepared and passed according to the wishes of the executive, represented chiefly by the treasurer and the chancellor of Exchequer, is the essence of the British as well as the Indian financial system.

In the U.S.A. things are very different. Before 1921, there was no coherent executive budget in that country. The various departments prepared their estimates, sent them to the department of Treasury which consolidated and sent them to the Congress without any security or co-ordination. In the Congress, in each house, the estimates for expenditure were considered by an Appropriation Committee which worked through 14 sub-committees, each concerned with a particular block of expenditure. Each sub-committee called before it the departmental officials to explain and defend their estimates, and after such reduction, alteration, or addition as it thought fit, it made a report to the parent (Appropriation) Committee containing its recommendation. That body put together the reports of the various sub-committees and presented them to the House of Representatives as its own recommendation. The House' voted the appropriations with such additions or alterations as it thought fit and then they were sent to the Senate to undergo the same procedure at the hands of that body and its Appropriation Committees. The Revenue proposals were considered by a separate Ways and Means Committee in each House and adopted without and attempt to balance them with the expenditure voted.

This chaotic system worked because, thanks mainly to the heavy protective tariff, the revenue proceeds in the U.S.A. generally always exceeded the expenditure requirements. This could not, however, continue indefinitely and even the U.S.A. began to feel and pinching effect of World War I. The result was the passing of the Budget and Accounting Act, 1921, which attempted to introduce certain reforms along the British lines. It set up a Bureau of the Budget (originally in the Department of Treasury but later transferred to the White House and now part of the President's Executive Office) to which now all the departmental estimates come for scrutiny and co-ordination. The Bureau calls the official representatives of the various departments, gives them a hearing and after such revision and review as it thing necessary, produces a unified and coherent budget more or less after the fashion of the British Treasury. This budget is transmitted by the President to the Congress as his executive budget. Departmental representatives are forbidden to plead before the Congressional Committees for the restoration of any cuts made in their estimates by the Bureau.

On account of the separation of powers, the American executive is neither represented in the Congress nor is it in position to exercise financial leadership over it. In each House, the demands are considered by an Appropriation Committee which works through 11 sub-committees in the House of Representatives and 10 in the Senate, each corresponding to one or more of the departments and functional activities of the Government. To co-ordinate the work of these sub-committees, it is now required that all their proposals must clear through the whole Appropriation Committee. Departmental officials appearing before these bodies are forbidden to plead for more than the President has provided for in his estimates. In spite of all this the fact remains that the Houses and their Committees can deal with the President's budget as they please. They are quire free to make additions, increase, or reductions in the demands as they come from the President with the result that by the time it emerges out of the hands of the Congress, very little of the original plan on which it was drawn in the Bureau of the Budget may be left in it. The American budget system is, therefore, still largely disintegrated and un-coordinated. Theoretically, the Appropriation Committees and Houses themselves are agencies of co-ordination but on account of the huge magnitude of the task and the various influences at work, they can achieve it but imperfectly. In recent years an attempt has been made to provide the Houses with a legislative staff agency to enable them to perform functions more effectively but it is doubtful whether any such improvizations can be a satisfactory substitute for the executive leadership like that in Britain and India.

THE EXECUTION OF THE BUDGET

A budget is of no use unless it is enforced, *i.e.*, revenue and expenditure are regulated according to it. Enforcement or execution of the budget is a responsibility of the executive because of grants of money are made by the legislature to it and it is also the agency authorized to collect the taxes.

Control of expenditure within the terms of the budget is a far more complex affair than the collection of revenue, and is budget execution, the primary emphasis is placed on it. The objects of control of expenditure are two, namely, (1) to see that it does not exceed the budgetary grant under and head, and (2) to ensure that it is not improper, extravagant, wasteful. The amounts voted in the budget are the maxima up to which the executive may spend for the specified purposes, and which must not be exceeded in any case without fresh legislative sanction. They do not mean that the executive may spend so much without due regard to necessity and economy. It is always implied that notwithstanding budgetary provision the executive shall spend on any object only the minimum amount absolutely necessary as an ordinarily prudent person does in private life.

The Machinery of Executive Control Over Expenditure

The machinery of executive control over expenditure differs in its details from country to country, but generally speaking, it consists of *(a)* the Finance Ministry or its equivalent by whatever name it may be known, and *(b)* the heads of various administrative departments and their principal lieutenants. We describe the machinery and the way it functions in India, Britain and the U.S.A.

The Finance Ministry and its Control Over Expenditure in India

We have alrcady noticed the role of the Ministry of Finance in the preparation of the budget estimates. To appreciate its functions in connection with the execution of the budget, particularly control over expenditure, it is necessary to bear in mind that the legislature makes the grants to the Government as a whole (technically to the President) and not to individual departments. The Finance Ministry, as the financial representative and adviser to the Government must therefore, be convinced about the advisability and soundness of the proposed expenditure before it allows the administrative ministry concerned to proceed with it. It is true that at the time of the preparation of the budget, the matter is discussed between the two ministries and included in the budget with the concurrence of the Finance Ministry but according to the existing practice, the consent given by the Finance Ministry at this stage is only tentative. This, of course, does not apply to the normal existing expenditure which is taken as a matter of course but new expenditure has to cross this hurdle. The reason why the concurrence of the Indian ministry of finance with proposals for expenditure over new schemes is only tentative at the preparatory stage of the budget was explained in one of the report of Estimates Committee. "At present," says this report, "the budget estimates for the following financial year are prepared towards the middle of the current financial year are broadly stated. The Budget Division of the Ministry of Finance receives the various proposals from the Ministries in one lump sum during one or two months towards the close of the financial year. Consequently, the Budget Division does not have sufficient time to examine the proposals in greater detail and to scrutinise each and every item carefully. The practice has therefore, been that the Budged Division applies broad checks and determines certain gross amounts for the various schemes without committing itself or the Ministry of Finance to their spending during the next financial year. The system is that whatever has been included in the estimates is merely with a view to get the vote of the House thereon and does not entitle the administrative Ministry to incur expenditure unless a detailed expenditure sanction has been issued by the Ministry of Finance.

This procedure means considerable delay in starting new schemes and is one of the most potent factors responsible for the slow progress of many of the development projects. Of course, the remedy lies in the administrative ministries preparing fully detailed schemes at the very outset so that the Finance Ministry may be able to give its sanction to them at an early date; and the minimum of post-budgetary checking and control may be necessary. Total elimination of such control is, however, neither possible nor consistent with the financial accountability of the Government to Parliament.

Apart form the control exercised by it in respect of new expenditure, the Finance Ministry performs a number of other duties also in connection with the carrying out of the budget. These are:-

(a) seeing that administrative ministries do not receive more fund, during the financial year than they can spend, and that they surrender unspent balances as early as possible before the close of the financial year,

(b) Supervising revenue collection through the Central Board of Revenue which collects the more important union taxes like customs, central excise, estates duties, and taxes on income,

(c) Sanctioning reappropriations beyond the competence of the controlling officers,

(d) Watching the progress of expenditure in the spending departments through periodic reports from them, and cautioning them when necessary, and

(e) Giving financial advice and guidance to the Administrative ministries generally.

The Organisation of the Finance Ministry in India

The Indian Finance Ministry consists of two Departments Revenue and Expenditure Department, and the Department of Economic Affairs, each under a secretary. The Revenue and Expenditure Department has three principal Divisions, namely, the Revenue Division, the Civil Expenditure Division, and the Defence Expenditure Division. The Revenue is responsible for revenue policy and collection. The Civil Expenditure Division is concerned with the scrutiny and sanctin of the expenditure of the various administrative ministries as described above, and also for determining the pay, allowances, leave and other general conditions of service of Government employees. It has 4 to 5 branches, each under a joint secretary, and each of these branches deals with the scrutiny and sanction of a group of administrative ministries. The joint secretary in charge of the branch functions as the financial adviser to the various administrative ministries attached to his branch. Under the joint secretary, there may be deputy and under secretaries. All these officers are authorised to accord sanction to the proposals of the Administrative ministries with which they deal, in a varying measure. The Defence Expenditure Division is concerned similarly with the scrutiny and control of defence expenditure. Its head is of the status of an additional secretary and is designate as Financial Adviser Defence. This division also prepares the budget of the Defence departments.

The Department of Economic Affairs also has three Divisions called the Internal Finance Division, the External Finance Division, and the Budget Division. Here we are concerned with the Budget division only. It is concerned with the preparation and consolidation of the budget (except railways), public debts, audit and Accounts, and placing of the appropriation accounts and Audit report before the Public Accounts Committee. While the Finance Ministry is the biggest executive authority in respect of sanction and control of expenditure, there is below it a regular hierarchy of sanctioning and controlling authorities made up of the administrative officers of various ranks. The sanctioning power vested in each of them is graded according to their rank in the hierarchy.

The Departmental Controlling Officer

Subject to the overall control of the Finance Ministry, the Head of each administrative department is designated as the controlling officer in respect of the expenditure occurring in his department. Money is actually spent by the officers of the administrative departments over the services they provide. These services embrace the entire country, and the officers conducting them are stationed in its various parts. Geographically, therefore, the expenditure of each department takes place at numerous places far removed from the capital and from one another.

The best method of doing this is that the entire allotment of the Department should be placed at the credit of its Head in the headquarters' bank and all departmental expenditure, no matter where it occurs, should be met with withdrawals from it. Thus, the Head by looking in his credit account at the bank can read and know at any time the progress of expenditure in his department under the various heads and sub-heads, and the balance of budgetary grant, and can apply such control as may be necessary. This is actually the system they have in England. The public funds are kept in the Exchequer account at the Bank of England. A royal order under the Sign Manual authorizes the Treasury, with the concurrence of the Comptroller and Auditor-General, to issue from the Exchequer account the amounts authorised by the Appropriation Act. The Treasury from time to time requests the Comptroller and Auditor-General to grant credits for lump sums and the latter, satisfied, that the amounts asked for are within the limits of the Appropriation Act writes to the Bank granting the credit asked for. Then, at the request of the Treasury the Bank transfers sums (within the amount of the credit) from the Exchequer to the supply account of the Paymaster-General, specifying the services in respect of which the issues are to be made. The Heads of the various departments obtain the funds required to meet their bills by issuing 'payable orders' on the Paymaster-General. The Heads of the Department maintain suitable registers to watch that the 'payable orders' issued by them against any head or vote do not result in the excess over budgetary grant under that head or vote.

But in India, the payments are not concentrated in this way in the hands of the controlling officers nor are they made from one source like the Bank of England. In this country as we shall see later, receipts and payments take place at some 300 and odd treasuries, one in each district, with branches at the sub-divisional centres. Payments at these treasuries are made on the certificate of numerous disbursing officers belonging to the various departments. The disbursing officers submit monthly accounts to the controlling officer of their departments, who gets these accounts classified and consolidated under the various sub-heads. These departmental accounts which are periodically reconciled with the accounts kept by the Accountant-General on the basis of fortnightly accounts received from the treasuries, enable the controlling officer to watch the flow of expenditure in his department against the budgetary grants and to apply the necessary control.

The Comptroller and Auditor-General of India, in spite of his designation, has no control over the issue of money from the consolidated fund of India. So long as the centers of payment remain dispersed as they are in our country, control at the very source of issues of money either by the Comptroller and Auditor-General or the controlling officer is impossible, and without such control at the source, excess over grants cannot be effectively prevented. "In India", said the Comptroller and Auditor-General of India in the course of a speech, "due to the very large number of treasuries in which Government payments are made, it is impossible in the existing conditions to keep track of up-to-date progress of expenditure either by the executive or by the Accounts authorities.

The remedy for this lies in the abolition of the Treasury system of payments, concentrating them at one source as in England and giving to the Comptroller and Auditor-General the control over issue of money from the Consolidated Fund of India. The vast size of our country and the comparatively underdeveloped state of banking facilities, have prevented this hitherto, but these obstacles have to be overcome if effective control over public expenditure is to be established.

❐

9

Performance of Budget

A Performance Budget is a challenge to the traditional budget system. It presents public expenditure in terms of functions, programmes and activities. It thus clearly differs from the line-item budget which emphasises staff, furniture, equipments, etc. In the words of Administrative Reforms Commission, a Performance Budget is "a technique for presenting government operations in terms of functions, programmes, activities and projects." Burkhead opines "Performance budgeting can be most appropriately associated with a budget classification that emphasises the things which government lays. Performance budgeting shifts the emphasis from the means of accomplishment to the accomplishment itself" The Mayor's Committee on Management Survey in U.S.A. explained 'programme budgeting' which practically speaking is the same concept in the words "A programme budget tells in advance what activities the departments and the government as a whole are authorised to carry forward in terms of expenditure" for a given year. "It emphasises the work to be done, not the number of clerks, pencils and paper to be used in doing that work." The Hoover's Commission of the U.S.A. also explains the concept lucidly in the following words "We recommend that the whole budgetary concept....... should be refashioned by the adoption of a budget based on functions, activities and projects; this we designate a 'performance budget'. Such an approach would focus attention upon the general and relative importance of the work to be done or upon the services to be rendered rather than upon the things to be acquired......

An analysis of the above opinions reveals the performance budgeting indicates a process that seeks the implementation and control of programmes through budget allocation. The governmental operations are presented in terms of functions, programmes, activities and projects. Such a functional classification of government transaction results in identification of government activities in the annual budget in the financial and physical terms. Thus a direct correlation of inputs and outputs is established and performance is assessed in terms of costs. The emphasis is shifted from the means of accomplishment to the accomplishments themselves. In fact the performance budgeting is concerned with the ends to be served by the government rather than the expenditure incurred on several objects.

All this leads us to conclude that a performance budget is prepared in functional categories, viz., education, health or agricultural development. Each functional category is then divided into programmes, for instance education may be divided into Higher Education, Secondary and Primary education. Each 'programme' is thereafter divided into 'activities, which, in turn, are divided into 'projects'. To be more precise, training of school teachers is an activity whereas construction of a school building is a 'project'.

Process of Performance Budgeting. Following are the phases of performance budgeting: *(i)* Establishing a functional classification of all governmental operations; *(ii)* Developing a system of cost-accounting and financial management which may accord with the functional classification; *(iii)* Establishing quantitative hours and yardsticks of performance and unit costs; *(iv)* Evolving under each programme and activity objective system of reporting and evaluation which in its turn provides timely feedback to the programme managers. The process of classification in performance budgeting follows following steps:

(a) Prepare a comprehensive list of all the objectives and scope of work of the Ministry/Department or undertaking;

(b) Lay down the programmes and activities in such a manner as would lend itself to treatment for allocation of funds from the priority point of view;

(c) Frame from this list a functional classification that indicates vividly the range of work of the Ministry, Department or undertaking;

(d) The programmes and activities be so classified as to facilitate the compilation of accounts and computation of costs. It may also facilitate the consideration of alternative courses of action for arriving at a specified goal of action.

The steps *(ii)* to *(iv)* of performance budgeting have already been discussed in earlier chapter on budgeting. However, a format of Performance Budget is referred as follows:

FORMAT FOR PERFORMANCE BUDGET

1. Introductory—objective organisation
2. Financial Requirements : (a) Programme; (b) Activity classification; (c) Sources of financing.
3. Explanation of financial Requirements.

(a)

Name of Activity	Actual	Devised Estimates (Current Year)	Budget Estimates (Next Year)

(b) Nature and purpose of Activity.

Physical work, inputs and outputs.

Workload factors, norms, yardsticks and standards.

—Progress during last and current year (Actural vs Target)

Explanation of variation.

Targets for next year.

Requirements for inputs, including staff, materials and equipment.

Detailed work plans and schedule.

ADVANTAGES OF PERFORMANCE BUDGETING

Following are some of the striking advantages of performance budgeting:

(a) It enables the correlation of the physical and financial aspects of every programme and activity. The existing budgetary system does not make such a correlation possible.

(b) It helps in affecting improvement in the procedure of budget formulation and reviewing the actual progress of programmes at all levels of governments.

(c) It leads to over-all efficient financial management and programmes and projects. It eliminates the callous waste of money that occurs during the closing months of the financial year to avoid the lapse of the financial grants.

(d) It helps improving decision making and management of programmes and objectives, an indirect help to the administrative authorities.

(e) It affixes the responsibility very precisely. It indicates who was responsible for what and earmàrks authority for executing the work for the next year.

(f) It facilitates the better appreciation and review of the objectives of the government, the direction of outlays and the results accruing out of these onlays, for the benefit of the legislature.

(g) It provides a clear and true picture of spending and revenue alternatives.

(h) It clearly shows as to what was done in the previous year and at what cost, both unit-wise and programme-wise.

The administrative Reforms Commission (1969-70) also visualised the following benefits of Performance Budgeting.

(i) It improves the formulation of the budget and facilitates the process of decision-making at all levels of government.

(ii) It enhances the accountability of the management and provides an additional tool to management control of financial operation.

(iii) It presents more clearly the purposes and the objectives for which the funds are sought and to bring out the programmes and accomplishments in financial and physical terms.

(iv) It helps in a better understanding and better review of the budget by the legislature.

(v) It renders performance audit more purposeful and effective.

Condition for the Adoption of Performance budgeting in India

A re-orientation becomes essentials for introducing a technique of such a complex nature as the performance budgeting. The important prerequisites necessary for the introduction of performance budgeting in India are pointed out as under :

(1) To Evolve Way for Effecting Measurement. Performance budgeting enacts the measurement and evaluation of the 'results' or 'yields' of a programme, but in India, in a sizeable part of government operations there are no 'end-products.' the concept may not be useful when applied. It is pointed out that "even in the cases where the end-products can be identifiied and quantified, there appears to have been no systematic effort at evolving work or perfromance units with a view to measuring the physcial progress or accomplishments with few exceptions like Public Works Department." According to the A.R.C. Working Group, "It may, however, be mentioned here that the idea of measuring workload is not altogether unknown in India. Apart from the P.W.D the O & M units of the ministries and the Staff Inspection Unit (previously Special Re-organisation Unit) of the Ministry of Finance, etc., have been engaged for quite some time in evolving workload factors, indices and ratios in respect of manpower utilisation and related aspects and have been adopting the technique of work study, work measurement etc........ These studies can be carried further and suitable yardsticks norms evolved in due course, for measuring the output and accomplishments."

In the field of government programmes and activities. Physical measurement may be of three types: *(i)* measures of achievement, reflecting 'the effect of the work and the achievement of objective or programmes; *(ii)* measures of 'yields' or 'results' reflecting the results of the work or output; and *(iii)* measures of workload in terms of volume of work, time and costs. In the productivity ratios can be developed in combination with data on the employment of labour, the time spent and the resources expended. This can be used to show results in terms of units.

(2) Advance Programming. It is essential for the success of performance budgeting to have a system of advance programming of the government operations on a long-term basis. It is pointed out that; "in the context of planned economic development, long-term planning with annual break-down is already invogue, indications already exist about operational task, times schedules, targets and other aspects." There is greater emphasis on the process of annual Plans today which makes it possible to frame 'budgetary requests adequately supported by necessary administrative planning and projection into the future."

(3) Representation of Total Cost. The existing cash accounting basis, it not necessary that the cost of a programme or acitivity as shown in the budget may represent the total cost of the programme or activity. To quote Working Group, "It has been recognised that, in the initial stages, accounts should not be unduly disturbed. Refinements such as accrual accounting, allocation of overheads like general administration and common services, etc., may also be deferred to a latter stage. The introduction of performance budgeting elsewhere has not been made contingent on shift from cash to accural basis. Moreover, the advantage to be gained by having total or fulll or accrued cost may not be commensurate with the cost and layout involved in a radical departure immediately from the long established accounting systems and practices."

(4) Functional Classification. System of performance budgeting requires that the outlay shown in the budget documents for any programme should represent the 'total cost of such programme of activity and should be available at one place.' This could be achieved only if all outlays are classified on a functional basis without considering the nature of the Departments/Organisations incurring them. This requirement is not feasible under the present circumstances.

(5) Concentration of Authority. Under the system of performance budgeting it is required that the execution of the budget and the authority carrying out the programmes must be located in one agency. In India this has been made possible, to a considerable extent by the extensive delegation of powers to the administrative Ministries/ Departments supplemented by the recent changes affected in the budgetary procedures. "With the greater delegation of the administrative Ministry with the budgetary process, the state of affairs will increasingly approximate to the ideal situation where the budgeting and administering agencies will be the one and the same. Also, if suitable norms and standards could be laid down in respect of a wider field of governmental activities as is inherent in performance budgeting and if the financial management skills could be developed in the administrative Ministries, they, with the aid of their financial advisers, will be able to formulate budgets in such a manner as to obviate the necessity of modification in a large measure by an outside agency, *i.e.*, Finance Ministry."

(6) Strengthening the Reporting System. Under performance budgeting, it is commonly stressed that there is a need to strengthen the reporting systems because an adequate system of performance reporting is an indispensable element of performance budgeting. "At present reporting is mainly in financial terms in the context of and on the lines of budgetary appropriations... With a view to relating financial progress with actual achievements, it is necessary that both the physical and financial aspects are interwoven into a single report against a background of time and cost and a projection into future commitments. Such a performance reporting at regular intervals is an indispensable aid to performance budgeting and expenditure control."

(7) Evolving Necessary Data. The introduction of performance budgeting makes it essential to evolve the necessary financial data through the accounting system. Whereas the existing accounting system would require, to be modernised if the decision-to introduce the technique of performance budgeting is contemplated.

To conclude in the words of Working Groups, "The introduction of performance budgeting in the existing circumstances and at this stage of the development of our institutions and procedures may be attended with some initial difficulties. But these difficulties should be capable of being resolved in a satisfactory manner, given the necessary motivation, resources and a spirit of cooperation. The benefits to be derived from the new technique should not be viewed in terms of costs involved, but have to be viewed in the larger context of securing benefits resulting from more effective control, greater efficency and allround improvement in governmental operations. The conversion to performance budgeting has to be viewed as a major step towards the improvement of the budgeting structure with a view to better comprehensibility and towards making budget a programme oriented document. Having regard to the significant changes involved, the installation process should of necessity, be carried out in a phased manner. In the nature of things, the introduction of this technique has to be an evolutionary process to be developed and extended gradually over a number of years."

The Management Approach in Budgeting

In the conventional system of budgeting, there is an emphasis on financial aspects of governmental operations. According to U.N.O.Publication. "The financial accountability to the legislature is usually the overriding consideration and this permeats the entire budgetary process. Emphasis is placed mainly on the observance of appropriation limits. Moreover, the object-cum-organisations classification of expenditures in the budget does not enable identification of programmes or projects and, furthermore, is not related to the cost of major inputs or the work performed. In other words, the system of budgeting does not provide information on what a government is actually doing and what it gets for the money spent. Of course, it may be possible to compile such information from departmental reports or other supplementary documents, but in many cases this information cannot be linked directly with financial data as they appear in a budget or in the accounts because it does not constitute a basis for budget management. The absence of pertinent information of this type reduces the usefulness of this budgetary approach even for purposes of legislative review and appropriation. The sanctions resulting from this process then tend to be accorded to policy objectives that are not explicit in the budgets".

In general the government budget includes certain entrepreneurial operations popularly known as departmental undertakings, in addition to normal administrative programmes and activities. It has been observed that, "the institutional separation of enterprise activities rests partly on management considerations, but this emphasis on management aspects, sound as it is, is rarely found in its application to public sector transactions included in a budget. A plan is essentially a blue-print for action while budgetary activity is mainly operational in nature. It would be, therefore, only logical to expect that management considerations should be of eminent importance in budgeting and that the budget should be so devised as to highlight the truely operational character, both physical and financial, of any given programme. Such is, however, not the experience in many developing countries. As a result, the operational character of government budget and its links with planning are largely obscured".

The efforts to correct the anomalies in the coventional system of budgeting has been the ground for the need, development adoption and use of performance budgeting. The primary consideration has been to bring to the fore management aspects in the budgetary framework and thereby to bring out the 'most significant economic, financial and physical aspects of the budgetary activity.'

The concept of performance budgeting was evolved in the U.S.A. and it has been thoroughly applied there. Although a programme based budget was in practice in various forms in some part of the U.S.A. The concept as it is understood now got a major recognition in view of the 'Hoover Commission's Report' in 1949. The commission, recognising that "the most important aspect in budgeting is the performance in respect of the work to be done or the services to be rendered and the cost involvement of such work/service," recommended that the whole budgetary concept of the Federal

Government should be refashioned by the adoption of a budget based upon functions activities and projects' and this was designated by the Commission as a 'performance budget'.

A.E.Buck's proposals supplemented the recommedations by the Commissions's Task Force Report. It was stated : "A programme or performance budget should be substituted for the present budget, thus presenting in a document of much briefer compass the government's expenditure requirements in terms of services, activities, and work projects rather than in terms of the things bought. Such a budget would not detract from congressional responsibility and should greatly improve and expedite committee consideration."

In a follow up action to the recommendations of the Hoover Commission the Federal Government in the U.S.A., took a policy decision to formulate its budget on a performance basis since 1951.

Performance Budgeting

Performance budgeting is a technique of presenting government financial operations in the forms of functions programmes, activities and projects. "Through such a meaningful classification of transactions, government activities are sought to be identifiied in the budget in financial and physical terms so that a proper relationship between inputs and outputs could be established and performance assessed in relation to costs." Thus the process of performance budgeting is not only a technique, it constitutes a new approach to budget formulation and execution. Since the costs and benefits are indicated side by side this technique helps in the decision making regarding allocation of funds for various programmes.

Performance budgeting has also been termed as a budgeting technique that emphasises "the budget as a work plan".

According to the Hoover Commission Report,"The Federal budget is as inadequate document, poorly organised and improperly designed to serve its major purpose; which is to present an understandable and workable finanacial plan for the expenditures of the government. The document has grown larger and larger each year as the Government's requirements have increased, but its general framework and method of presentation have not changed." Accordingly the Commission recommended that "the whole budgetary concept of the Federation Government should be refashioned by the adoption of a budget based upon functions, activities and projects" and designated this the "performance budget".

Difference Between Performance Budgeting and Conventional Budgeting

Performance budgeting is a better and forward step. "The previous periods of almost universal use of unmodified object of expenditure budgeting (convensional budgeting) was incongruous with announced objectives of making the budget a management tool". The two types of budgeting technique different in scope and their content.

(1) Performance budgeting, shifts emphasis from the budget 'as a means of accomplishment to the accomplishments themselves', and concerns itself basically with the objectives set out by the government and not on the outlays incurred on several projects. 'An important aspect of the technique of performance budgeting is the precise detailment of the job to be performed or services to be rendered and a realistic estimate of what that job or service will cost.'

(2) Preparation of a performance budget is based on 'functional categories and their sub-division into programmes, activities and projects rather than being prepared in terms of organisational units and the objects of expenditure.' "The object classification shows what government purchases but not why; accordingly, it does not show the nature of governmental programmes or accomplishments under these programmes."

(3) A performance budget formulated in terms of costs and yields enables management control 'by bringing out the programmes and accomplishments in financial and physical terms' closely interlinked into one detailed document.

Under performance budgeting, the whole area of governmental operations are divided into functions, programmes, and activities/ projects. 'A function represents a major division of the total efforts of the government such as Education, Health, Agriculture, Industry, etc. Programmes are broad categories within a function that identify the end-products or accomplishments towards the fulfillment of the objectives of a function. They broadly reflect the responsibilities of major organisational units of the government.' Activities constitute the collection of homogeneous types of work in a programme with a purpose to contribute towards the accomplishment of the programmes. 'The term project is generally used to distinguish such activities as are of a captial nature.' Thus, after World War II, attempts to make the management approach really effective were intensified, and "performance budgeting" was urged: There was nothing new about the concept, for it meant emphasising the budget as a "Work Plan".

Performance Budgeting and Programme Budgeting

Some distinction has been pointed out in the past between a programme budget and a performance budget, but the Hoover Commission did not seem to consider them as different concepts. "There is no precise definition for performance budgeting; it has come to mean something different in every jurisdiction which puts it into operation. In particular, there has been a tendency to make programme budget and performance budget synonymous terms, and this has contirbuted a good deal to the terminological confusion. In attempt to clarify what is meant here by programme and performance, definitions will precede organisational and hierarchal lines. For present purposes, programme will be defined in relation to a higher level of organisation than performance. A programme embraces a number of performance untis. Programme and performance may also be distinguised according to their time dimension. Budgeting programme are inherently forward-looking, a projection of the economic and social policies of a government. Performance must be based on the past on record of prior accomplishment. In the preparation of budget estimates programme determinations should precede and set the framework in which the measurement of performance can be undertaken."

A United nation Manual on Programme and Performance Budgeting has however made a useful distinction between programme budgeting and performance budgeting. "In programme budgeting, the principal emphasis is on a budget classification in which functions, programmes, and their sub-divisions are established for each agency, and these are related to accurate and meaningful financial data. Performance budgeting involves the development of more refined management tools, such as unit costs, work measurement, and performance standards. Of course, the measurement of work, both in a physical and financial sense, presumes an already formulated set of work units which can be derived only when programmes and their sub-divisions are first established. In this case, performance budgeting is an all-inclusive concept embodying programme formulation as well as measurement of the performance of work in the accomplishment of programme objectives."

Objectives of Performance Budgeting

Its main objects are:

(a) to coordinate the physical and financial aspects of every programme or activity;

(b) to improve budget formulation, review and decision-making at all levels of management in the government machinery;

(c) to facilitate better appreciation and review by the legislature;

(d) to make possible more effective performance audit;

(e) to measure progress towards longterm objectives as envisaged in a development Plan; and

(f) to integrate the annual budgets and development Plans."

In our country, having a planned economic development, there is a major place for the public sector which constitute a major step towards accelerating economic growth, the technique of performance budgeting has its own advantages. The major advantage lie in the fact that 'it serves to bring together the financial and physical implications of each programme, facilitating thereby programming, decision making, review of the progress and control for the management,' directed towards a better, definite purposeful and intelligible presentation of govenment's financial activities to the legislature.

Performance budgeting seeks to focus attention on the size of the programmes to be implemented. The purpose of this technique of budgeting is to identify the services and the cost of particular services. It emphasises the functions of the government in terms of programmes and projects. The essence of performance budgeting lies in the explanation of the activity pattern and work programmes of the department to which it relates. Its one more purpose is to facilitate comparative evaluation of programmes in terms of cost and benefit.

❑

10

Budgeting for Economic Development

Literally the word budget means a leather bag or satchel to carry official papers in. From that association, it came to mean those papers themselves, more particularly the papers containing the financial proposals for the year.

In its current sense, the term budget means the plan of the expenditure and of revenue to balance that expenditure, of usually a public authority. We say 'usually', because private concerns and individuals, also Many have their budgets, and we do speak of the budgets of the business concerns, of family budgets of this or that class of people, or of particular persons. The budget need not always be annual. There many be a long-term budget covering many years, or a short-term monthly or even weekly budget. In public administration, however, we are concerned with the budgets of governmental authorities only and it is almost the universal practice to prepare these budgets on an annual basis.

The term budget connotes both the financial plan presented to the legislature for its sanction, and the sanctioned plan as it emerges after being passed by the legislature. In India, the word budget is sometimes used as an equivalent of the estimates or the expenditure only, *e.g.*, when we speak of the 'budget' of a department. In England, the use of the word is generally restricted to the revenue or taxation part of the financial plan, only. In the U.S.A. the term 'budgeting' is used to connote the entire financial process consisting of the preparation of the budget, its enactment by legislature, its execution, accounting, and audit.

The Financial Year

The basis of the budget preparation is the financial year, but the dates of its commencement are different in different countries. In India, England, and most of the Commonwealth countries it begins on 1st April and ends on the 31st March, but the corresponding dates in the U.S.A., Australia, Italy, Sweden, etc. are 1st July and 30th June,and in France and a number of other continental countries, the 1st January and 31st December.

It has been suggested that for India the present fixation of the financial year is unsuitable and it would be better to have it from 1st November to 31st October, or from 1st January to 31st December. Ours is a predominantly agricultural country where the crops and hence the financial outlook are mainly dependent on the south west monsoon. Budget preparation for the ensuring financial year commencing on April 1, has to begin some time in August or September of the current year when the complete state of rainfall is not known.

Long-term Budgeting

Usually public budgeting is annual because it enables the legislature to exercise a closer control over the activities of the Government than would be possible if a budget for many years were voted. It is, however, contended that a country's needs for a single year cannot be intelligently budgeted for, without consideration of its long-term needs. Many of the improvements needed, *e.g.*, the strengthening of defences extension of communication, economic and industrial development, etc., are costly and cannot be effected within a single year. Long-term budgeting is, therefore, essential to make suitable provision for these. Though in some American jurisdictions budgeting for two years or so prevails, this cannot be really called long-term budgeting which in effect, is only another name for financial planning over a number of years to finance the development and improvements required. In this sense all these countries which have adopted the policy of planned development do have long term budgeting of a kind. The first and second five-year plans of India with their targets of Rs. 2,000 and about 5,000 crores of expenditure and the ways and means of meeting it are nothing but long-term budgets of this kind.

Long-term budgets or plans do not involve actual voting of appropriations for the entire period of the plan by the legislature though it may be called upon to approve the plan in principle and broad outline, nor do they include detailed estimates of expenditure. They are rather a forecast of the outlay required.

The steps in formulating a long-term budget are the following:

(1) To determine and forecast the needs of the country over a period of several years, and the outlay required to meet them.

(2) To explore the possible sources—taxation, savings borrowings, etc.—of raising the amount of outlay required.

(3) To prepare a balanced programme for the entire period, which should contain the various items of development agreed upon, and should also be flexible enough to permit modifications according to the prevailing circumstances.

(4) To arrange the various improvement projects in order of their relative priority.

(5) To incorporate in each year's annual budget a portion of the long-term budget according to the time-schedule, and to get it duly passed by the legislature to do the necessary revision for the future year's programme in the light of the prevailing circumstances, and to add the forecast for an additional year for the one which has been transferred to the current budget.

Thus, the long-term budget may always cover a fixed number of years, from 3 to 10 as desired. Every year, one year's programme will become part of the current year's budget, and one future year's programme will be added to make up for the transfer.

Single vs. Plural Budgets

Most of the Governments have a single budget incorporating the financial estimates of all their departments. The advantage of it is that the overall financial position of the Government, as a whole, is revealed. If there be a number of department wise budgets, some of them may show a surplus and others a deficit so that the net situation for the government as a whole may not be known except by complicated calculations and adjustments. It is the practice of some countries like France, Germany, Switzerland, and India, however to have two budgets—one for the administrative departments and the other for commercial enterprises such as railways. India has had a separate railway budget since 1921 when the Acworth Committee recommended that the Indian railways should be run on business lines. The advantage of the arrangement is that a business approach to railway policy is facilitated, and the railways can keep their profits for their own development subject to the payment of fixed annual contribution to the general revenues of the country.

The allotments of funds for other business enterprises of the Indian Government, however, form part of its general, budget figuring as certain lump sums therein. For the rest, these undertakings prepare their own budgets in an autonomous fashion. The budget of the Damodar Valley Corporation has to be laid (but not passed) before the Union Parliament and the legislatures of two participating states—Bihar and Bengal.

The Economic and Social Implication of the Budget

In the olden days when the philosophy of laissez-faire governed the activities of the state, the budget was looked upon merely as a devise for securing orderliness and method in management of the state finances. Economy in expenditure and the imposition of as little burden on the tax-payer as possible were regarded as its chief merits. Today, the state is no longer expected to confine itself to the neutral role of an umpire holding the ring for the competing individuals each trying for his own prosperity and well-being as best as he may. Under the complex conditions of the modern industrial society, the state has been assigned a definitely positive role in securing national prosperity and welfare. With this change of attitude towards the state, there has come a new conception of the budget also as a major instrument of economic and social policy. Though the instrumentality of an appropriately constructed budget, a number of economic and social objects may be realized, particularly.

(a) increasing of production,

(b) redressing the inequalities in the distributions of income and wealth,

(c) combating inflation caused by war or other crisis, and

(d) securing full employment for the people as part of the goal of the welfare state.

The budget can step up production by protecting and subsidizing industry and agriculture. It can redress inequalities in the distribution of income and wealth by the increased taxation of the large income on a graduated scale, imposition of inheritance taxes and death duties, and by using the money thus obtained for the provision of free or cheap social services like education, health, housing, etc., for the poorer sections of the community. It can fight inflation caused by the vast issue of paper money during war and other crises by withdrawal of the portions of money from the hands of the people through heavy taxation and borrowing thus curtailing their purchasing power.

The manipulation of the budget to secure one of the above objects is a complex operation requiring expert technical knowledge and experience of economic and financial matters and reliable data and statistics not only of the governmental income and expenditure but of the entire national income and expenditure, both in the public as well as the private sectors. This new technique of the budget preparation has been installed in England now for about a decade and the way for it is being prepared in India also by compilation of annual reports on national income, the first of which was published in 1951.

Some Principles of Budget Making

Long experience of the leading countries of the world suggests certain principles, to which budget making should conform. Of course none of these is of such absolute validity as to permit no departure from it in any case, but normally their observance is considered essential for sound budgetary practice. The more important of these principles are the following:

(1) Normally the budget must be a balanced one.

(2) Its estimates should be on a cash basis.

(3) Estimating should be closed.

(4) The form of estimates should correspond to the form of accounts.

(5) Its revenue and capital portions should be kept distinct.

(6) Budgeting should be gross and not net.

(7) The Rule of the lapse.

1. The first principle is that the budget should be balanced, *i.e.*, the estimated expenditure should not exceed the estimated revenue or income. This is the well-known rule of private finance with which every one of us is familiar, *i.e.*, one must keep within one's income if one is not to go bankrupt. Public finance differs from private in certain important particulars, specially in the greater elasticity in the matter of revenue which can be increased, when necessary, to meet extra expenditure, but there is a limit to this, and a state which habitually budgets for more expenditure than the revenue available, would be courting bankruptcy in the long run.

When the amounts of expenditure and revenue in a budget are equal or nearly so it is called a balanced budget. If the expenditure is less than the anticipated revenue, it is a surplus budget. If the expenditure is more than the estimated revenue, it is called deficit budget.

Certain newer trends of economic thought, however, consider deficit budget in certain circumstances not only excusable, but also necessary. They look upon the deficit budget as an instrument of 'compensatory fiscal policy' which alone can cure the ills from which the modern capitalist economy is prone to suffer periodically. The argument is as follows: Capitalism is based on the free competitive enterprise of private individuals and corporations. Such enterprise is run for the sake of profit. It turns in this direction or that according to the pull of the profit. The result is over-production in certain sectors, followed by slump and under-employment which reduce the purchasing power of the people and make the depression progressively deeper and more widespread. To fight such depression, what is required is to create more work and income for the people. The State can do it by increased governmental expenditure on public works, etc., and finance such expenditure through deficit budgeting. A balanced budget gives back to the people one way or another the same amount which it takes from them in the shape of taxation or borrowing. Its effect on private economy is, therefore, nil. A deficit budget, on the other hand, provides for more expenditure than the anticipated revenue filling the gap between the two by the issue of uncovered paper money.

Deficit financing has thus now become a recognized method of fighting trade depression. It is also resorted to, to meet the huge expenditure of war and of development plans. It is, however, not safe to indulge in it beyond a certain point, for its effect is inflation which if left unchecked, results in soaring prices and serious depreciation of the currency system of the country.

2. The principle of the cash basis of the budget means that its estimates of expenditure and income should relate to what is expected to be actually spent or received during the year, and not to liabilities or demands which incurred or which accrue within the year under reference, but are to be met or realized in some other year. For example, if certain sums on account of arrears of tax relating to the year 1954-55 are realized in the year 1955-56 they should be shown in the receipt estimates of the latter year and not of the former. Same

way, if the liability for any payments was incurred in the former year but was actually met in the latter year, it should be shown in the expenditure estimates of the latter year only. In Britain, the U.S.A., and India cash budgeting of this type obtains.

In sharp contrast to this, there is the system of revenue budgeting obtaining in the continental countries like France. Under this system the budget estimates of a financial year are based on the liabilities of payment and demands for revenue according to that year, regardless of when they may actually be made or realized. In the example given above the arrears of revenue relating to the year 1954-55 would figure in the receipts of that year, even though they may be actually realized in the year 1955-56. So, also, about expenditure.

The advantage of the cash budgeting is that it enables the final preparation of accounts of a financial year to be done soon after its close, but its drawback is that it does not reveal the true financial picture for that year. But deferring the payments due to a future year, surplus instead of deficit may be shown in the present year's budget, which is misleading. The revenue type of the budget is free from this defect but it involves long delay in the preparation and presentation of the final accounts.

3. The third principle of budget-making is that the distinction between recurring expenditure and income on the one hand, and capital payments and receipts on the other; should be maintained, and the two should be shown in two separate parts of the budget known as the current or revenue budget and the capital budget. Receipts from loans, deposits, sale proceeds of property, etc., are occasional and not recurring, and so are also,on the expenditure side, capital outlay on works, debt payment, paying back the deposits, etc., The consequence of not keeping the recurring and capital items separate would confuse the financial picture. Current expenditure might, in that case, be met out of the loan funds and a balance, or surplus might be shown when really there is a deficit. So, the revenue and capital parts of the budget are kept distinct and balanced separately, and the overall surplus and deficit is found out by taking both into account.

4. The fourth principle is that budgeting should be gross and not net. This applies equally to accounting also. Gross budgeting means that all the transactions both of receipts and expenditure should be fully shown, and not merely the resultant net position. Neglect of this rule results in the short-circulating of financial procedure, laxity of financial control; and incomplete accounts. If a department with an estimated expenditure of 4 lakhs, and receipts of 2 lakhs budgeted on a net basis, it would go to the legislature with a request for grant for 2 lakhs only thus depriving the legislature of its control over half of its expenditure which it met out of its receipts.

In certain exceptional cases where expenditure of receipts may be merely nominal, *e.g.*, in case of expenditure by the Union Government on account of a state to be reimbursed subsequently by the latter, these are not entered into the budget as that would artificially swell the expenditure and income figures. In Britain the so-called 'appropriations in aid' furnish examples of net budgeting.

5. The fifth budgetary principle is that estimating should be as close *i.e.*, exact as possible. There should neither be gross over-estimating or gross under-estimating. If there is over estimating of expenditure, unnecessarily heavy taxation may have to be imposed on the people to raise the amounts. If there is under-estimating, the whole budget may be thrown out of gear when it comes to execution. Close estimating is achieved by taking past three years' average figures of receipts and expenditure under various heads as the starting basis, and making appropriate variations due to special circumstances which can be foreseen.

An absolutely exact estimating is, however, a counsel of perfection rarely realized in practice. It is a common experience that expenditure has an uncanny way of going above the estimates, while revenue has the opposite trick of falling below the estimate. Hence, the practical precept is to be rather liberal in estimating expenditure; and conservative in the estimate of income. This is a sound rule within certain limits, but serious deviations of the actuals from the estimates are considered reprehensible and should not be allowed to occur. Itemized estimates are an aid to close budgeting while lump sum estimates tend often to be wide of the mark.

6. The sixth principle of budget-making relates to its form which should correspond to the form of accounts *i.e.*, the budgetary heads should be the same as those of accounts. This facilitates budget preparation, budgetary control, and the keeping of accounts. In India, the form of the budget is prescribed by the Finance Minister after considering any suggestions made by the Estimates Committee.

7. The seventh and last budgetary principle is the rule of lapse. This means that any part of the grant not spent within the financial year expires at its close and cannot be kept over for the future. No reserve funds can be built up without statutory authorization.

The rule of lapse is essential for the effective financial control. If the unspent balance of one year were available for expenditure in future years, departments could live on their accumulated balances for at least some time and would, to that extent become independent of the legislature's control. But the rule is inconvenient from the point of view of economical planning of expenditure.

GOOD BUDGETARY PRINCIPLES

Budget thus, being an effective instrument of financial and work management must conform to certain budgetary principles. There are no rigid principles for budget-making but the following ones have been framed on the basis of long experience of the leading countries and it is desirable that they should be observed for sound budgeting.

Budget Formulation is the Responsibility of the Executive

As the Chief Executive is responsible for running the administration, he is in the best position to say what funds are required for it. It should, therefore, be the duty of the Chief Executive to formulate the Budget. But the Budget framing is a stupendous task,and he must, therefore, be aided and advised by a body of specialists. In India, the Ministry of Finance, in England the Treasury and in U.S.A. the Bureau of Budget, help their respective Chief

Executives in the budget-planning. In Parliamentary governments there exists the well accepted principle "that no demands for grants can be made except on the recommendation of the Executive". The principle also makes it clear that it is the function of the executive alone to prepare the budget. The Parliament can decrease or refuse the demands presented to it by the Executive but it cannot increase them. This principle is of great merit because the Chief Executive being the actual expending authority is the better judge of how much money is required for a particular purpose and if more is given to the Executive than what it needs, it cannot be made responsible for money it did not need. That would obviously lead to wastage and extravagance.

Budget should be a Balanced One

The Budget should be a balanced one, *i.e.*, the estimated expenditure should not exceed the revenue or income. When the amounts of the expenditure in a budget are equal or nearly so of the income accrued it is called a balanced budget. If the expenditure is less than the anticipated revenue it is a 'Surplus Budget' and if the expenditure is more than the anticipated revenue, it is called a 'Deficit Budget'. "The balancing of the budget", says Mr. P.K. Wattal, "Is the first requisite of financial stability and occupies the same place in the financial administration as the maintenance of law and order in the Executive administration. On the other hand, unbalanced budgets are bound sooner or later to weaken the faith of investors and lead to monetary inflation, which if uncontrolled will terminate in national disaster." An occasional deficit budget, however, need not cause worry as there are bound to be deficit in periods of planning for economic development.

Estimates should be on a Cash Basis

The principle of the cash basis of the Budget means that it should be prepared on the basis of actual receipts and expenditure expected during the year not on the basis of receipts which are to be realised in some other years or the expenditure which is ordered in that year but is likely to be incurred in the next financial year, *e.g.*, if certain sums on account of arrears of tax relating to the year 1959-60 are relaxed in the year 1960-61, they should be shown in the receipts estimated of the latter year and not of the former.

Budgeting should be Done on the Basis of Gross and no net Income

Budget should persent a clear-cut picture of the gross and not the net income of the country. Both the receipts and expenditure should be fully shown in the Budget and not merely the resultant net position. For example, if there is a department with an estimated expenditure of Rs. 25 lakhs and receipts of 20 lakhs it should show in the budget both the expenditure and receipts and not merely 5 lakhs only. If the department prepares the estimates on the net basis, it would mean that it would approach the legislature for grant of 5 lakhs only and hence deprive the legislature of its control over the expenditure of 20 lakhs, which is met out of its receipts.

Estimating should be, as far as Possible, Exact

Estimates provided in the budget should be, as far as possible, exact. There should be neither too much of over-estimating nor underestimating. While money should be provided for all necessary expenditure, the amount provided for should be the absolute minimum. If there is over-estimating of expenditure, people are unnecessarily heavily taxed and if there is under estimating, the whole budget may be thrown out of gear when it comes to execution. It is a tendency on the part of the departments in India to under-estimate their expenditure, although there are clear instructions to the Heads of all the Ministries, that they should try to achieve economy and avoid waste as far as possible. According to Sri Ashok Chanda, this tendency to over-estimate spending capacity arises from two causes: firstly it is assumed that the Finance Ministry will in any case reduce the allotment requested and, therefore, it is better to ask for more and secondly, the inclusion of schemes and large provisions creates both politically and administratively an impression of efficiency and energy in the sponsoring ministries." Close and exact estimating can be achieved by taking past three average figures of the receipts and expenditure under various heads as the starting basis and making appropriate variations due to special circumstances which can be foreseen.

Annuality of the Budget

The principle of annuality is one of the most important principles of budgetism. It means that the budget should be prepared on an annual basis. In other words, it means that the legislature should grant money to the Executive for one year. A year is a reasonable period of time, for which the legislature can afford to give financial authority to the Executive. It is also the minimum period which is necessary to execute the financial programme. But annuality of the Budget does not mean that there should be no long-term planning. All those countries which had adopted the policy of planned development do have long-term budgeting, but these long-term plans do not involve actual using of appropriations for the entire period of the plan by the legislature though it may be called the approve the plan in principles and broad outlines as is done in the case of our Five Year Plans.

Rule of Lapse

The annuality principle of budgeting also implies that money left unspent during the year for which it was sanctioned must lapse to the Public Treasury and the Government cannot spend is unless re-sanctioned to the next year's budget. This rule of lapse is essential for effective financial control. If the unspent balance of one year could be carried over for expenditure in future year, it would make the departments independent of the control of the legislature till the time their accumulated balances are spent. But this rule is defective from the point of view of economical planning of expenditure. The departments knowing that if they do not utilize grants they shall lapse, have no incentive for economy and therefore, towards the end of the financial year they spend it lavishly with little regard to its urgency or utility.

Treasury Control

The legislature authorizes the government to spend money, but it does not direct them how to spend it. That is the job of the government itself. The best system of direction and internal control can be seen in the working of the British Treasury in England where it concerns itself not only in regard to preparation of budget but also exercises day-to-day supervision over the flow of finances to the operating agencies.

Executive Discretion

The executive must be given sufficient discretion in the matter of allotment of appropriation if it is to exercise supervision over the activities of the spending departments. M. Reue Stourum has rightly said, "The pilot incharge of steering a vessel is the only competent judge of the position and of the speed he has need to give his sails because he alone is posted in such a way as to know the force and the direction of the winds and the currents, which may hinder or delay his movements." The legislature should provide for broadly defined functions of the spending agencies and the executive should be left alone in the matter of determining the precise means of operation to achieve the purpose set forth by law. It should possess the power to make re-appropriations from one minor head to another. It should also have the power and means to meet financial emergencies.

Single Budget

Lastly, it is also an important principle of Budget making that the government should have a single budget incorporating all revenues as well as expenditures of the government. A single budgets presents to the people a clear cut picture of the financial transactions of the government as a whole. But if there are a number of department-wise budgets, some of them may show a surplus and others a deficit. It will not thus be possible to know the net financial position of the government as a whole except by complicated calculations and adjustments. On the basis of this principle it is also wrong to prepare Extraordinary Budgets for special purposes. An exception to this principle of unity of Budget is, however, sometimes made in some countries including India when separate budget is prepared for commercial enterprises such as Railways. India has had a separate budget for Railways since 1924. The Railways are free to keep their profits for their own development after they had made their own contributions to the general revenue.

The principles of budgeting as indicated above are followed in every country with some minor differences of details. In India, we are acting upon them in the true sense as will be borne out from a study of the Budgetary Process.

PERFORMANCE BUDGETING

The performance budgeting was first experimented in the municipal governments in the United States. It was the functional organisation of these governments which facilitated the movement towards performance budgeting. The cities of Richmond and New York were pioneers in this field. The term 'performance budget' was originally coined by the First Hoover Commission in the United States in 1949. The commission recommended the adoption of a budget based upon "functions, programmes and activities" the three ingredients of a performance budget. Such a budget involves casting budget categories in functional teams as opposed to objects of expenditure. It also involves providing work cost measurements of facilitate efficient performance of prescribed activities reducing, as far as possible, the work cost data to discrete measurable units. It is designated to be a reflection of what the government was doing how much, and at what cost. The focus of attention is the ends to be served by the government rather than the amount of money spent.

The traditional pattern of budgeting which worked in India and other countries till recently, served the purpose of fiscal accountability. The traditional budget is merely a document for parliamentary control. In this the entire expenditure is presented through a series of demands for Grants. Every Department or Ministry presents one demand for its own requirements and separate Demands for each of its subordinate organisations. Hence the Demands for Grants follow the organisational pattern. The details in each of these Demands are on the basis of object-wise classification *i.e.* equipment, materials, establishment charges etc. The traditional budget pattern developed in the '18th and 19th centuries and was mainly conceived in financial terms. The sole object of the budgetary system was accountability of funds. The emphasis was placed, on the development of a uniform system of object expenditure (input) accounts that could be routinely audited to prevent misuse of public funds. It has been called the 'object of expenditures budgeting.' It is also called 'incremental budgeting' because in this process the existing base is identified first, and then come the proposed departures by way of increments to transfer the present into the future.

Since budgeting is tied to a base, each building block estimates the cost of what it is already doing plus the cost of the increments it wants. The objectives of governmental programmes such as an indication of the purpose for which the outlays are proposed, the economies of the administrative operations, or the relationship between resources and operations are not indicated in the traditional budget and do not get clearly identified in the budgetary process. In the 1940s and 1950s the concern shifted to issues of efficiency. So the performance budgeting techniques were developed. According to Jesse Bürkehead, a performance budget is one "which presents the purposes and objectives for which funds are requested, the costs of programmes proposed for achieving these objectives, and quantitative data measuring the accomplishments and work performances under each programme".

Performance budgeting derives its ethos and much of its technique from costs accounting and scientific management. In the literature on performance budgeting, budgeting is described as a tool of management" and the budget as a "worth programme." Thus performance budgeting is management oriented; its principal thrust is to help administrators to assess the work-efficiency of operating units by *(a)* casting budget categories in functional terms, and *(b)* providing work-cost measurements to facilitate the efficient performance of prescribed activities. Generally, the method of performance budgeting is particularistic, the reduction of work-cost data into discrete, measurable units.

Performance budgeting is generally understood as a system of presentation of public expenditure in terms of functions, programmes, performance units that is, activities projects etc., reflecting primarily the governmental output and its cost. Through budget allocations, implementation and control of programmes are sought to be achieved. The emphasis shifts from the means of accomplishment to the accomplishments themselves. Its main concern is the ends to be served by the government, this technique lays emphasis on precisely defining the work to be performed and a correct estimate of what that work will cost therefore a performance budget is prepared in functional categories", as for example health, agriculture. Each function is divided into "programmes", and the programmes are subdivided into "activities".

The U. N. Manual for programme and performance budgeting has defined these terms thus : Functions represent broad groupings of operations that are directed towards accomplishing a major purpose of government *e.g.* health, education etc. Programmes refer to broad categories within a function that identify the products of major organisations; for example education may be divided into higher, secondary and primary education. An activity is a more limited division of action geared towards the attainment of the goals of an operating programme or sub programme. It involves processes for which an intermediate or a low-level administrative unit is responsible. It consists of several specific operations forming part of a process aimed at achieving a particular result. For example, training of teachers in primary education programme is an activity. A project refers to a series of works in an investment programme or sub-programme for the formation of capital goods. It is carried out by a production unit capable of functioning independently.

The various components of performance budgeting and its supporting systems include:

(a) formation of objectives;

(b) programme/activity classification;

(c) norms, yardsticks and standards;

(d) accounting classification;

(e) management accounting;

(f) decentralised responsibility structure;

(g) delegation of financial powers; and

(h) reporting and review performance.

Stages of Performance Budgeting

Performance budgeting can be introduced at any level, that is, branch department or national level. What is important is that the system at the lower level must be organically related to the system at the next higher level. That means that it should be derived from and in turn support the higher level system. The performance budgeting system can be discussed under the following heads.

1. Objectives. As far as possible, the objectives of individual programmes are clearly spelt out in quantitative and measurable terms, setting them against long-term aims and goals of the government.

2. Analysis. That means that the long-term strategy and the short-term tactics for achieving the objectives are considered possible alternative programmes identified, the costs and benefits of the alternative programmes worked out and the programmes selected.

3. Organising. The roles of different organisation in achieving the specified objectives are demarcated. The financial rules and accounting system are remodeled to effectively implement the programmes.

4. Budget/classification. The programmes taken up for implementation are classified with reference to a classification system. The idea is to facilitate allocation of resources to related programmes.

When the budget is prepared on the basis of the above; it must go through the prescribed procedure of presentation approval of implementation.

5. Evaluation. Criteria for evaluating the programmes with reference to the objectives are evolved. The proper information and reporting systems on financial, physical and economic data relevant to the programmes are installed for monitoring the programmes during execution, and evaluating them on completion.

Objectives of Performance Budgeting

Working Group of the Administrative Reforms Commission of India said that the primary purposes of the performance budgeting are:

(a) to correlate the physical and financial aspects of every programme or activity;

(b) to improve budget formulation, review and decision-making at all levels of management in the government machinery;

(c) to measure progress towards long-term objectives as envisaged in the plan;

(d) to bring annual budgets and development plan closely together through a common language;

(e) to facilitate better appreciation and review by the legislature; and

(f) to make possible more effective performance audit.

The Administrative Reforms Commission of India in its report on Finance, Accounts of Audit in 1968 stated that a Performance Budgeting, which in essence, is a technique for presenting Government operations in terms of functions, programmes, activities and projects, seems among others, to achieve the following important objectives:

(a) to present more clearly the purposes and objectives for which the funds are sought and bring out the programmes and accomplishments in financial and physical terms;

(b) to enhance the accountability of the management and at the same time to provide an additional tool to management control of financial operations;

(c) to help a better understanding and better review of the budget by the Legislature;

(d) to improve the formulation of the budget and to facilitate the process of decision making at levels of Government; and

(e) to render performance audit more purposeful and effective.

The Commission emphasised that planning and budgeting should be brought much closer than had been the case in the past. It may also be added here that the annual budgetary process will have to incorporate within itself the decentralised planning function. This will strengthen the planning process.

Advantages of Performance Budgeting

Performance budgeting has several advantages,

(1) Record keeping along functional lines would help to bring act the variance between budgeted and actual costs. That will help management to check on the work accomplished against work assigned. In case wide variations in the performance ratios are noticed, remedial action may be taken,

(2) Given the desire and drive for efficient management of governmental organisations. Performance budgeting could serve as a convenient tool of management. It helps administrators to prepare their budgets on the basis of what they hope to accomplish,

(3) It serves both as a tool for recovering the efficiency of existing operations and their results and as a system of feeding the data for planning future services,

(4) It upgrades the budget decision-making process by throwing up the requisite information on cost of work accomplishments appropriate for various levels of operation,

(5) It makes legislative review, control and policy-making more meaningful and makes budget informative and understandable to the taxpayer,

(6) It should be an excellent instrument for translating long-term plan's & programmes into reality,

(7) Performance classification helps improve public relations by providing clearer information for a rational public appraisal of responsible government,

(8) Thavaraj sums up that performance budgeting helps "to bring about an organic integration of planning, programming and budgeting, provides for more effective controls, makes legislative control more meaningful, helps to gear the process of decentralisation of authority in conformity with responsibility and helps to improve public relations". He further observes that "it is certainly not a panacea for administrative ills. But, in the hands of skillful administrators, it should produce impressive results."

No doubt there will be some repetition, but it will be useful to quote Sastri on advantages of Performance budgeting. He observes, "Performance budgeting system with its emphasis on explicit specification of objectives should...help inculcate a certain discipline in the public enterprises to make advance projections of the demand for their products, the prices at which they might be able to sell, the costs they are likely to incur and the profits/losses they are likely to make. This will, at the same time, enable them to identify the likely shortfalls in the utilisation of capacity and the levels of efficiency which they hope to reach in respect of the various production processes and input uses like labour and machine productivities. Such a system will help and, in turn, be helped by the central planning authorities to remove bottlenecks and deficiencies, to correct demand and price deficiencies in planning, to plan for optimum utilisation of national resources—capital, capacities, natural resources and manpower, and to improve productivity and efficiency at the national level."

Requisites for Performance Budgeting

Performance budgeting in order to be effective, requires certain conditions to be satisfied. First there must be clarity of objectives in the organisation. The absence of clear cut objectives would mean that the programme would lack direction; the yardsticks of measurement will be imprecise and not indicative of the mission; the expected outcome would be vague and therefore the performance measurement would be difficult. Second, the activities must be amenable to quantitative measurement. The performance measurement is futile in quality dominated activities like diplomacy, social welfare, community services. In fact many of the activities performed by the government departments suffer from these handicaps. Those activities which do not produce tangible output are not easily amenable for measurement. Third, how for the output is homogeneous and the process is repetitive. Homogeneity facilitates counting with the help of standard measures. Fourth, there should be variability of the output and direct costs which are attributable to the various levels of operation. The greater the variability of cost and output at operating levels the greater will be the need for performance measurement. Fifth, whether the programme is susceptible to violent fluctuations on the input and/or the output side. Where the input is unstable.

Problems of Performance Budgeting

The introduction of Performance Budgeting may sometimes be faced with certain problems or difficulties. First, as said in the preceding paragraphs, functional classification is the first and basic step to Performance budgeting, but political & organisational reality may sometimes abstract clear categorisation which is most useful for classification purposes. Therefore the first problem is of identifying appropriate and adaptable functional categories. Second, Performance budgeting does not solve the greatest problem in decision-making, and that is the comparative evaluation of projects, functions or activities unless it is supported by cost-benefit analysis. But cost benefit analysis is far from perfect, particularly in such cases where the indirect and intangible costs & utilities are involved in a big way. Third, the classification developed may sometimes be too broad to reveal significant programmes and activities of the agencies to serve as a firm basis for budgetary decisions and management. Fourth, there is a possibility that important programme and management considerations may be relegated to the background because of the tendency towards over decentralisation and over simplification of appropriation structure and consolidation of functional categories for purely budgetary purposes.

In conclusion it may be said that what is important in performance budgeting is not so much the use of sophisticated economic, statistical or accounting techniques of quantification and measurement but the shaping of a critical and questioning attitude. What is it we are trying to do? What are the different ways of doing it? Which is the most effective & least cost way? How do we ensure that results are achieved. What is the feedback mechanism? What are the premises on which the objectives were based and programmes formulated? Do they continue to be valid?

Performance Budgeting in India

The demand for the introduction of performance budgeting in India was first made in 1954 during a debate in Lok Sabha. Later this demand was made from time to time. The Estimates Committee of Parliament in its twentieth report (1957-58) recommended that "Performance cum-Programmes System of Budgeting would be ideal for a proper appreciation of the schemes and outlays included in the budget, especially in the case of large scale development activities. Performance budgeting should be the goal which should be reached gradually and by progressive stages without any serious budgeting dislocation". The Estimates committee followed it up at various points of time by restating its recommendation and asked that public undertakings be asked to prepare performance-cum-programme statements. In 1961 the Government of India issued instructions to public undertakings to the effect that they should prepare the above named statements besides business type budgets for submission to Parliament.

Recommendations of foreign specialists, and the efforts of the Indian Institute of Public Administration and the Planning Commission also contributed to the movement for performance budgeting. The Administrative Reforms Commission recommended to the government that, starting with the 1969-70 budget and in two years, performance budgeting should be introduced in all departments and organisations of the government which are in direct charge of development programmes. The Government did not stick to the time table. It took a decision that performance budgeting should be introduced by all developmental departments in a gradual manner. Even earlier than this, the Ministry of Finance had prepared a document entitled 'Performance Budgets of Selected Organisations 1968-69', which covered alternative presentations of the budgets of four ministries/departments, and which was presented to Parliament in April 1968 as a supplement to the conventional budget documents. Since then performance budgets have been prepared for gradually increasing number of departments. By 1977-78 about 32 developmental departments of the Government of India had been covered under the scheme. This process is continuing. Several State Governments also have started preparing performance budgets in development departments.

PREPARATION OF BUDGET IN INDIA

The preparation of their Budget involves the following operations which follow in the order given below:

(1) Preparation of the preliminary estimates by the disbursing officers.

(2) The scrutiny and review of these estimates by the controlling officers.

(3) Scrutiny and review of these revised estimates by the Ministry of Finance.

(4) The final consideration of the consolidated estimate by the Cabinet.

(5) Scrutiny and review of the revised estimates by the Accountant General and the Administrative Department.

(1) Preparation by the Disbursing Officers. The work in connection with the preparation of the Budget begins 6 to 8 months before the commencement of the next financial year. Since the Indian financial year begins from the 1st of April every year, the work of budget preparation starts in the month of August-September. The Accountant-General sends prescribed forms for the estimates of revenue and expenditure separately to the Heads of various departments in the month of July or August. The Heads of Departments send those forms to the disbursing officers—Heads of the local offices who prepare the preliminary estimates. The task of preparing the estimates is the most important one. In the works of Mr. P.K. Wattal, "It is not a simple arithmetical exercise in striking out averages of previous years and putting in a safe figure which would not look exactly like repetition of the last year's performance. Behind figures lie grime realities of administration. The circumstances of no one year are exactly similar to those of the previous year and yet they are not quite dissimilar". Every care should therefore be taken in the preparation of the estimates. While preparing the estimates, the local officers are to fill in four columns of the prescribed from:

(i) Actuals of the previous year,

(ii) Sanctioned estimates for the current year,

(iii) Revised estimates for the current year, and

(iv) Budget estimates for the next year.

Sometimes there remains much difference between the budget estimates and the actual amount spent or required to be spend. This is mainly due to two important factors. Firstly, the estimates are prepared some 18 months earlier, and secondly, Indian economy is a gamble in monsoon and the estimates are prepared much before the advent of monsoons. Besides as Mr. Ashok Chanda puts it, "the preparation of estimates on new projects at the time of their inclusion in the budget proves in most cases to be difficult... The estimates given have often to be based on mere expectations and no nothing concrete and positive."

(2) Scrutiny and Review of Estimates by Controlling Officers. The Local officers send the estimate to their respective controlling officers of Head of Departments for scrutiny and review.

The scrutiny is purely of an administrative type. The controlling officer has to judge the relative importance of the proposals from the various branches and section of his department for new expenditure in the light of the possible grant for the department as a whole. He has therefore to accept some of them and reject others.

(3) Scrutiny and Review by the Accountant-General and the Administrative Department. After the estimates forms have left the desks of the controlling officers, part I of the estimates which relates to revenue and to standing charges like permanent establishment, travelling allowances etc., is submitted to the Accountant-General and the General Administration Department for scrutiny and review. The General Administration Departments exist in State Governments. Besides the general review, the Accountant-General's Office is also required to prepare estimates under debt, deposit and remittance heads.

(4) Scrutiny by the Ministry of Finance. The estimates thus received from the various departments are scrutinised by the Ministry of Finance and after revision and modification, are consolidated together into the Budget of the Government as a whole. In the words of Mr. P.K. Wattal, "the scrutiny applied by the administrative Department. The administrative department is responsible for the policy of the expenditure or its necessity or general propriety but the Finance Department is mainly concerned with economy and is therefore entrusted with the duty of keeping the demands of the departments within the funds available. The unresolved differences of opinions between the administrative departments and the Finance Department are submitted to Government (Cabinet) for decision". The scrutiny of the estimates by the Ministry of Finance is done from the financial point of view, that is to effect economy, and see to the availability of funds. The operation of the scrutiny by the Ministry of Finance in regard to new expenditure, *e.g.*, over a new social service or the existing activity in new direction, is fully revealed from the nature of following questions if applied on them.

(a) Is the proposed expenditure really necessary?

(b) If so, how have we so long done without it? Why now?

(c) What will it cost and wherefrom is the money to come?

(d) Who will go short as a consequence of it?

(e) What is done elsewhere?

(f) Are new developments likely to render it unnecessary? And so on.

The Ministry of Finance then prepares an estimate of income and expenditure of the government of India. On the basis of the estimated expenditure, proposals regarding fresh taxes are made in the budget. In other words, the budget is divided into two parts—the Income side and the Expenditure side.

(5) Approval by the Cabinet. The Finance Minister examines the budget estimates somewhere in January and in consultation with the Prime Minister prepares his financial policy with regard to taxation etc. After that has been done, the budget is submitted to the cabinet for joint consideration. It is so done, because it is the cabinet which is responsible for laying down the general course of policy. When the Cabinet has approved the budget, it is ready for being introduced in the Parliament.

The Contents of the Budget. The Indian Budget which is called the "Annual Financial State" consists of two parts:

(a) Budget speech of the Minister of Finance, and

(b) Budget Estimates.

Budget Speech. The speech of the Finance Minister gives information relating to the general economic conditions of the country, the financial policy to be followed by the Government, the explanation for the difference between the budget estimates and the revised estimates of the current year and explanatory memoranda, which explains the reasons for variations in the current year's original estimates. The budget speech of the Minister is an event of great importance in the annual activities of the nation.

Budget Estimates. The Indian Constitution enjoins upon the President of India to present to Parliament the "Annual Financial

Statement" showing separate estimates for expenditure charged on the Consolidated Fund of India and expenditure charged on "Public Accounts" of India. Article 112 mentions the following expenditures as charged on the Consolidated Fund of India:

(a) The emoluments and the allowances of the President and other expenditure relating to his office.

(b) Salaries and allowances of the Chairman and the Deputy Chairman of the Council of States and the Speaker and the Deputy Speaker of the House of People.

Non-Votable items.

(c) Debt charges for which the Government of India is liable, including interest, sinking fund charged and other expenditure relating to the raising of loans and the service and redemption of debt.

(d) (i) The salaries, allowances and pensions payable to, or in respect of Judges of the Supreme Court.

(ii) The pensions payable to, or in respect of Judges of any High Court which exercises jurisdiction in relation to any area included in the territory of India or which at any time before the commencement of this Constitution exercised jurisdiction in relating to any area included in a Province corresponding to a State specified in part A of the First Schedule.

(iii) The pensions payable to, or in respect of, Judges of the Federal Court.

(e) Salary, allowances and pension payable, to, or in respect of the Comptroller and Auditor-General of India.

(f) Any other expenditure declared by the Constitution or by Parliament by law to be so charged."

(g) Any sums required to satisfy any judgment, decree or award of any Court or arbitration tribunal.

The items mentioned above are non-votable, although the Parliament can discuss them. All other expenditures which are paid out of the Consolidated Fund are voted by the Parliament.

SPECIAL FEATURES OF INDIAN BUDGET SYSTEM

No Single Budget. In India, the Budget is called "the Annual Financial Statement." India does not have one single budget for the whole of the country. Rather, it has a number of budgets. The State Governments have their own separate budgets and the Central Government has its own. Even the Central Government has two budgets, viz. the General Budget and the Railway Budget. The Railway Budget deals with the income and expenditure of the Railways in India and is prepared by the Railway Ministry while the General Budget which deals with the estimates of all other operating agencies is prepared by the Finance Ministry. and is introduced in the Parliament by the Finance Minister. The General Budget is introduced about one week before the Railway Budget. The separation of the Railway Budget from the General Budget was made in 1924 with a view to safeguarding the stability of the General Budget as the railway estimates were subject to huge fluctuations by their very business like nature. The Railways are required to make an annual contribution to the general revenues, which, at the present, is fixed at 4 per cent on the capital invested on the building of Railways as computed every year.

Demands presented in two Categories. Another interesting feature of our Budget system is that the demands are presented in two categories. In one category are placed the demands which are chargeable on the Consolidated Fund of India and hence non-votable. Such demands are in regard to the salaries of the President, Judges of the Supreme Court and High Courts, Comptroller and Auditor-General of India, Chairman and other members of the Public Service Commissions etc.

Audit and Accounts Combined in one Department. Another important and interesting feature of our budget system is the complete centralization of the Audit and Accounts functions. The Audit and Accounts Department functions under the constitutional authority of the Comptroller and Auditor-General of India and hence, is independent of the Executive branch of the Government, Central or State. The Department of Audit and Accounts not only audits the accounts of the Central Government but it is also responsible for the audit and accounts of the State Governments. In this regard, the Department occupies a unique position in India.

Contingency Fund. Besides the Consolidated Fund in which all the incomes of Central Government are deposited, the Constitution also makes a provision for the establishment of Contingency Fund of India directly under the President of India. The object of this Fund is to provide for unforeseen emergencies pending parliamentary authorization. The money to this fund is provided from different sources from time to time. The need for such a type of fund was definitely of paramount importance for a country like India where the success or failure of budget depends upon the uncertain monsoons. The Government might have contemplated huge income from the land revenue but actually the Government may have to incur large expenses on flood relief etc. in case of the excess of the monsoon.It is, therefore, to meet such contingencies that the constitution has authorized the Parliament to establish a Contingency Fund.

COMPTROLLER AND AUDITOR-GENERAL OF INDIA

Origin of the office of Comptroller and Auditor-General. The Comptroller and Auditor-General of India is the head of the Indian Audit and Accounts Department of India. This office came into being in 1919, when the first Auditor-General was appointed by the Secretary of State under the Montague-Chelmsford Reforms Act. The Auditor-General in India was then made responsible to the secretary of state and held office during His Majesty' pleasure. He was thus made independent of the Government of India whose accounts he had to audit. The Government of India Act of 1935 gave him a constitutional recognition. Our new constitution also under Article 141, makes provision for such officer redesignated as the Comptroller and Auditor-General of India. He is thus an officer having a constitutional sanction.

Independence of the Office. The Comptroller and Auditor-General is the guardian of Public Finance and he is to see that not even a Paisa of it is spent without the authority of Parliament. In order that he may perform his functions properly, it is necessary that he should be independent of the Executive. He has accordingly been given status equal to that of the judge of Supreme Court. The independence of his office has been secured by making following provisions in the constitution. He is appointed by the President of India. He holds office for a period of six years without any age restrictions, draws the same pay as a judge of Supreme Court and is entitled to a special rate of pension. Though appointed by the President, he can be removed by him on grounds the misbehaviour and incapacity only when an address is presented to him by each House of the Parliament supported by majority of the total members of the house present and voting. His salary and emoluments have been made a charge on the Consolidated Fund of India and the conditions of his service cannot be altered to his disadvantage during his term of office. To the same end, he has been made ineligible for any further office under the Union or State Government after retirement.

It may be mentioned here that an exception has been made to the last condition in case of Mr. A.K. Chanda former Comptroller and Auditor-General of India by appointing him as the Chairman of the Third Finance Commission. The propriety of this appointment has been questioned on the floor of the Lok Sabha. It has been contended that the office of the Chairman of the Finance Commission was nothing short of a government appointment and militated against the spirit of the constitution which envisaged that high official like the Supreme Court judge and the Auditor-General should be free from the allurements of the executive after retirement. The government is of the view that the Chairmanship of the Finance Commission is neither an office of profit nor a further office the holding of which has been prohibited by the Constitution, as it did not carry any salary except four allowances. It was an independent office and the Finance Commission was not within the control of Government of India. There are, therefore, no question of his being lured by the offer. No doubt Mr. Chanda is one of the fittest persons to hold his position, but it was feared that by simply satisfying a legal quibble or by being right in technical manner the Government was not satisfying the objectives before the constitution makes."

Duties and Power of the Auditor-General. The duties and powers of the Comptroller and Auditor-General are laid down in the Audit and Accounts Order of 1936, as adopted by the Indian (Provisional Constitution) Order 1947 Article 149 of our constitution provides that Parliament shall lay down through an act the duties and powers of the Comptroller and Auditor-General but it has not been done so far and, therefore, he derives his powers from the above mentioned orders.

1. His Accounting Functions

(i) Accounting and Audit is a central subject. The Comptroller and Auditor-General was, therefore, vested with statutory duties and powers over both the audit and accounting of all the financial transaction of the Union and the States. He performed the work of Audit and Account of local bodies also in regard to all States except Madras, U.P. and Punjab who made their own arrangements of this work. But the accounts of Defence and Railways and accounts relating to transaction in U.K. are beyond his purview.

The Comptroller and Auditor-General has a headquarter organization in Delhi and there are officials of Accountant-General in each State. There are also specialized organizations under him, like the office of the Accountant-General Post and Telegraphs.

(ii) He was also empowered to prescribe the form in which the accounts of the Union and of the States were to be kept, which also included the power to give any direction with regard to methods and principles in accordance with which any accounts are to be maintained.

(iii) He had also the duty of preparing each year's accounts showing the annual receipts and disbursements for the Federation and States and to submit the same to the respective governments. His duty also extended to prepare and to submit to the President a general financial statement relating to the accounts of each year showing balances and outstanding liabilities and such other information as may be required by the President.

Later on through Comptroller and Auditor-General (duties, powers and conditions of service) Act 1971 such powers of

Comptroller and Auditor-General were defined on March 1976. President of India issued an ordinance relieving him of the responsibility of compiling the accounts of the Union and the States at once or through stages. The ordinance was replaced by the C and AG Act, 1971. The act thus separated Audit from accounts both at the Centre and in the States.

2. His Audit Functions

(i) In his capacity of Auditor-General, he is responsible for auditing the accounts of Government of India and those of the States. He is to ascertain whether money as shown in the accounts as having been disbursed was legally available for and applicable to the purpose to which it had been applied.

(ii) He is also to furnish such information and assistance to the Federal Governments or the governments of states as may be required for the preparation of Annual Financial statements.

(iii) It is also his duty to audit all transactions of the Federation and of the States relating to debts, deposits, remittances etc. all trading, manufacturing and profit and loss accounts etc. maintained by any department of the Federation or of the States.

(iv) Lastly he is to prepare an Annual Report for each of the governments whose accounts are audited. The audit report contains the comments of the audit-authority on the correctness or otherwise of the expenditure and other financial transactions. The report particularly points out the more important financial irregularities like cases of budgetary grants being exceeded, failure to obtain the necessary sanction for expenditure, non-compliance with rules and regulations, cases of improper and wasteful expenditure and of misappropriation and embezzlement. He then submits the report in the case of the centre to the President and in the name of State to the Governor who are required by the constitution to cause to be laid before their respective legislatures.

Paul H. Appleby commented upon (being not satisfied) the function of the Comptroller and Auditor—General in following words:

"The function of the Comptroller and Auditor-General in India is in large measure an inheritance from colonial rule; it upholds that rule was an integral part of it. It greatly restricted the Indians who served the Government. These restrictions were sought by the government's in situation of administration largely concerned with police and taxation functions and not engaged in rapid pursuit of welfare state objectives."

"Following is the extract from the Constitution."

Comptroller and Auditor-General of India

148. 1. There shall be a Comptroller and Auditor-General of India who shall be appointed by the President by warrant under his hand and seal and shall only be removed from office in like manner and on the like grounds as a Judge of the Supreme Court.

2. Every person appointed to be the Comptroller and Auditor-General of India shall, before the enters upon his office, make and subscribe before the President, or some person appointed in that behalf by him, an oath or affirmation according to the form set out for the purpose in the Third Schedule.

3. The salary and other Conditions of Service of the Comptroller and Auditor-General shall be such as may be determined by Parliament by law and, until they are so determined shall be as specified in the Second Schedule:

Provided that neither the salary of a Comptroller and Auditor-General nor his rights in respect of leave of absence pension or age of retirement shall be varied to his disadvantage after his appointments.

4. The Comptroller and Auditor-General shall not be eligible for further office either under the Government of India or under the Government of any State after he has ceased to hold his office.

5. The administrative expenses of the office of the Comptroller and Auditor-General, including all salaries, allowances and pensions payable to or in respect of persons serving in that office, shall be charged upon the Consolidated Fund of India.

6. Subject to the provisions of this Constitution and of any law made by Parliament, the conditions of service of persons serving in the Indian Audit and Accounts Department and the administrative powers of the Comptroller and Auditor-General shall be such as may be prescribed as rules made by the President after consultation with the Comptroller and Auditor-General.

Part V—The Union

Duties and Powers of the Comptroller and Auditor-General

149. The Comptroller and Auditor-General shall perform such duties and exercise such powers in relation to the accounts of the Union and of the States and of any other authority or body as may be prescribed by or under any law made by Parliament and until provision in that behalf is so made, shall perform such duties and exercise such powers in relation to the accounts of the Union and of the States as were conferred on or exercisable by the Auditor-General of India immediately before the commencement of this constitution in relation to the accounts of the Dominion of India and of the Provinces respectively.

Power of Comptroller and Auditor-General to give directions as to accounts.

150. The accounts of the Union and of the States shall be kept in such form as the Comptroller and Auditor-General of India may, with the approval of the President, prescribe.

Audit Reports

151. (1) The reports of the Comptroller and Auditor-General of India relating to the accounts of the Union shall be submitted to the President, who shall cause them to be laid before each House of Parliament.

(2) The reports of the Comptroller and Auditor-General of India relating to the accounts of a State shall be submitted to the Governor of the State, who shall cause them to be laid before the Legislature of the State.

❒

11

Tax Administration in India

Sometimes, the government faces the problem whether a certain expenditure should be met out be raising taxes or by raising loans. Heavy taxation as well as reckless borrowing may ruin the financial structure and may bring misfortunes to the community as a whole. The general principle followed in financing public expenditure is that the normal or ordinary and recurrent expenditure should be financed out of taxes while non-recurrent and productive expenditures should be met out of loans. This general principle has to be analysed. The government should raise as much taxation annually as the nation can bear, to defray extra-ordinary or abnormal expenditure, as far as possible from this source. The great advantage of a tax, as compared with a loan, is that the former never leaves any charge behind it in the form or repayment of principal to disturb subsequent budgets. Gurley and Shaw have emphasised that mounting volume of public debt is necessary featrue of the financial structure of the economy.

(a) Taxation is a burden on the current income, while borrowing implies curtailment of future power of spending.

(b) Taxes comes from the annual incomes and involve curtailment of present enjoyments, while a loan comes from savings and reduces the available funds for production in private sector.

(c) A tax is compulsory contribution, while a loan is generally voluntary. The pressure of a tax is immediate, while that of loan is imposed on future.

(d) The burden of heavy taxation may not be equitable, but the burden of loans is diffused over a long period.

(e) The taxes exercise a solitary and wholesome check on the tendency of an individual to go for extravagent expenditure; while loans may give an expectation of increased, income in future, that expectation of an increased income in future may make an individual extravagant in present.

This does not mean that loan finance should out rightly be rejected.

Advantages of Public Debt and Demerits of Taxation

For financing wars and recovery of the economy from war effects, public debt is the most convenient alternative to taxation. It is difficult, may impossible, to raise enough resources speedily from taxation from these purposes. For long term projects necessary for economic development, long term public debt offers a convenient method of financing as compared with taxation. Projects such as irrigation, social overhead capital, railways, big steel plants etc., can be constructed with the help of long term borrowings.

Taxation has three limitations. *(i)* it has to be on a large scale which is impractical; tax resource is inadequate *(ii)* it has adverse effects on ability to work, save and invest. It has also a disincentive effect on savings and investment. *(iii)* Besides, it reduces consumption, thus, reducing the effective demand.

Raising of long-term public debt, is, thus, preferable to taxation for financing long term projects.

Disadvantages of Public Debt and Merits of Taxation

A major disadvantage of public debt financing is the obligation to pay a fixed rate of interest and the principal. There is no such obligation in the case of taxation. Besides, government loans are held by the rich people who receive interest on these loans and are entitled to receive the principal amount. The rich, thus becomes richer/and thus, the public debt increases inequality of income and wealth.

Taxation is a powerful weapon to reduce inequalities of income and wealth when they fall heavily on the rich e.g., progressive income, taxes and heavy indirect taxes on luxury goods. However, a properly utilised public debt can benefit the weaker sections through increased output and employment. For curbing inflation, it is necessary to withdraw the excess purchasing power from the economy. For this taxation is a better method than public borrowings.

The rules to finance an abnormal outlay for non-economic purposes may be summarised as below:

(1) As far as feasible and practicable current expenditure should be met out of the annual receipts and with the increase in expenditure, taxation should also increase.

(2) When the abnormal expenditure is expected to last for a number of years, tax structure should be adjusted to meet it.

(3) When there is non-recurring expense of a large amount, it should be financed through borrowing.

(4) This principle will not work where an equitable distribution of the increased taxation cannot be secured or the productiveness of various taxes would have to exceed or heavy taxation would be politically inexpedient. Taxation has to be supplemented by loans.

financing of Public Enterprises in India

The finance function is the primary function of an enterprise—public and private. Without sufficient finances, the operation of the enterprise and expansion programmes cannot be carried out efficiently.

In public enterprises, the responsibility of providing necessary funds is of the government. But other sources are also used for financing the projects and programmes of public enterpirses. The major sources of finance for the industrial and commercial enterprises in public sector are as follows:

(1) Equity and loans from the government,

(2) Internal resources,

(3) Capital market (both for loans and equity),

(4) Loans from public financial institutions,

(5) Government grants and subsidies,

(6) Arrangement for working capital,

(7) Foreign investments,

(8) Public deposits,

(9) International Borrowings.

(1) Equity and Loans from the Government

(i) Equity. Equity capital is the main base of an enterprise. The whole of equity capital is contributed by the government in departmental public enterprises. In government companies incorporated under the Indian companies Act, the government is to invest at least 51 per cent of the equity capital of the company. In case of public corporations, the government meets their capital requirements as and when necessary.

Initially, the government provides the resources to a public enterprise except in the case of nationalised ventures which generally have their own funds to begin with.

In India, a few public enterprises which were earlier in private hands, countinue to have a small portion of its equity capital in private persons, for example, the National Paper and Newsprint Ltd., the Praga Tool Ltd., the Fertilisers and Chemicals Travancore Ltd., and the State Bank of India. There seems to be no specific policy of the government to buy back these small private holdings.

The government may also invite the public at large to participate in equity capital of public enterprise. Upto now the government has allowed private equity holding only in Scooters India Ltd., where 35 per cent of the equity capital has been subscribed by the public.

(ii) Loans. A part of the capital requirement of a public enterprise is generally provided by the government in the form of term loans. The rate of interest on these loans vary according to the period of loan depending upon the redemption yields of the Government of India and the bank rate. The government has adopted a rule of thumb to maintain loan equity ratio at 1 : 1.

The interest on loans is a charge on the profits of the company. It adversely affect the profitability of the enterprises especially when the period of construction and gestation is sufficiently long. The rates of interest on loans are decided from time to time. Special considerations as to rates of interest are taken into account in special circumstances. A rebate of 1/2 per cent is given in all cases, for timely payment of interest and principal and a penal interest at 2½ per cent on overdue instalment is charged. Normally, loans beyond 15 years are not given except with prior concurrence of the Department of Economic affairs in the Ministry of Finance and in no case loans beyond 30 years are granted.

(iii) Equity Vs. Loans. The decision of loan-equtiy mix in the capital structure of a public enterprise is taken by the government which emphasises uniformity without considering the nature of the public enterprise. A distinct advantage of equity is that the public enterprise is not under an obligation to pay return on the amount as it is in the case of loan provided to it where it is a charge on the profitability of the concern. The loan is not in the interest of a public enterprise where the period of construction and gestation is long enough and even thereafter, the payment of interest may wipe out all or a large amount of profits. Dividend on the other hand can not be claimed as a matter of right.

The government generally prefers loans to equity from two reasons:

(i) the amount of interest is an income to the government and helps it in meeting its obligations, and

(ii) the interest paid on loan forms part of the cost of production of goods and services by the public enterprises and hence can be charged from the buyers of goods and services.

Conversion of Loans into Equity. In 1970, the government decided to organise the capital structure of public enterprises in order to reduce the interest burden. It was decided that the whole of expenditure on township should be financed through equity. In some other cases where gestation period was long the government revised its formula of having an equal proportion of loan and equity and have converted some of the loans into equity. The total conversion of loan during 1971-72 was Rs. 212 crores, and this was done with a view to widening the equity base of public enterprises. The government countinues with the scheme of converting loans of public enterprise into equity.

(2) Internal Resources or Ploughing Back of Profits

Ploughing back of profits for expansion and development work is a well recognised practice in private sector enterprises. The practice is also followed in surplus generating public sector enterprises. In Indian public sector enterprises depreciation reserve is the main source of retaining profits. In 1973-74, the figure of retained profits in central manufacturing units was to the tune of Rs. 154 crores and Rs. 387 crores were utilised out of retained earnings during the year. During 1977-78, 96 public enterprises generated internal resources to the turn of Rs. 731 crores out of which Rs. 457 was on account of depreciation reserve. Upto the end of 1977-78, 59 public enterprises had deployed Rs. 2,579 crores in fixed block out of their internal resources that comes about 29.5 per cent of their total gross block. During 1983-84, 116 public enterprises generated Rs. 3282 crores as internal resources of which Rs. 1,641 crores was depreciation, 75 public enterprises had financed acquisition of their assets of Rs. 9,450 crores out of their internal resources. This constitutes about 35.6 per cent of their gross block at end of March, 1984.

Public enterprises can retain more profits to finance their project easily by not declaring divided for two or three years because the government is the only major shareholder and therefore no problem will arise.

(3) Capital Market for Raising Funds

Public enterprise cannot go to the capital market for raising funds (through equity or Bonds) without the prior approval of the government which is not often sought and given. However a few exceptions are the Scooters India Ltd., (for equtiy) and HMT (for debentures). Financial Institutions, most often, use this source of capital supply and had collected large amount of fund through this source. In May 1985, the government announced that some selected public enterprises would be allowed to go to the capital market. The rate of interest shall not exceed 14 per cent or 10 per cent (Tax-free) on these bonds. The interest on tax-free bonds will be free form Income Tax. Some public enterprise which have issued bonds under the scheme are NTPC, and Mahanagar Telephone Nigam.

The newly set-up Indian Railway Finance Corporation Limited (Set-up in December, 1986) has also been permitted to raise resources from the capital market by issuing 10 per cent tax-free railway bonds.

(4) Loans from Public Financial Institutions

Commercial banks and public financial institutions also provide assistance to public enterprises. Commercial banks generally meet the short-term working capital requirements of public enterprises. Financial institutions advance short and long-term loans at public enterprises. Prior to 1971, public enterprises were not allowed to raise funds from public financial institutions. But in 1971, public financial institutions were authorised to assist public enterprises on the same lines as to private units. The total amount of outstanding cash-credit, advance drawn by public enterprises from commercial banks and other was Rs. 6719 crores as on 31st March, 1984. Public enterprises, suffering losses get it difficult to meet their working capital needs from banks.

(5) Government Grants and Subsidies

Where a public enterprise acts non-commercially under the instructions of the governemnt to meet certain social objectives, the losses suffered by the public enterprise on such non-commercial operations are distinctly met by the government. Such assistance from the government to meet the specific losses of the operation is called grants and subsidies. For example, the Indian Airlines receives subsidy from the government for operation of certain routes at the request of the government. Likewise, the Food Corporation of India also receives subsidy from the government to supply articles at a fixed price at the point of sale because the cost incurred in much higher than the price fixed by the government.

(6) Arrangement for Working Capital

The short term working capital needs are financed by commercial banks by advancing loans or fixing the limit for cash credit. Apart from commercial banks, the government also meets the short term and long term working capital needs of public enterprises. It public enterprises fail in getting advances or meeting their working capital requirements, they approach the government for short term loans. The duration of these loans 2-3 years but in no case ecceeds five years. As on 31st March, 1984, Rs. 1,174 crores were outstanding from 47 public enterprises as working capital loan from the central government. Internal resources are also permitted to be used for meeting the working capital requirement after meeting the capital expenditure requirements of the enterprise.

(7) Foreign Investments

The government policy is not in favour of foreign equity investments in public enterprises unless necessitated in larger public interest. The government, however allowed foreign equity participation in Madras Refineries and its associated venture, the Madras Fertilizers. Foreign equity investment of small value exists, mainly due to historical reasons, in the Indian Telephone Industries. A few public enterprises which were earlier in private sectors have been allowed to continue with foreign equity of small value. As on 31st March, 1984.

Madras Fertilisers had the highest share of foreign equity i.e., Rs. 6.69 crores out of a total of Rs. 13.65 crores i.e., about 49 per cent.

(8) Public Deposits

Accepting public deposit is very popular in private sector. Unsecured deposits are accepted by private sector enterprises at a much lower rate the bank lending rates for a period ranging from one to three year. Earlier, the public enterprises were not allowed to accept public deposits like private units. But in 1980-81, 19 selected public enterprises have been allowed to mobilise funds throught public deposits. Upto December, 1983, such deposits exceeded Rs. 433 crores.

(9) International Borrowings

Indian public enterprises have also started raising funds from international money market either on their own or through some public sector bank. Asia's biggest over international loan was raised by the National Aluminium Company from Rs. $ 680 m. The other public enterprises are ONGC ($ 200 m. Euro-doller loan), S.B.I. ($ 30. for financing foreign requirements of public enterprises) I.C.I.C.I. total loan raised in foreign markets equivalent to 48 m U.S. dollars. It may be of interest to note that each loan in assisted in the foreign market on its own marit depending upon the image of the company in the eyes of foreign investors.

ROLE OF PUBLIC DEBT IN A DEVELOPING ECONOMY

Borrowings from the public can be another important source of capital formation in underdeveloped countries. This device is better than taxation. Taxation implies forced saving; borrowing is voluntary. The tax payer is never happy in paying a tax, for he does not expect to get his money back. A lender on the other hand, gives his money on loan of his own accord to receive it back along with interest after a stipulated period. Unlike taxation borrowing does not adversely affect incentives to save and investment. The lure of interest is always there to increase the incentives instead. Public borrowing act as an anti-inflationary measure by mobilising surplus money in the hands of the people in a developing economy. A successful public borrowing programme can be a useful tool of economic development by diverting resources from unproductive channels i.e., real estates, jewellery, gold etc., to productive channels. Public-borrowing is resorted to for specific development projects like power generation, irrigation works, roads, railways etc. Thus it is useful method of financing development projects.

After taxation, public borrowings are the second most important source of public revenue. It is different in nature from taxes, since all borrowings from the public must be repaid. Repayment will require the raising of resources in future when the time comes. On account of this obligation of repayment, it is customary to regard public borrowing as merely an exercise of fund raising for the government while taxation is the income proper. The governments can raise public debt either in the form of a voluntary loan or in the form of a compulsory loan. Voluntary loan is secured by the government by issuing various types of bills and securities on the money markets. Such borrowing is very common in both developed and developing countries since the public expenditure is rising at a much faster rate that the income through taxes. In the absence of better alternatives to meet this deficits the governments are obliged to raise loans. The developing countries require massive resources for carrying out the programmes of development. Therefore, logic of incurring such loans is that they help in the development process and build up the repaying capacity of public authorities. For example, construction of roads, railways, canals and other irrigation works installation of power plants, buidling up of heavy and capital goods industries etc., through public loans is justified since such expenditures are productive and help in building up the capacity to repay the loans. Expenditures on schools, hospital buildings etc., are not directly productive but are highly beneficial to the society. Their benefits are likely to accrue to many future generations as well. Therefore, it is advocated that they should be financed through public debt. Financing them from taxation will place heavy burden on the present generation while the benefits will accrue to a number of generations. Therefore, raising of resources to meet such expenditures through public loan is desirable. Even otherwise, the low level of national income and savings provides a limited scope for higher taxation while demands for public expenditure are ever increasing. To meet over increasing deficit in public expenditure and tax revenue, reliance on public borrowings is also increasing in developing countries.

The scope for voluntary loans is very limited in developing countries because the general level of income is very low resulting in a low level of savings. Therefore the governments of developing countries have to raise compulsory loans at times. Such loans are also raised in severe inflationary conditions in order to restrict the total spending power in the hands of the people. In the usual form of compulsory loan, bonds are issued by the government for period ranging from five to ten years havings tax free interest payment. Employees, contributions to national social security or provident funds is also a form of compulsory lending, since contributions to such funds and compulsory. The money goes to the government and the employees gets his share only on retirement or on the occurrence of certain specified events. An example of compulsory loan is the Compulsory Deposit Scheme introduced by the Government of India in 1974. The objective of the CDS were (i) restraining conspicuous consumption in cases of persons in the higher income brackets and (ii) generating additional resources for the government.

Money can be borrowed either within the country or from outside it, that is from foreign markets. Government generally prefers to borrow within the country so the interest that they have to pay might not go to foreign countries and adversely affect their balance of payment position. But when money at cheap rate is available in a foreign market or when it is difficult to obtain it in internal market government do borrow in foreign market. Besides, Government may resort to foreign borrowing when it is indispensable for the economic development of the country to purchase capital goods in the foreign market. Here, it has to be seen that the foreigner may not have an undue hold on the destiny of the country.

If the borrowed money is invested on any project which is likely to yield some money income at a future date, as for instance, irrigation, railway etc., it is known as productive debt. When the borrowed money is invested for a purpose which yields no monetary income, it is known as unproductive debt of the country.

Public debt is comparatively a modern phenomenon, which may be said to come into existance with the development of democratic form of government in the world. During the days of monarchies, the kings and emperors used to build State hoards which were full of gold and jewels: All income was deposited in this hoard and all money was spent out of it. During an emergency, like war, money was spent out of State hoards, which sometimes used to become empty. However, there are case when the kings borrowed money on their personal credit. In this way, public debt plays a creditable rule in the economic development of a country like India, particularly by the creation of social and economic overheads—the basic requirement of development, which the private enterprise do not take up because neither they are willing nor they are capable of investing a huge amount and then waiting for long for profit.

❐

12
Planning Commission

India became free at a time when our national resources were meagre and the need of the hour was to most fruitfully and purposefully employ all the present available resources for nation's advancement. It was with this object in view that our policy makers thought of having an independent Planning Commission.

Evolution of Planning Commission

Some of our thinkers make us believe that idea of having a planned economy for India came as early as in 1876 when Dadabhai Naoroji wrote his 'Poverty of India'. The idea however, gained ground when Late M. Visvesvaraiya wrote his 'Planned Economy of India'. In 1938 Indian National Congress set up a National Planning Committee under the presidentship of Late Pt. Jawahar Lal Nehru. The work of the committee was however, hampered due to the outbreak of Second World War. In the meanwhile Sir Ardeshir Dalal of Bombay did some spade work under the Department of Planning and Development which was set up in 1944. In 1946, an Advisory Planning Board was set up by the interim Government of India. It was headed by Shri K.C. Neogi and among other members were Dr. Zakir Hussain, Dr. K.T. Shah, G. L. Mehta, Meghanand Saha and Sir Shanti Swarup Bhatnagar. The Board was to review the planning already done, to make recommendations about co-ordination and improvement of planning and to recommend about objectives and priorities. It was also to make recommendations about future machinery of planning. The Board was of the view that there should be a single and compact authoritative organisation. It should be responsible directly to the Cabinet and concern itself to the whole field of development. The organisation was to be called Planning Commission. The Board was of the view that it should consist of members and no minister should be member of the Commission. In view of the Board, the chairman of the Commission should be a person with general experience of public affairs. It should include persons from industry, science, technology etc.

Functions of the Planning Commission

Much had been expected from the Planning Commission in India, though unfortunately the commission has not come up to the expectations of the people. The commission, broadly speaking, is responsible for giving plans both for the centre as well as the states. Since our plans run over a period of 5 years, it is expected that the commissions will also give yearly plans to the States as well as central government. It is also supposed to have periodical assessment of the success of the plans vis-a-vis evaluation of targets fixed and achieved. One of the functions of the commission is to "make an assessment of the material, capital and human resources of the country, including technical personnel, and investigate the possibilities of augmenting such of these resources as are found to be deficient in relation to nation's requirements." The commission has also been assigned task of fixing the targets and determine priorities and allocate resources of achieving those priorities. It will also suggest means, methods and machinery which will execute plans and the way in which hindrence, which come in the way of planning, could be removed. The commission is also supposed to make "Such interim or ancillary recommendation as appear to it to be appropriate either for facilitating or discharging of the duties assigned to it : or on a consideration of the prevailing economic conditions, current policies, measures and development programmes; or on an examination of such specific problems as may be referred to it for advice by central or state government for facilitating the discharge of duties assigned to it."

Composition of the Planning Commission

Composition of Planning Commission is another serious problem with which not only India but all countries of the world, which have resorted to planning, are faced. Whether the commission should consist of only non-official experts or the politicians is one problem. It is said that the former are experts in their field and thus can give impartial and unbiased plans most suited to the needs and necessities of the nation. But it is felt that the disadvantage of such a commission will be that it will not have the patronage of the government which may not find it possible to always implement the recommendations of the commission. The advantage of the latter method is that there will be complete and perfect co-ordination and co-operation among those who formulate programmes and those who execute them. But the greatest disadvantage of the system is that the targets will be fixed with political and regional considerations and may not be acceptable to the nation as a whole. Thus both the systems have their own advantages and disadvantages. Late Prof. D.R. Gadgil once observed, "It is the power complex of the Planning Commission or its members, their natural desire to exercise power and patronage like ministers that are chiefly responsible of the neglect by the commission of its main functions and for a needless extension of its activities over many irrelevant fields.

For quite some time an eminent economist Dr. D.R. Gadgil was the Deputy Chairman of the commission. The members of the commission enjoyed very high status. After the mid-term elections in 1970, it was felt that due to ever-changing political complex of the country, it was essential that in the Planning Commission, there should be a political personality. Such a personality will on the one hand, have its impact on the State Chief Ministers and on the other hand, will forge its view point in the cabinet and at other central levels. Accordingly the Planning Commission was reconstituted. Then a cabinet minister rank politician made as Deputy Chairman. In 1977 when Janata government came to power again an economist, Prof. D.T. Lakadawala was made Deputy Chairman but in 1980 he was replaced by a politician. At present an economist is Deputy Chairman of the commission (Prime Minister continues to be the Chairman).

In India however, a questions has often been raised is as to whether the Prime Minister should at all be associated with the

Planning Commission any longer as its chairman. The Estimates Committee of Parliament in its 21st report presented to the Lok Sabha observed, "While the Prime Minister's formal association was absolutely necessary during the formative stages and while he would still have to provide the guidance and assistance to the Planning Commission so as to facilitate the success of planning, it is a matter for consideration whether it is still necessary for him to retain a formal connection with the Planning Commission." Discussing the matter of co-ordination between the Planning Commission and the government, the committee observed, "This can, however, be affected by the minister being invited to attend the meetings of the commission when a subject with which he is concerned is discussed. The co-ordination with the cabinet can also be maintained by a representative of the commission attending the meeting of the cabinet when a matter of interest to the Commission is considered." Due to our changed political conditions, the country has however decided that a minister of the cabinet rank should be actively associated with planning process.

Administrative Reforms Commission and Planning Commission

Administrative Reforms Commission is one of its reports came to the conclusion that no minister should be associated with the Planning Commission. For two reasons, Firstly every minister is already over busy with administrative and parliamentary work and secondly his association can leave an impression with non-Congress government led states that their interests are being under estimated whereas those of congress(I) led states are being over estimated. But this view of ARC has not been accepted and the ministers are being associated with planning commission.

Method of Working

In spite of the fact that the Commission is divided into different divisions and each member has so me specific walks of life and branches of economy to deal with, the commission works as one body. All policy matters as referred to the commission and are also decided and considered by the commission as one body. Divisions which the commission has created are only a matter of convenience. The members of the commission work almost on the principle of collective responsibility. Though they may have internal differences, yet they do not bring them on the surface while discussing or expressing their opinions both inside and outside the cabinet.

ORGNISATION OF PLANNING COMMISSION IN INDIA

Planning Commission is required to plan for the whole country and in that it maintains a very heavy establishments. It works through divisions and branches. It has several advisory bodies attached to it.

Organisation of Commission

"The commission is a very huge organisation and as such it is essential to organise its working into different divisions and sub-divisions. Broadly speaking the commission has three main branches namely the *(i)* Programme Advisers Division *(ii)* The General Secretariat and *(iii)* The Technical Division. There is also financial division, food and agricultural division, trade, communication and commerce divisions and also employment social services division. The Programme Advisers, advise the commission regarding availability of resources, fixing of targets and the methods of their achieving them. Then is the General Secretariat which has further divided itself into four branches namely *(a)* Administrative Branch, *(b)* Plan Co-ordination Branch, *(c)* General Co-ordination Branch and *(d)* Information and Publicity Branch. The administrative branch deals with the administrative activities of the commission. Co-ordination branches deals with such matters as co-ordinating the activities of various departments of the commission including providing information and publicity matters for the use of the public. The technical divisions may be divided into general divisions and subject divisions. Some of the important divisions deal with Education, Health, Labour and Employment, Food and Agriculture, Natural Resources, Transport and Communications, Cottage and Small Scale Industries, Scientific and Technical Manpower Division and so on.

There is also public co-operation division. This division is responsible for winning the co-operation of the people in so far as planning programmes are concerned. The social services division is primarily concerned with problems relating to depressed classes of the society. Rural Reconstruction and Uplift Division looks after local institutions and organisations so that rural man power is properly organised and used.

Resources and Scientific Division plans proper use of land, jungle, water energy and mineral resources and also helps development committee and on national resources. Guidance about long term planning is given by Perspective Planning Division.

National Development Council

Main aim and object of the Planning Commission is to fix targets for social and economic development of the country. This can, however, be done only when there is close co-operation and co-ordination between the centre and states on the one hand and the Planning Commission on the other. In order to achieve this object in 1952, National Development Council (N.D.C.) was set up. This consists of about 50 members including the chief ministers of all the states as its members. It also includes Home, Finance, Defence and Planning Ministers of the Union Government as members. The council is a very powerful body having such powerful and high level persons as members, that it has virtually become a Super-n Cabinet. It is presided over to the Prime Minister. It has ever taken decisions on such important matters as the raising of food targets unilaterally without consulting the Food Ministry. The council was, however, established to strengthen and mobilise national resources, to promote common economic policies throughout the country and also is securing rapid and balanced development of all part of the country. The Council is supposed to review the working of the plans and suggest ways and means for achieving targets and filling the gaps wherever necessary.

Since the council has large membership, therefore, in order to make its working effective it has set up a standing committees which also includes chief minister of states.

Programme Evaluation Organisation

Programming is as important as the evaluation of Programming. Without proper evaluation there are no methods of knowing the achievements and failures. It was with the end in view and primarily with the object of knowing the achievements in the field of community development that with the help of Ford Foundation, Programme Evaluation Organisation was set up in 1952. The organisation is an autonomous body but works under the overall supervision and control of Planning Commission and in close co-operation and co-ordination of the ministries of Government of India. It provides statistical data and information about social and economic changes which our villages are witnessing. It gives authentic information about the methods which have proved effective and have also proved their utility thus bring to notice steps which have been accepted or rejected by our village folk.

Need of Evaluation in India

It is very essential that every work must be properly evaluated. In India where the resources are scarce need for evaluation is still more essential. Our evaluation has shown that our plan targets are unrealistic. These have lagged for behind in actual practice, practically in the field of creation of employment, rate of production growth and vital sections of economy. It was due to these reasons that plan had to be halted. During Janata regime rolling, plan system was introduced but this given up when in 1980 Congress (I) came to power. Evaluations is on going process in India and very necessary as well.

Committee on Plan Projects

The committee was founded in 1956 on the recommendations of the National Development Council. It is headed by the Home Minister and its members include Ministers for Planning and Defence. A minister of the central government whose subject is to be discussed is also invited. Joint Secretary, is its ex-officer secretary. The Committee investigates about the functioning of important projects and suggests ways and methods for observing economy in the execution of Plan projects. It is also supposed to suggest methods for bringing efficiency and promptness in the disposal of pending projects. It is a committee of National Development council. It conducts studies of specific problems through specially appointed teams with a view to raising efficiency and introducing economies, particularly in construction costs. It investigates working of projects on the field itself.

Research Projects Committee

The committee is responsible for scrutinising all research projects which are received in the Planning Commission for financial assistance. Usually financial assistance is given only to organisations and institutions and not to individuals.

It consists of leading economists of the country and also includes eminent social scientists. It is responsible for initiating research on social and economic problems which confront the nation. It works in collaboration with research institutes and undertakes collaborative research programmes.

Some other Advisory Bodies

Of course National Development Committee on Plan Projects and Research Programme Committee are some of the important bodies of the Planning Commission, but in addition, there are other advisory bodies as well. These are Committee on Irrigation and Flood Control, Committee on Public Co-operation, Committee on Public Goods, Committee on Foreign Agreements and so on. The Commission also appoints several working groups at the beginning of each plan. Their reports form the basis both for the formulation and finalisation of the reports not only in the beginning but while finalisation of reports. The view point of important organisations in the public sector is always taken into consideration. These include the Federation of Indian Chamber of Commerce and Industry.

In this way the Planning Commission takes the view point of all sections of the society before it finalises its reports.

FEATURES OF PLANNING IN INDIA

Planning Commission was officially set up in 1950, and as such it is only 36 years old. During this period the impact of planning on administration has clearly been felt. Our whole administration views every project from one angle namely whether it is a planned project and non-planned project. Usually administration does not hesitate to sanction funds for planned projects, whereas there is hesitation for sanctioning non-planned projects.

Significant Features of Planning in India

One of the significant and distinguishing feature of our planning is that it is based on public co-operation. In the words of authors of First Five Year Plan, "Public co-operation and public opinion constitute the principle force and sanction behind planning." Since this feature is significant in the sense that administrator is to always remember that planning has the approval of the people and as such any disregard to the principles enunciated in the planning will be affrontation of public opinion. It is evident from the fact that at every stage states are associated with working of planning.

The another significant feature is that planning in India touches each level of society. We have Central Planning Commission. Then the states have their own planning boards. Then there are district and block councils which plan at their own level. At the village level planning is done by Panchayats. Thus planning is not something which means enforcement by administrators from above.

Then another feature is that Planning Commission has no constitutional status but it came into existence only with an executive order.

Still another feature is that our Commission works through committees and working groups. It has many advisory committees attached to it. These are committees on *(i)* Irrigation *(ii)* Flood Control *(iii)* Public Co-operation and *(iv)* Capital Goods etc. Similarly it has set up many working groups which deal with *(a)* Agriculture *(b)* Steel *(c)* Industrial Machinery *(d)* Community Development *(e)* Education *(f)* Fertilisers etc.

The Planing Commission's another salient feature is that it consults the representatives of trade, industry and private sector undertakings.

Administration and Planning

Planning inspite of its not having any constitutional status, is playing a very big role in our administration. Its role in administration is evident from the fact, that some of our senior statesmen have called it as super cabinet. In the view of Finance Commission, Planning Commission has narrowed down its scope. Chairman of Fourth Finance Commission P.J. Rajamanner said that, "It is the setting up of the Planning Commission that has in practice restricted the scope and function of Finance Commission.

Then the Planning Commission has also shown its impact of centre-state relations. Financial policies of the central government with respect to states are determined on the recommendations of Planning Commission and schemes approved by it.

One of the objectives of Planning Commission is to determine basic values and decide objectives of community., Thus the guide-lines are provided by the commission and the administrators are only to ensure that the objectives once decided are achieved.

Administration is also required to pool resources both in terms of domestic savings and foreign, exchange, for the execution of projects which have been approved by the Commission.

In planning, administrator now cannot move in a free manner. He must take the view point of the planners into consideration. In this way free hand of administrator is restricted by the planners. While discussing the impact of planning on administration it has been said. "Although it has neither constitutional nor statutory authority yet it has come to exercise significant influence over the formulation of public policies even in matters other than of economic development."

Criticism of Planning Commission. Planning Commission has come under heavy criticism. One of the criticisms advanced is that it is working on Parkinson's law and thus its machinery has become top heavy which is not conducive to efficiency. Then another criticism is that in actual practice its plans had no relation with realities. The gap between the targets and achievements being so wide that after Third Five Year Plan, a recess in planning became inevitable to bridge the gaps. Then its also said that Planning Commission has forgotten its advisory role and instead of being only an adviser, it has always tried to impose itself on the government and that too without any clear decisions and firm views. A study made by the Indian Institute of Public Administration pointed out that whereas rate of national growth has slackened that of the Commission has increased beyond all proportions. It has also been pointed out that the Commission has usually not been constituted to have on its strength persons having background of business and industry.

Since Prime Minister and senior Ministers are members of the Commission, therefore, Administrative Reform Commission has rightly pointed out that "Unfortunately over the 17 years, the Planning Commission has in some measures, carried the reputation being a parallel cabinet and sometimes super-cabinet. One of criticism advanced is that the Commission is fantastically applying text book maxims. It has failed to manifest the qualities of a brain trust organization.

Recommendations of Administrative Reforms Commission

Administrative Reforms Commission which went into the working of the Planning Commission recommended that:

1. The Commission should not involve itself into executive functions and decisions. It should confine itself to the preparation of plans.

2. It should prepare annual evaluation plan reports which should be approved by the parliament.

3. Prime Minister, Finance Minister and Planning Minister should work in close co-operation with each other, but ministers should not be appointed as members of the Commission.

4. The number of members of Commission should be restricted to 7 only and all should preferably be full time members. At the most two members may be part-time members. The members should be appointed on the basis of their experience and expertise. Each member should be for a fixed period of 5 years but arrangements be so made that all members do not leave the Commission simultaneously.

5. The status of a member should be that of a Minister of State, where as that of the chairman, that of a Minister of cabinet rank.

6. On all important matters Commission as a whole should take decisions.

7. The working of the Commission should be so streamlined that it provides the triple needs of analysis, thinking and planning.

❑

13

Finance Commission

Political Freedom in 1947 paves the way for economic transformation and social justice. Vast agricultural irrigation and mineral resources lay unexploited and the available scarce resources needed rational allocation among competing demands. Planning offered the only way to achieve a rapid and balanced growth within the framework of well-defined national priorities. The Government of India accordingly appointed a Planning Commission in March 1950 to prepare a blueprint of development taking an overall view of the needs and resources of the country.

Objectives

The first Five Year Plan(1951-52 to 1955-56) had a two-fold objective. Firstly, it aimed at correcting the disequilibrium in the economy caused by the war and the partition of the country. Secondly it sought to initiate simultaneously a process of all-round balanced development which would ensure a rising national income and a steady improvement in the living standards over a period of time. Since the country had to import 47 lakh tons of foodgrains in 1951 and there were inflationay pressures in the economy, the Plan accorded the highest priority to agriculture, including irrigation and power projects, and 44.6 per cent of the total outlay of Rs. 2069 crores in the public sector(later raised to Rs. 2,356 crores) was allotted for their development. The Plan aimed at increasing the investment from the level of 5 per cent to about 7 per cent of the national income.

In December 1954, Parliament declared that the broad objectives of economic policy should be to achieve the "socialist pattern of society." Under the socialist pattern of society, the basic criteria for determining the lines of advance were to be not private profit but social gain and greater equality in incomes and wealth. It was stressed that socialist economy must be efficient, progressive in its approach to science and technology and capable of growing steadily to a level at which the well-being of the mass of population can be secured. The Second Five Year Plan(1956-57 to 1960-61), therefore, sought to promote a pattern of development which would lead to the establishment of a Socialistic society in India. In particular, it stressed that the benefits of economic development should accuse more to the relatively less privileged sections of society and there should be a progressive reduction in the concentration of income, wealth and economic power.

This Plan Aimed at. *(i)* an increase of 25 per cent in the national income; *(ii)* rapid Industrialisation with particular emphasis on the development of basic and heavy industries; *(iii)* a large expansion of employment opportunities; and *(iv)* a reduction of inequalities in income and wealth and a more even distribution of economic power. The Plan aimed at increasing the rate of investment from about 7 per cent of the national income to 11 per cent by 1960-61. With an outlay of Rs. 4,800 crores in the public sector (of which Rs. 3,600 crores was the investment outlay) and Rs. 3,100 crores in the private sector, the plan laid particular stress of industrialisation, such as increased production of iron and steel and of heavy chemicals including nitrogenous fertilizers and development of heavy engineering and machine-building industry.

The Second Plan was followed by the Third Five Year Plan(1961-62 to 1965-66) whose principle aim to secure a marked advance towards self-sustaining growth. Its immediate objective was to: *(i)* secure an increase in the national income of over 5 per cent per annum, and at the same time, ensure a pattern of investment which could sustain this rate of growth during subsequent plan periods; *(ii)* achieve self-sufficiency in foodgrains and increase agricultural production to meet the requirements of industry and exports; *(iii)* expand basic industries like steel, chemicals, fuel and power and further industrialisation could be met within a period of ten years or so mainly from the country's own resources; *(iv)* utilise to the fullest possible extent the manpower resources of the country and ensure a substantial expansion in employment opportunities; and *(v)* establish progressively greater quality of opportunity and bring about reduction in disparities of income and wealth and more even distribution of economic power. The national income was to increase by about 30 per cent from Rs. 10,540 crores in 1960-61 to about by Rs. 19,000 crores by 1965-66(at 1960-61 prices) and per capita income by about 17 per cent, from Rs. 330 to about Rs. 335 during the same period.

Outlay and Investment

Against the revised outlay of Rs. 2,356 crores in the public sector in the First Plan the actual expenditure amounted to Rs. 1,960 crores. In the Second Plan against the provision of Rs. 4,800 crores in the public sector the actual expenditure amounted to Rs. 4,672 crores while the private sector-achieved an investment of Rs. 3,100 crores. The third plan provided for an outlay of Rs. 7,500 crores for the public sector. Against this the actual expenditure in the public sector amounted to Rs. 8,577 crores. In the private sector there was an investment of over Rs. 4,000 crores.

Achievement during the Three Plans

Fifteen years of planning resulted in all-round progress of the economy despite occasional set-backs. Notable expansion took place in basic facilities like irrigation, power and transport and valuable mineral deposits were opens up to feed industries, small and large. During the First Plan owing largely to the increase in agricultural production, the national income went by 18 per cent as against a target of 12 per cent. In the Second Plan, the increase in the national income was 20 per cent as against a target of 25 per cent and during the Third Plan national income(revised series) at 1960-61 prices rose by 20 per cent in the first Four years and registered a decline of 5.7 per cent in the last year. Per capita real income in 1965-66 remained the same as it was in 1960-61 owing to a 2.5 per cent growth in population.

Agricultural production increased by about 41 per cent during the first two Plans. In the Third Plan, the performance of agriculture was not satisfactory. In 1965-66 and 1966-67, there were widespread drought conditions and agricultural production fell sharply. This not only slowed down the rate of growth of the economy but also increased our dependence on food imports. During the Third Plan the country imported 250 lakh tons of foodgrains. We had also to import 39 lakh bales of cotton and 15 lakh bales of jute.

The net output in organized manufacturing industries nearly doubled during the first two plans. The share of the public sector industries in it went up from 1.5 per cent at the beginning of the First Plan to 8.4 per cent at the end of the Second and much of this increase was in key industries like steel, coal mining and heavy chemicals. In the Third Plan, the production of organized industry increased by 8 to 10 per cent annually during the first four year but the rate of increase declined to 5.3 per cent in the last year of the plan due to dislocation caused by Indo-Pakistan conflict and disruption in the flow of foreign aid. Over the Third Plan, as a whole, the growth rate of organized industries was 8.2 per cent against a target of 11 per cent. A notable feature, however, was the continuous increase and diversification of production capacity specially in steel and aluminium, machine tools, industrial machinery electrical and transport equipment, fertilizer, drugs, pharmaceuticals and petroleum products. All this contributed to the strengthening of the industrial structure.

There was a marked progress in the extension of health and educational facilities. Expectation of life at birth increased for 35 years in 1980-51 to 50 in 1971. School enrollment increased from 235 lakhs in 1950-51 to 663 lakhs in 1965-66. Special programmes, devised for amelioration of the conditions of the scheduled castes and scheduled tribes, brought them multifarious benefits and strengthened their position.

Annual Plans

The Third Five Year Plan was followed by three Annual Plans 1966-69. The situation created by the Indo-Pakistan conflict, two successive years of severe drought, devaluation of the currency, general rise in prices and erosion of resources available for Plan purposes had delayed the finalisation of the Fourth Five Year Plan. During the period, three Annual Plans were formulated within the framework of the Draft Outline of the Fourth Plan. They took into account the conditions prevailing at that time. The State of the economy and the non-availability of financial resources for Plan purposes kept down the size of development outlays during this period.

The outlay by major heads of development in the Annual Plans was as follows(Rs. crores): Agriculture and allied sectors 1,666.6; Irrigation and Flood Control 457.1; Power 1,182.2; Village and Small Industries 144; Industry and Minerals 1,575.0; Transport and Communications 1,239.1; Education 322.4; Scientific Research 51.1; Health 140.1; Family Planning 75.2; Water Supply and Sanitation 100.6; Housing, Urban and Regional Development 63.4; Welfare of Backward Classes 68.5; Social Welfare 12.1; Labour Welfare and Craftsmen's Training 35.5 and other Programmes 123.5. The total outlay during the three years amounted to Rs. 6,756.5 crores.

Financing of the Annual Plans

Item	Latest estimates		
	Centre	States	Total
1. Domestic budgetary resources	2,397	1,251	3,648
2. Balance from current revenues at 1965-66 rates of taxation	184	119	303
3. Surplus of public enterprises at 1956-66. Fares Freights and Tariffs	215	194	409
4. Railways	(–)112[1]	–	(–)112
5. Others	327	194	521
6. Additional taxation including measures increase the surplus of Public enterprises	611	299[1]	910

7. Loans from Public(net)[2]	384	335	719
8. Small savings	125	80	355
9. Annuity deposits, compulsory deposits, Prize bonds and gold bonds	65	–	65
10. State provident funds	176	125	301
11. Miscellaneous capital receipts(net)	637	(–)514[3]	586
12. Budgetary receipts corresponding to external assistance(net)	2,426	–	2,426
13. Other than OL 480	1,507	–	1,507
14. PL 480 assistance	919	–	919
15. Deficit financing	644	38	682
16. Aggregate resources (1+12+15)	5,467	1,289	6,756
17. Central assistance for State plans	(–)1,763	1,763	–
18. Resources for the plans (16+17)	3,704	3,052	6,756

Fourth Five Year Plan

The Fourth Five Year Plan(April 1969 to March 1974) was presented to Parliament on May 18, 1970. It aimed at accelerating the tempo of development in conditions of stability and reduced uncertainties. It proposed to introduce safeguards against the fluctuations of agricultural production as well as the uncertainties of foreign aid.

Perspective of Development (1969-1981). According to the twelve-year perspective of which the Fourth Plan forms a part, the national income is expected to grow at a compound rate of about 6 per cent per annum, with rise in agricultural production of 5 per cent a year and annual expansion of around 9 per cent in the net income from mining manufacturing and construction. The rate of increase in population is expected to decline from 2.5 per cent a year to 1.7 per cent in 1980-81. This implies a drop in the birth rate from 39 thousand to 25. As a result, the per capita income would rise by over 3.5 per cent per annum as against 1.2 per cent a year since the inception of the Five Year Plan.

The rate of growth of the national income, visualised above would call for an increase in the investment-income ratio from 11.3 per cent in 1968-69 to 17.18 per cent by 1980-81. As the objective is to dispense with the net foreign aid by that time export earnings would have to expand at 7 per cent a year if the growth in non-food imports is to be limited to 5.5 per cent per annum. This also implies the steeping up of domestic savings rate from 8.8 per cent to 18 per cent in 1980-81.

The government sector would account for nearly three-fourths of the improvement in the aggregate saving rate and its own saving to national income ratio would rise from 1.4 per cent to 8.2 per cent. Even in public consumption expenditure is allowed to expand at the rate of growth of national income (*i.e.*, 6 per cent), with 8.9 per cent annual increase on public expenditure in health education and social services, and increase of 4.5 per cent a year on defence and non-development consumption outlays, the taxation effort required to achieve government saving target would raise the tax-income ratio from less than 13 per cent in 1968-69 to about 18.5 per cent in 1980-81.

The rising government expenditure on education, health and social services would improve the living-standards of the masses.

Objectives. The Fourth Plan aims at increasing the standard of living of the people through measures which also promote equality and social justice. The Plan lays particular emphasis on improving the condition of the weaker sections and the less privileged, especially through provision of employment and education. Efforts are also to be directed towards reduction of concentration and a wider diffusion of wealth income and economic power.

In more concrete terms, the major objectives of the Plan are as follows:

(i) to obtain annual rates of growth of over 5.5 per cent in the national income, of 5 per cent in agricultural production and of 8 to 10 per cent in industrial production;

(ii) to achieve these overall and sectoral rates of growth in the national income to raise the investment-income ratio from 11.3 per cent in 1968-69 to 14.5 per cent in 1973-74.

(iii) reduction in foreign aid net of debt charges and interest payments to about one half of the current level at the end of the Fourth Plan ; this would require a sustained increase of about 7 per cent a year in exports and limitation of non-food imports to roughly 5.5 per cent per annum. Elimination of concessional imports of foodgrains under PL 480 by 1971;

(iv) requirements of overall resources and policy decision as to the quantum of foreign aid would imply stepping up of saving income ratio from 8.8 per cent in 1968-69 to 13.2 per cent in 1973-74. This works out to a marginal saving-income ratio of 28 per cent.

Fourth Plan together with the achievement in 1969-70 and 1970-71 and the anticipated achievements in 1971-72.

Outlays: Size and Pattern

The Fourth Plan envisage a total outlay of Rs. 24,882 crores, comprising Rs. 15,902 crores in the public sector and an investment of Rs. 8,980 crores in the private sector. The public sector outlay includes Rs. 13,655 crores as investment in both the sectors for the creation of productive assets thus amounts to Rs. 22,635 crores.

The estimates of development outlays do not include most of the expenditures by local bodies financed out of their own resources or on maintenance of services and institutions established during earlier Plan which would be provided for in the normal budgets.

Resources

Out of the Fourth Plan public sector outlay of Rs. 15,902 crores, the Centre was expected to mobilise Rs. 12,796 crores Rs.

9,296 crores for its own Plan and Rs. 3,500 crores for transfer to the States and Central assistance for their Plans. The States were to mobilise the remaining Rs. 3,106 crores to make up the total of Rs. 6,606 crores of resources for the State Plans.

A reassessment of the resources for the public sector Plan has been undertaken as part of the mid-term appraisal of the Fourth Plan. Based on the experiences of Plan financing during the first three years, the reassessment places the five-year estimate of resources for the public sector in Plan at Rs. 15,898 crores—Rs. 12,128 crores to be mobilised by the Centre and Rs. 3,770 crores by the States. As compared to the original Plan estimates, it shows a decrease of about Rs. 736 crores for the centre whereas the share of the States is expected to go up more or less by the same amount. The Central assistance for State Plans has been kept at the same level as originally envisaged. However, since Himachal Pradesh has become a State since January 1971, the total for all States (including Himachal Pradesh) has now been shown at Rs. 3,567 crores as against Rs. 3,500 crores in the original scheme of financing the Plan.

Table gives the original as well as revised estimates of financing the public sector and private sector Plan outlays.

Resources for the Private Sector

(Rs. in crores)

Item	Fourth Plan period	
	Original	Revised
Private savings	14,160	16,235
Drafting by public sector	(–)5,695	(–)6,732
Retained savings	8,465	9,503
Net inflow of funds from abroad	30	(–)257
Resources available for private investment	8,495	9,246

FIFTH FIVE YEAR PLAN

Plan Implementation. In every plan the problems of implementation have been discussed and general remedies have also been suggested. Some of the basic weaknesses in the process of implementation have been identified from time to time. Thus the Administrative Reforms Commission, the National Commission on Agriculture, the Irrigation commission and a large number of reports of Special Committees, task forces and evaluation studies have brought out in detail the structural procedural and institutional weakness and suggested specific remedies. In spite of this, there has been no significant improvement in the level of performance.

It is proposed in this Chapter to make some departures from the past and after stating with the general and specific problems of implementation are, to indicate in some detail what has been done during the Fourth Plan period and what is proposed during the Fifth Plan to improve the implementation process.

The problems of implementation arise out of weaknesses at all levels of the implementing machinery starting with Government departments at the Centre and the States, through the various non-secretariat organizations, autonomous Corporations, Boards and other authorities down to the organizations in the fields at the project, district of village level.

Improving the apex implementation machinery of Government at Centre and States, is perhaps the most important of these tasks as it must spearhead the reform of the implementation process at lower levels. While the steps taken or proposed to overcome the problems of implementation of the Plan in the various sectors below the apex level tend to be specific to those sectors the steps required in regard to the Government departments themselves are broadly the same regardless of which sector of the plan they are responsible for.

Government Departments

Statement of Objectives, Policies, Agencies and their Functions. Although the broad targets for the Five-Year Plan are laid down, the apex bodies usually have not in the past broken them up at the start of the plan into concrete targets for the various implementing agencies below them and set them in a pre-determined yearly/ quarterly time-frame. It is intended that as early as possible in 1974, this will be done by all the apex/implementing agencies.

Likewise, the policies that are required to be adopted to meet these targets need to be enunciated clearly and in good time. As soon as possible, any additions or modifications to agencies that may be required to execute the plan should be identified, their functions clearly specified, any inter-relationships of these agencies defined and the means to be adopted for coordinating them should be spelt out.

Organizational Structure of Government Departments and their Manning. The development of the organizational framework has not kept pace with the increasing variety and complexity of the job that state and Central Governments have taken on. Rigid compartmentalisation in fields which require a high degree of integrated multi-disciplinary activity, excessively wide or narrow spans of control, lack of clear lines of responsibility, inadequate delegation of authority, and improper relationship and positioning of line and staff functions have all hindered plan implementation.

Some of the steps that have been taken or are proposed at the level of the State and Central Governments are:

1. Commissions with a high degree of autonomy have been set up for atomic energy, electronic and space and their chiefs invested concurrently with the status and power of Secretaries of Government.

2. A Board type set up similar to the Railway Board has been provided for Posts & Telegraphs.

3. The chairman of the Central Water & Power Commission and the Director General Council of the Indian Council of Agriculture Research have been given the status and powers of Secretaries to Governments in the Ministries of Irrigation & Power and Agriculture respectively.

4. The Chairman of the Steel Authority of India Limited—who is holding company for public and private sector steel plants and the attached mines which supply essential inputs to them is also the Secretary to Government in the Ministry of Steel.

5. Specialists have been increasingly inducted into the higher level of secretarial administration to enable their effective participation in policy-making, programming for review of implementation.

As recommended by the Administrative Reforms Commissions, Internal Finance Advisers have been appointed in each Ministry/Department or for a group of Ministries/Departments making competent financial advice available internally to them. A revision of the status of these officers to make them more effective is under examination.

The following steps are under implementation:

As recommended by the Administrative Reforms Commissions (ARC) important changes are being introduced in the system of work in the central secretariat to secure rational distribution of work within a ministry with manageable charges and unity of command at all levels.

– reduction in the number of levels of consideration.

– switch-over to the desk officer system.

– flexibility in structuring pattern to match the tasks to be performed.

– reduce nothing to essential matters.

– introduce aids to efficiency like the functional file and care indices for important matters, mechanisation and computerisation of complex reference/information system.

Procedures. The need for greater decentralisation of power and delegation of authority is again regularly commented on in previous Plan documents. Significant steps have however recently been taken in this regard. Substantially larger powers for expenditure have been delegated to Corporations and other autonomous bodies for example SAIL has been authorised to undertake capital expenditure up to 10 crores without reference to Governments.

Authorities delegated to administrative ministries can be redelegated to subordinate authorities regarding re-appropriating budget provision creating posts incurring contingent and miscellaneous expenditure and writing of losses.

The general approach being taken is that authority should be delegated to the maximum possible extent rather than the minimum necessary. This also applies to delegation of powers from the Centre to the States particularly in such areas as National highways maintenance where the States can act as agencies of the Centre.

Likewise, number of other recommendations regarding restructuring relationships between different agencies of Government and public sector undertakings with a view to speeding up procedures, giving the undertakings greater responsibility and accountability and still ensuring that Government retains adequate checks and controls, are under examination.

To summarise, of the 527 recommendations concerning the Centre made by the Administrative Reforms Commissions, decisions have been taken on nearly 400 and the remainder are under various stages of processing. Likewise the remaining 51 recommendations concerning the State are in various stages of consideration and implementation. In addition to these, several other steps that have been taken or are under consideration to improve organizational structures and reduce procedural delays.

While a significant amount of work has been and is being done in restructuring departments of Government at the Centre and State and reducing procedural delays much process has yet to be made.

An early start will be made by setting up monitoring and evaluation cells for each major industry in Central Departments of

Government. Likewise expertise will have to be built up or inducted in developing and operating data banks, planning and project evaluation, pricing, licensing and other policy-making and coordinating R & D. All of these tasks are too complex to be left to one or two individuals and require multi-disciplinary groups drawn from operating organizations. There is no doubt that these groups would add a little to governmental overheads but if they are carefully recruited and properly directed, their cost would be a negligible fraction of what they could save the country. Similar steps need to be taken by State Governments.

The Sixth Plan

The then ruling party (Janata) could not frame any plan for 1978-83 period and instead formulated a rolling plan. After two years Janata Government collapsed and the Congress launched regular Sixth Plan for 1980-85. The Plan stood for the alleviation of poverty. Hence it aimed at achieving of economic and technological self-reliance, reduction of poverty and weeding out of unemployment, development of indigenous energy sources, improvement of the quality of life of the poorest through the minimum needs programme, minimisation of inequalities of income and wealth through better redistribution and population control. The Plan involved all segment of people for development purpose.

Appraisal

An analytical study of the Plan indicates that the economy went up by 5.4 per cent per annum though the target of growth in national income was 5.2 per cent. The development of agriculture and services exceeded the target as 3.8 to 4.3 per cent in agriculture and 5.5 to 6.6 per cent in services. In manufacturing and mining sectors performance has not been up to the mark *i.e.*, 6.6 per cent to 3.7 per cent. This performance adversely affected agriculture and service sector. The saving rate come down from 24.5 per cent to 23.3 per cent. Power shortage remained the hurdle though output of commercial energy was a bit improved. Basic industries suffered a decline.

The Seventh Plan (1985-90)

It was initiated on April 1985 and was designed for the period 1985 to 2000. It attached highest priority to productive employment. Efforts were also made to shaken the rate of population growth and raise the national level of the people. Energy planning was an important part of long term planning.

Objectives

It emphasised the policies and programmes which could augment food-grains production increase, employment opportunities and raise productivity. The growth rate of gross domestic product was kept at 5% during the plan.

The generation of productive employment was aimed at by launching an attack on grinding poverty, rampant in employment and regional imbalances. A substantial economy in the resources was conceived. These improvements could be effected through the increase of human resources, greater relactivity in the development and use of domestic technological capabilities, fast introduction of new technologies in agricultural, factories and offices greater emphasis on capacity utilization and better project implementation and pursuing policies which could reduce costs of production in industrial sector.

In the VIIth Plan the plan outlay was kept at Rs. 1,80,000 crores at 1984-85 price level. Gross investment in the private sector was to be Rs, 1,68,148 crores. It meant a total investment of Rs. 3,22,366 of which 94% was to be financed from domestic resources. Evidently the Public sector outlay amounted to be Rs. 2,22,169 crores.

An Appraisal

Many of the targets were exceeded. It may be due to economy in 1989-90. In agriculture and industry, the annual growth rate went up to 4.5% and 8.5% respectively. Mining and quarrying and electricity generation showed a growth of 5.7 and 9.1 respectively. It fell short of Plan targets substantially. It was to some extent compensated by due to increase in manufacturing output to the extent of .8 per cent (*i.e.*, from 8% to 8.8%). It may be possible out that a big gap between income and expenditure of the government was responsible for fiscal deficits. Imbalances between aggregate demand and domestic output resulted in inflation. Moreover the fiscal deficits of the government was financed by running down of foreign exchange reserves or through fresh external borrowings, entailing attendant problems.

VIIIth Plan (1992-97)

Abnormal circumstances overtook the country due to appalling poverty rampant, unemployment, rapid decline in living standards in 1991. Hence the Congress Government postponed the VIIIth Plan to 1992. The Plan envisioned decentralization of plan process involving re-orientation and priorities of Planning, its process and mechanism. The masses were to be associated with the planning and its implementation was envisaged through democratic decentralization and a closer linkage of the Planning Commission with the Planning organization.

The Plan aimed at ensuring the needs of the masses and improvement in the quality of their life. Hence planning promotes rapid over-all development and diversification of the economy and strengthen infrastructural base. It caters to the needs of ecologically sustainable development.

The Plan's outlay is almost double the VIIth Plan in public sector outlay, actual enhancement is only 52%. As regards the resource mobilization the Planning Commission has stressed the necessity of financial discipline both at the Centre and in the States to reduce fiscal loss and curtail unproductive expenditure. Besides it has emphasised efficient management of public sector units and nationalization of developmental schemes.

Highlights of the Plan (1992-97)

In the recent past we were on the brink of economic disaster. Our's was a shattered economy. The present Finance Minister—Dr.

Manmohan Singh— an eminent economist brought the nation out of economic morass. He made a departure from the fast socialistic practices and adopted policy of liberalization. Measures such as tightening of monetary policy to counter inflationary pressures and curtail in governmental expenditure were adopted for effecting fiscal discipline. Policy pertaining to foreign investment was restructured. All this has been done to make our economy viable, and consistent with global economic environment. Thus 8th Plan has become a vehicle of development and an instrument to meet ever mounting fiscal deficit and also critical situation in the balance of payments and contain high rate of inflation.

Its main highlights are as follows:

(i) Provision of a new orientation to planning inconsonance with the new thrusts in economic policy and ensuring of public sector investment.

(ii) To curb the fundamental weakness in India's balance of payments situation to avoid disrepute of Indian economy.

(iii) Ensuring the price stability for the smooth functioning of the economic system.

(iv) Deficit financing to be kept at par with a reasonable degree of price stability.

(v) Improved fiscal management to effect more savings of the Government.

(vi) The above principle in view following objectives are to be achieved: *(a)* Generation of adequate employment; *(b)* Checkmating population growth; *(c)* Eradication of illiteracy through universalization of primary education for people between 15 to 35 years of age; *(d)* Safe drinking water and primary health care facilities; *(e)* Self-sufficiency in food and production of surplus for export; *(f)* Improvement of infrastructure *viz.*, transport, communication and irrigation for growth process.

The financial investment is to be Rs. 7,98,000 crores and outlay of Rs. 71,000 crores. It necessitates massive domestic effort as outflow from abroad is to be only 16% of G.D.P. Public sector investment is to be 45.3%. Public sector investments at the rate of 10% of G.D.P. is to be from borrowings out of savings of household to the extent of 70.4%, 9.71 per cent from the rest of the world and balances from its own savings. It is expected that the new economic policy has been instrumental in salvaging the country's sunken economy considerably during short span of time.

RECOMMENDATIONS OF 8TH FINANCE COMMISSION

Eighth Finance Commission was headed by Mr. Y. B. Chavan, a former Finance Minister of Government of India recommended that a total of Rs. 494 crore be given to nine states during the period 1984-85as a grant-in-aid in order to enable these to meet the revenue deficits. It also recommended that Sikkim may also be given share from Union excise duties including excise duty on electricity and additional duties in lieu of sales tax. Another recommendations of the Commission was that the recovery of Savings loans given to the state governments which was held in abeyance during the period 1979-80 to 1983-84 may be deferred to 1984-85.

The Commission was of the view that existing arrangements regarding to finances of relief expenditure by the states affected by national calamities may be continued during the year 1984-85. It however, did not make any specific recommendations for providing expenditure on financial proposals for upgradation of standards of administration for the improvement of capital assets.

The Commission stressed that it was necessary to make real assessments for the grants-in-aid to be provided under Article 275 of the Constitution.

The grant-in-aid to be given to the states as mentioned above recommended by the Commission, is shown in the Table given below:

The recommendations of the Commission clearly show that these are in favour of the States and these have an impression that it

Name of States	Amount in Grant (Rs. in crore)
Assam	38.17
Himachal Pradesh	91.15
Jammu & Kashmir	114.85
Manipur	56.08
Meghalaya	40.27
Nagaland	81.12
Sikkim	11.96
Tripura	53.34
West Bengal	7.89

wishes that the centre should meet revenue deficits of the states to enable these to come over financial difficulties.

RECOMMENDATIONS OF NINTH FINANCE COMMISSION

Ninth Finance Commission was constituted under Article 280 of the Constitution. It was headed by Shri N.K.P. Salve, M.P. Its other members were D. Raja, J. Chelliah, Lal Sethanwala and Mahesh Parsad was its Member Secretary. In its final report of 1989-90 submitted to the President on 29th July, 1988, the Commission recommended devaluation of Income Tax, Union Excise Duty etc. The government accepted these recommendations.

In its interim report it recommended the transfer of Rs. 13668 crore to the states for 1989-90, the last year of 7th plan, as follows:

Tax Head	Income in Crore (Rs.)
The net income tax	2990.38
Share in basic excise duties	6408.00
Share in basic excise duties in deficit states	810.10
Share in additional excise duty	1496.36
Share in tax on railway passenger fares	95.00
Non-plan deficit grants-in-aid	984.06
Grants for upgradation of administration	171.67
Margin money	169.55
Grants for special problem states	551.55

These problem states were:

Arunachal Pradesh, Assam, Goa, Mizoram, Himachal Pradesh, Jammu & Kashmir, Manipur, Meghalaya, Nagaland, Orissa, Rajasthan, Sikkim and Tripura.

Out of the total transfers recommended Rs. 11,785.64 crore was by way of tax devaluation and rest by way of grants. Besides the Commission also recommended a relief of Rs. 184.98 crore in repayment of principal and Rs. 236.75 crore in interest repayment in 1989-90 in respect of drought loans to some states and special loan to Punjab.

The Commission has recommended the continuance of scheme recommended by the Eighth Finance Commission. It provides that the Centre would provide 50 per cent of the margin money as grants-in-aid under Article 275(1) of the constitution. It has also recommended moratorium on interest payments and repayments of principal due in 1989-90 of the Central loan given to states by way of additional plan assistance towards relief expenditures on account of unprecedented drought during the years 1986-88.

Though the Finance Commission in its own way tries to see that financial dependence of the states on the Centre is considerably reduced yet the fact is that this dependence is increasing day by day because each state is trying to become over-ambitious in providing facilities to the people in the shortest possible time.

❐

14

Government Audit and Accounts

ACCOUNTING AND AUDIT

Accounting means keeping a systematic record of financial transactions whether of a public authority or private concern or individual. Accounting is important in several ways. In the first place, it is an indispensable means of exercise of financial control. Without accounts, it is impossible to know how much was received or how much was spent and for what purpose, and in absence of such knowledge, there can be no control. It is only through systematic accounts supported by vouchers and receipts that the legality and honesty of the transactions can be determined. Secondly, accounts are important by way of record of what was received and paid. Such record is essential to prevent the neglect of demands of dues and double payments, through forgetfulness. Accounts are thus, to large-scale financial transactions of public authorities what memory is to small-scale individual transactions.

Through accounts the authorities can know whether a particular activity or programme of the Government is self-supporting or involves a burden on the public exchequer, and if the latter, whether it should be continued or expanded or not. Scientific budget preparation would be impossible without the help of accounts. The estimates would be guess-work and wide of the mark. As we have seen, the estimates have to be prepared on the basis of several sets of figures relating to past years.

The form of Governmental Accounts. The form of Governmental accounts differs from the business and commercial accounts, because the objects of the two are different. Business and commercial accounts are so kept as to facilitate the preparation of the balance sheet showing profit or loss, and assets and liabilities. Government activities are not run for profit, but for service to the people. Here there is no question of profit of loss or a balance sheet to show them. The object of Governmental accounting is to furnish data to show whether the provisions of the budget as voted by the legislature have been observed or not, *i.e.*, whether expenditure has been kept within the budgetary limits and revenue has been collected according to it or not. The Government accounts, therefore, follow the budgetary form *i.e.*, they are kept under the same heads and sub-heads as those of the budget. Commercial type of accounts may, however, by kept for specified business and commercial undertaking of the Government, and in their case the balance sheet may also be prepared.

In India the form of the accounts of the Union as well as of the States is prescribed by the Comptroller and Auditor-General of India, with the approval of the President. The form of the budget is such as the Finance Minister may, after considering the suggestions, if any, of the Estimates Committee, settle.

The Account-keeping Agency in India. According to the theory of Financial Administration, keeping of the accounts should be a function of the executive authorities. Since the legislature grants moneys to the executive and the latter spends, it is but right that the executive should keep and render account of what it spends. In Britain the Head of each department, as we have seen, is nominated, as the accounting Officer in respect of his department, and each department keeps its own accounts.

In India, the duty of keeping the accounts of the Union (except the Railway and the Defence Accounts) as well as the States devolves upon the Comptroller and Auditor General of India and his staff. Under the Comptroller and Auditor-General there is in each state an Accountant General in whose office the accounts of the transactions (Union as well as State) taking place within the territorial limits of that state are kept. Railway accounts are kept by the Financial Commissioner for Railways, and defence accounts by the Finance Ministry through the Financial Adviser (Defence) and the military Accountant General.

Separation of Accounts from Audit

This combination of the accounting and audit functions in the hands of the same agency has come down from the days of the British rule and is now about a century old. It is a relic of those days when the legislature had no control over the finances, and the executive was all-in-all. It is no longer compatible with the present constitutional set-up of the country under which the Parliament has been given the supreme power of control over the national finances. An independent audit of the accounts kept by the executive is the principal tool of parliamentary financial control. If, however, the audit agency is also responsible for keeping the accounts, then it means that it audits accounts kept by itself. This is highly objectionable in principle, and has been rightly condemned by Auditors General one after another. The evils of the combination of the Audit and accounting functions were summed up by Mr. Narhari Rao, the first Comptroller and Auditor General of independent India in a note submitted by him to the Public Accounts Committee. "The present arrangements," said this note, "under which the spending authorities are not responsible for the maintenance of a complete and up-to-date account relating to the transactions for which they are responsible and the duty of compiling and maintaining these accounts rests upon an outside authority, namely, Indian Audit Department, is wholly inconsistent with the various responsibilities of the spending departments, namely, effective control over their financial transactions and the discharge of their responsibilities to Parliament to keep within the budget grants and appropriations. Indeed, existing arrangements blur the responsibilities and are highly defective. The separation of audit from accounts and the organization of the necessary accounting machinery under the administrative departments with a view to removing these serious defects and the enforcement of effective exchequer control are essential and overdue, and I, as Comptroller and Auditor General, attach the greatest importance to these reforms being carried out after the minimum interval required to introduce the necessary organizational changes.

The Simon Commission had also commented adversely on the combined system of audit and accounts in India and steps were taken to separate the two in U.P., N.W.F.P., and some Central Government departments some time before 1931, but the attempt was given up in the following years for reasons of economy. The Auditor General admitted that the separation would mean some additional cost but the resulting improvement in financial and audit control would more than compensate for it. He promised that for effecting the separation, he would be able to provide a considerable part of the Accounts Organization for the Union and the States from his own present organization, retaining for himself a comparatively small portion of it for purposes of audit.

This movement for separation of accounts from audit attracted serious attention from time to time. The Comptroller and Auditor General's (Duties, Powers and Conditions of Service) Act passed in 1971, visualised the need for separating accounts from audit. In 1973, a sub-group of the Cabinet Committee on Administration came to the conclusion that the existing system of payment and accounting was outmoded. It recommended the integration of the payment & accounting functions with administrative responsibility. Their scheme of departmentalisation envisaged the Secretary of the department as the Chief Accounting Authority with responsibility for accounting. It recommended that the accounting organisation should be placed under the Financial Adviser to the Ministry, usually of the rank of the Additional Joint Secretary.

Under an Act of Parliament passed in 1975, the Government of India launched the scheme of departmentalisation of accounts in three phases beginning from April 1, 1976. It was completed by Oct. 1976. The requisite accounting personnel were transferred from the Comptroller and Auditor General's establishment. The revenue accounting work was also taken over from April 1, 1977.

Under the new scheme, the Chief Accounting Authority for all transactions of the Ministry and its attached and subordinate offices, is the Secretary of the Ministry who is assisted by the Financial Adviser in the discharge of his responsibilities. The secretary as the

CAA has total and over all responsibility for the efficient working of the payment and accounting set up. On behalf of the CAA the Financial Adviser is responsible for:

(a) the preparation of the budget of Ministry & its departments;

(b) arranging payments sanctioned by the Ministry;

(c) consolidation of the accounts for the ministry as a whole;

(d) the preparation of Appropriation Accounts for the grants controlled by the Ministry;

(e) ensuring accuracy of accounts and efficiency of operation;

(f) the introduction of an efficient system of management best suited to the functional requirements of the Ministry and its departments. The Financial Adviser is assisted by the Principal Accounts Officer; other Accounts officers and requisite staff.

The Accounting Process in India. It has been mentioned in a preceding paragraph of this chapter that the treasuries scattered all over the country at sub-divisional and district headquarters are points at which public account starts. The district or the head treasuries classify the receipts obtained and payments made by them, the sub-treasuries under them for the Union Governments and State Government (within the limits of which they exist) separately under the various heads and sub-heads of accounts. They send these accounts with the supporting vouchers to the Accountant General at the State headquarters. The Accountant General and his staff consolidate these accounts received from the various treasuries on the monthly and annual basis. It is not, however, simply consolidation. The treasuries situated in one state may have received money or made payment on behalf of another state, or Government of India, or there may have been inter-departmental transactions within the same Government. These have to be duly adjusted so as to bring out the final position under each grant and appropriation.

The departmental authorities, for the purpose of controlling their expenditure so as to keep within their budgetary grants, maintain their own accounts. These are compiled from the copies of the vouchers and receipts of collections and disbursements which the sub-offices and officers of the department are required to send them in respect of moneys deposited by them or in their behalf, or payments authorized by them from the treasuries. They reconcile these accounts periodically with those kept by the Accountant General to eliminate possible errors. The departmental accounting is, however, only of a rough and ready kind for purposes of watching and controlling the flow of receipts and expenditure. "This improvised method", says Mr. Narhari Rao, "never worked satisfactorily and it completely broke down during the war."

The Final form of Accounts in India

The Comptroller and Auditor General's department prepares the final accounts of the Union and State Governments in two forms—"The Appropriation Account" and the 'Finance Account.' The 'Appropriation Account' is an account comparing the total grants, original and supplementary, made by Parliament for particular purposes for a financial year with the actual expenditure incurred for these purposes during the year. The Public Accounts Committee examines this account. Subsidiary accounts such as the profit and loss accounts and balance sheet of the commercial undertakings of the Government stores accounts works accounts, etc., and appended to the Appropriation Account to give details of expenditure concerning these, because such details do not figure in the Appropriation Account itself.

The Finance Account is a comprehensive accounts of the receipts and expenditure of the Government (Union or State), classified under the various heads and sub-heads of the budget.

Besides these, the Audit and Account department also prepares a General Financial Statement called the 'Combined Finance and Revenue Accounts of the Central and State Governments', giving a summary of the accounts of the Union and of all the State Governments for the preceding financial year, and showing their balances and outstanding liabilities.

AUDIT

Audit means an examination of accounts with a view to determine the correctness of these accounts and of the transactions they embody. The test of correctness applied may be one of formal legality only, or also of economy and propriety. A thorough-going audit should be an audit.

(a) against laws, rules, and regulations,

(b) against sanctions,

(c) against canons of financial propriety, and

(d) against appropriations as voted in the budget.

Of these criteria (a) to (c) seek to judge the legality, *i.e.*, conformity of the transactions to the requirements of budget provisions, and laws, rules, etc., which may be applicable, while canons of financial propriety are intended to check improper and wasteful expenditure. Some of the canons of financial propriety are the following namely.

(1) Every public servant should exercise the same vigilance and care in respect of expenditure of public money as an ordinarily prudent person would, in respect of his own money, *i.e.*, expenditures should not be more than the occasion demands,

(2) No authority should sanction or order expenditure directly or indirectly to its own advantage,

(3) Public money should not be spent for the benefit of a particular individual or section of the community unless *(a)* the amount of expenditure involved is insignificant, or *(b)* a claim for the amount has been decreed by a Court of law, or *(c)* the expenditure is in pursuance of a recognized policy or custom, and

(4) The amount of any allowance to meet expenditure of a particular kind, *e.g.*, travelling allowance should be so determined as not to become a source of profit to the recipient.

Audit of Governmental accounts in all countries is largely a legality and honesty audit, *i.e.*, it largely confines itself to seeing that expenditure is in conformity with the law and rules, and is supported by adequate vouchers. It is a highly controversial matter as to who should be the ultimate judge of the propriety and economy of expenditure—the audit or the administrative officer. Authoritative opinion inclines in favour of the latter, as administrative officer is in direct touch with the circumstances in which the expenditure has to be incurred, and he is also responsible for carrying out the Governments' policy. It is said that the primary object of government is not account-keeping but to look after the welfare of the people, and so considerations of audit and accounts must be subordinated to those of public policy. Also Audit's contact with a transaction is only indirect, *i.e.*, through vouchers, and papers and after the lapse of considerable time since the date of transactions.

Audit in India. Audit of Government accounts (including the accounts of the States) in India is a Union subject and is entrusted to the Comptroller and Auditor-General of India who is empowered to audit all expenditure from the revenues of the Union or States incurred in India or outside; all their transactions relating to debt, deposit, remittances, etc. all trading, manufacturing and profit and loss accounts and balance sheets kept under the order of the President or Governor; and receipts and stock accounts with the approval of the President or Governor or when required by these. Indian audit is governed not by law, but by an executive order—the Government of India Audit and Accounts Order 1936 as adapted under the Indian (Provisional Constitution) Order of 1947. In Britain there is statutory provision for audit under the Exchequer and Audit Act 1921, and so also in the U.S.A. under the Budget and Accounting Act 1921. Legislation on the subject is needed in this country also to bring audit provisions in line with new constitutional set-up.

Audit in India is primarily concerned with expenditure. Its concern with receipts is limited to those items only which it may be required by the executive to undertake, or may undertake with its approval. At present the receipts of Railways, Posts and Telegraph, and Customs only are subject to audit, while other receipts including those from Income-tax are not. The reason for this is that originally the British audit from which the Indian system was copied had a limited scope in respect of receipts and revenue departments in India were headed by very senior officers of I.C.S. whose work in respect of collections, governed as it was by special codes and laws, did not lend itself easily to the ordinary kind of audit. In England things have moved forward since then under the Exchequer and Audit Act 1921, the British Comptroller and Auditor-General is empowered to examine all receipts.

Audit should really be an arm of the legislature to assist it in seeing that its wishes and decisions as expressed in the budget are respected. In Britain the Comptroller and Auditor General is considered to be a parliamentary officer and the audit conducted by him is on behalf of the House of Commons. In India, practically the position is the same. The Constitution accords a thoroughly independent position to the Comptroller and Auditor-General and requires that his reports relating to Accounts shall be laid before each House of Parliament, but technically, the audit is conducted on behalf of the Executive and its reports are submitted to the Executive.

Finally, Indian audit is primarily a legality audit. The Government of India Audit and Accounts Order under which it is conducted requires the Comptroller and Auditor-General "to ascertain whether moneys shown in the accounts as having been disbursed were legally available for and applicable to the purpose to which they had been applied and whether the expenditure conforms to the authority which governs it." We have referred to the reason why audit does not usually go into the question of merits of expenditure. In doing so it is liable to encroach on the sphere of the administrators and produce friction between itself and them. In the U.S.A., the Comptroller General's advance decisions seeking to control details of departmental expenditure have led to much controversy between him and the administrative departments. Indian audit is not, however, precluded from investigating into or commenting upon the impropriety, wastefulness, or extravagance of expenditure where there is a prima facie case for doing it. Now we have a Public Accounts Committee to assist Parliament in the exercise of its powers of financial control. It is the duty of the committee, among other things, to draw the attention of Parliament to causes of improper, wasteful or extravagant expenditure, and the committee looks to audit to point but such cases to it.

The Audit Organization in India

As mentioned above, the audit and accounting functions in India were combined in the hands of one organisation, the Indian Audit Department, headed by the Comptroller and Auditor-General of India.

The Comptroller and Auditor-General of India is appointed by warrant under the hand and seal of the President of India. Though appointed by the executive, he cannot be removed from office except on an address of each of the Houses of Parliament as in case of the Judges of the Supreme Court. To buttress his independent position further, his salary and emoluments have been made a charge on the Consolidated Fund of India, and the conditions of his service cannot be varied to his disadvantage during his term of office. To the same end, he has been made ineligible for any further office whether under the Union or the State Governments. Audit to be reliable and useful must be conducted by a thoroughly independent authority. So the Indian Comptroller and Auditor-General has been accorded a fully independent status. His appointment is for a period of five years or till the age of superannuation whichever may be later. The staff working under the Comptroller and Auditor-General is also accorded independence in respect of its audit work by the provision that no disciplinary action against them can be taken without his concurrence.

The Headquarters office of the Comptroller and Auditor-General consists, besides himself of three Deputy Comptroller and Auditors-

General. Apart from the headquarters organization the Indian Audit and Accounts Department is divided into four classes of field officers, namely,

(1) the Civil Audit and Accounts offices,

(2) Post and Telegraph Audit and Accounts Office,

(3) Railway Audit offices, and

(4) Defence Services Test Audit offices Classes.

(1) and (2) are combined audit and accounts offices, while classes (3) and (4) do purely audit work. Accounts for railways and defence departments, as we have seen, are maintained departmentally. The offices of Auditor of Indian Accounts in the U.K. and of the Audit officer in the U.S.A. also are under the Comptroller and Auditor-General.

The Civil Accounts offices in the States are headed by Accountants General who have under them a large staff of deputies and assistants. For postal Audit, there is an Accountant General, Posts and Telegraph, who has under him a Deputy Accountant General, Posts and Telegraph, for each of the postal circles. Army and railway audit are headed by Director of Audit (War and Supply), and Director of Railway Audit respectively.

In some of the States audit of the Accounts of local and certain other semi-governmental bodies also is under the Indian Department while in others the State governments have a separate audit establishment for these purposes.

The Audit Report

Audit results in the certification of the Accounts by the Comptroller and Auditor-General as correct subject to such comments and remarks as he may choose to make, and in the preparation of an audit report for each of the Governments whose accounts are audited. This report is presented in case of the centre to the President, and in case of the States to the Governors. These heads are required by the constitution to cause these reports to be laid before their several legislatures. The legislatures refer the reports to their Public Accounts Committees of which there is one at the centre as well as one in each of the States, for examination of the report.

The audit reports contain the comments of the Audit authorities on the correctness or otherwise of the expenditure and other financial transactions. Particularly, they point out the more important financial irregularities the cases of budgetary grants being exceeded, over or under, budgeting failure to obtain the necessary sanction for expenditure, non-compliance with rules and regulations, cases of improper or wasteful expenditure, and of misappropriation and embezzlement.

AUDIT IS A WATCH-DOG OF DEMOCRACY

In a demoratic from of government the supreme authority with regard to financial policy is vested in the Legislature which determines the raising and spending of money. However, the function of the Legislature does not end with the voting of supplies and expenditure, but it has also to see that the money granted by it has been properly spent or not. In a demoracy the control of Parliament over public expenditure is complete and to ensure its complete control it has to see that the appropriations were spent by the executive for the purpose for which they were granted. This is ensured by the provision of audit of public expenditure by an independent statutory authority, the Comptroller and Auditor-General and the subsequent examination of his report by a Parliamentary Committee.

In the words of Robert H. Montogomery, "Auditing is a systematic examination of books and records of a business or other organization in order to ascertain or verify, and to report upon the facts regarding its financial operation and the result thereof." James Charles Worth defines audit "as the process of ascertaining whether the administrator has spent or is spending which appropriates money." Thus audit means the examination of accounts with a view to determining of their correction. It is the control of financial operation on behalf of legislature. Thus it may be used in two senses. While in a narrow sense it means the examination of the correctness of accounts, in the broad sense it embodies the determination of validity and honesty of the transactions as well. Audit of the government accounts is a legality cum-honesty audit. While auditing, the auditor has to see that the expenditure is not beyond the amount appropriated; that all the legal and other formalities provided by the financial rules were completed before the expenditure was incurred, that supporting vouchers and receipts show the same amount as is laid down in the records. Adult has been defined as a scrutinising agency. "An audit is conducted in order to discover and report to the legislative body any unauthorised, illegal or irregular expenditures, any financial practices that are unsound, and whether the administration has faithfully discharged its responsibility." He has also to see that the expending authority kept in view the principles of financial property while incurring the expenditure.

The system of legislative control over public finance first arose in England where it was the result of a gradual process than a creations. During the reign of King John the Parliament insisted that they should have the control of receipts and revenues whereas the discretion with regard to expenditure was the prerogative of the Crown. The Stuart Autocracy made the parliamentarians more exacting and they began to claim a share in the control of public expenditure as well. With the passage of democracy more and more powers passed into the hands of Parliament from the Lords and the Monarch with the result that parliamentary control over expenditure was established. The present Audit system was established under the Exchequer and Audit Department Act of 1834 and provision was made for a Standing Committee on Public Accounts in 1861 by the House of Commons.

Object of Audit

If we critically analyse the objects and functions of Audit it would become clear that Audit is the watchdog of national revenue. Formerly, audit was conducted only in case of expenditure to ensure that money was spent in accordance with the appropriation grants. But today audit is confined not only to expenditure. It embraces all financial transactions whether for receipt or payment. Its purpose is to ensure that the money which has been collected and expended is in occurrence with the provision of the Finance and Appropriation Acts passed by the legislature and that there is no fraud or embezzlement. Audit thus protects its master from thieves and dacoits. Without audit it would not be possible to discover the embezzlement of money. Moreover, audit not only checks embezzlement or fraud it has also to examine the wisdom, faithfulness and economy applied by the official in making the expenditure. Today it is no longer sufficient that appropriations should be applied to purposes approved, it is more important that these should be avoided. In the words of an American writer, "The Main objective of audit is to fix the accountability of the officers of the government for any illegal, improper or incorrect payments made resulting from any false, inaccurate or misleading certification made by them as well as for any payment prohibited by law or which did not represent a legal obligation under the appropriation fund involved."

Functions of the Audit

In brief, the functions of audit are to see that :-

(i) expenditure is not beyond the amount of allotment,

(ii) all legal and other formalities provided by the financial rules were completed before the expenditure was incurred;

(iii) supporting vouchers and receipt show the same amount as is shown in the records;

(iv) the canons of financial propriety were observed while the expenditure was made;

(v) extravagance has been avoided;

(vi) money has been wisely spent;

(vii) all the money has been collected which was to be collected in accordance with the Finance Act.

From the functions of Audit enumerated above it may be concluded that Audit is an important watchdog maintained by the legislature to prevent fraud in expenditure and to ensure economy and wisdom in public expending. It may also be borne in mind that audit is the servant of the legislature. The auditor-General, who is the head of the Audit Department submits his Report to the Legislature which studies it and takes necessary steps against officials responsible for unauthorized and unwise expenditure. Hence Durell calls the Comptroller and Auditor-General as the agent of the parliament. Osber Peaks call him as the "guide, philosopher and friend." It need hardly be emphasized that the Auditor-General should be independent of any executive control if he is to discharge his functions without any fear or favour. It is very important that public money should be properly spent and that utmost care should be taken to prevent fraud or embezzlement.

Accounting System in India

The function of accounting is usually vested in the spending agencies of the Government but in India, it is a peculiar phenomenon that accounting has been separated from the control of the Executive and is vested in the Audit and Accounts Department of India. The duty of keeping the accounts of the Union (except the Railways and Defence accounts) as well as of the States devolves upon the Comptroller and Auditor-General of India, and his staff. The general rules and forms for keeping the accounts are formulated by the Comptroller and Auditor-General. He is assisted in his task of accounting and auditing by an Accountant in each State.

Stages of Account Building in India

There are four stages in the building up of accounts in India;

1. The Initial Entry. The initial accounts are maintained at each Treasury. The Treasuries keep the accounts of receipts and payments of the money both for the Union and State Government separately under the various heads and sub-heads of accounts.

2. Classification of Accounts by Accountant-General. All the Treasuries send the accounts maintained by them with the supporting vouchers to the Accountant-General of their State by the first of the next month. The Accountant-General and his staff classified those transactions, *i.e.*, they mark each item of receipts or payments according to the account to which it relates.

3. Compilation of Accounts. After classification comes the stage of compilation and consolidation of the accounts. The Account Officers compile the accounts receipts from the Treasuries and from the departmental officers. The departmental officers receive the copies of the vouchers and receipts of collections and disbursements from their sub-officers and after consolidating them, send them to the office of the Accountant General to compare them with those received from the Treasury. The Account Officers send the accounts thus consolidated, to the government concerned by the end of the following month.

4. Annual Compilation of Accounts by the Auditor-General. Last comes the stage of the annual compilation of the accounts of the union Government and State Government by the Auditor-General of India. He prepares his finance accounts showing the annual receipts and disbursements for the Union and each State. Besides this, he also prepares a general financial statement called the Combined Finance and Revenue Accounts of the Central and State Governments giving the summary of the accounts of the Union and of all the State Governments for preceding financial year and showing their balances and outstanding liabilities.

5. Audit. The last stage in the execution of the budget is audit. The Parliament should not be content with appropriating money for specific purpose but it should also be able to supervise expenditure in order to ascertain whether the executive has spent it in accordance with her wishes or not. It is, therefore, necessary that some authority should check expenditure on behalf of the Legislature. This Function is performed by audit. The audit department is headed by the Comptroller and Auditor-General. His functions are not merely to ensure that the appropriations made by Parliament have not exceeded by the executive without a supplementary vote or that the expenditure conforms to rule but also to satisfy himself on behalf of Parliament as to its 'wisdom, faithfulness and economy. The Comptroller and

Auditor-General is the agent of the Parliament. He submits an annual report of his work to the Parliament.

Audit and Accounting—Difference

Audit in simple words, means the examination of the accounts with a view to determining their correctness and of the transactions they embody. In the words of Robert H. Montogomery. "Auditing is a systematic examination of the books and the records of a business or other organisation in order to ascertain or verify, and to report upon the facts regarding its financial operation and the results there of." Audit has been defined by James Charles Worth,"as the process of ascertaining whether the administrator has spent or is spending its funds in accordance with the terms of the Legislative instrument which appropriated money." Audit is thus a means of enforcing accountability of the administration to the Legislature in financial matters and therfore constitutes control of financial operations on behalf of the Legislature.

Audit as a system of Legislative control over public finance first arose in England and it was more the result of a gradual process than a creation. In the first place Parliament insisted during the reign of King John that they should have the control of receipts and revenues and the discretion with regard to expenditure was considered to be a prerogative of the Crown. But the Stuart autocracy made the Parliamentarians more exacting and they began to claim a share in the control of public expenditure as well. As more and more powers passed from the hands of the king of Parliament, gradually the present practice was established which gave the Parliament complete control over expenditure also.

Formerly audit was conducted only in case of expenditure and that only to ensure that money had been spent in accordance with the appropriation grants. But at present it is conducted for all financial transactions, whether for receipt or payment to ensure that money which has been collected and expended is in accordance with the provisions of the Appropriation Act passed by the Legislature and that there is no fraud or embezzlement. The present audit goes a step further also, to examination of the 'wisdom, faithfulness and economy' applied by the official in making the expenditure. It is no longer sufficient that appropriations should be applied to purposes and should not be exceeded without parliamentary approval. It is more important that these should be wisely and economically expended and that extravagance and waste be avoided. In the words of an American writer. "The main objective of audit is to fix the accountability of the officers of the Government for an illegal, improper or incorrect payment made resulting from any false, inaccurate or misleading certification which did not represent a legal obligation under the appropriation or fund involved."

Difference between Auditing and Accounting. Auditing and accounting are very closely related yet there exists a great difference between the two. According means keeping a systematic record of financial transactions whether of a public authority or of a private concern or of an individual. Unless accounts are properly maintained it is impossible to know how much was received and how much was spent and for what purpose. In the absence of such knowledge there can be no control. It is only through systematic accounts supported by vouchers and receipts that legality and honesty of the transactions can be determined.

Accounting is thus concerned with ensuring that the money requisitioned by a department is provided in the budget and that money is used by the department only up to that sum which is permitted by the budget and that the expenditure is in accordance with the law passed by the Parliament. The audit goes a step further. It has to see that the expenditure is in accordance with Appropriation Act, that the amounts are correct and all payments and receipts of money are supported by documents and vouchers. It detects errors and frauds and exercises a check on misappropriation and mismanagement. Audit thus begins where accounting ends.

Secondly, the keeping of the accounts is the function of the Executive authorities spending the amount and auditing that of the Legislature. Those who spend the money must keep accounts and be responsible for the fact that what they have spent was within the grants made by the Legislature. The auditors are not to keep the accounts. Their functions should be only to audit the accounts maintained by the spending authorities. Only then it can perform its audit duties efficiently. If the spending departments are given the discretion to adopt different methods of accounting it would make the task of audit difficult.

Definition of Audits its Functions and Objectives

Audit developed in the nineteenth century and now it has become an indispensable part of parliamentary control over finance. "An audit is an examination and verification of the accounts after transactions are completed in order to discover and report to the legislative body any unauthorised, illegal, or irregular expenditures, any financial practices that are unsound and whether the administration has faithfully discharged its responsibility". Audit enables an external control over administration and it intends to enforce accountability of provision of an independent examination of all financial transactions."

James Charles Worth defines audit "as the process of ascertaining whether the administrator has spent or is spending its funds in accordance with the terms of the legislature instrument which appropriates money." Thus audit means the examination of accounts with a view to determining of their correction. It is the control of financial operation on behalf of legislature. Thus it may be used in two senses. While in a narrow sense it means the examination of the correctness of accounts, in the broad sense it embodies the determination of validity and honesty of the transactions as well. Audit of the government accounts is a legality cum-honesty audit. While auditing, the auditor has to see that the expenditure is not beyond the amount appropriated; that all the legal and other formalities provided by the financial rules were completed before the expenditure was incurred, that supporting vouchers and receipts show the same amount as is shown in the records. Audit has been defined as a scruitinising agency."An audit are completed in order to discover and report to the legislative body any unauthorised, illegal or irregular expenditures, any financial practices that are unsound, and whether, the administration has faithfully discharged its responsibility." He has also to see that the expending authority kept in view the principles of financial propriety while incurring the expenditure.

The system of legislative control over public finance first arose in England where it was the result of a gradual process than a creation. During the reign of king John the Parliament insisted that they should have the control of receipts and revenues whereas the discretion with regard to expenditure was the prerogative of the Crown. The Stuart Autocracy made the parliamentarians more exacting and they began to claim a share in the control of public expenditure as well. With the passage of democracy more and more powers passed into the hands of Parliament from the Lords and the Monarch with the result that parliamentary control over expenditure was established. The present Audit system was establishment under the Exchequer and Audit Department Act of 1834, and provision was made for a Standing Committee on Public Accounts in 1861 by the House of Commons. There has been remarkable extension in the power of the Comptroller and Auditor General in England since the Exchequer and Audit Departments Act of 1866; by the passing of the Exchequer and Audit Act, 1921. "As comptroller of the Exchequer he controls entries and issues of public money to and from the Exchequer Account, and as Audit or he audits departmental accounts and submits the Appropriation Accounts to Parliament. His statutory function is to ensure that all expenditure is properly incurred *e.g.*, that no payments are made which go beyond and relevant statutory authority, and that Treasury sanction has been obtained wherever necessary. In addition, however, he has been encouraged by successive Committees on Public Accounts to examine departmental expenditure with a view to drawing the attention of the Committee to any cases of apparent waste or extravagance."

Objects of Audit

Audit is the watchdog of national finanace. Formerly, audit was conducted only in case of expenditure to ensure that money was spent in accordance with the appropriation grants but now audit is confined not only to expenditure but it embraces all financial transactions whether for receipts or payments.

Its purpose is to ensure that the money which has been collected and expended is in accordance with the provision of the Finance and Appropriation Acts passed by the legislature and that there is no fraud or embezzlement. Audit thus protects its master from thieves and dacoits. Without audit it would not be possible to discover the embezzlement of money. Moreover, audit not only checks embezzlement or fraud it has also to examine the wisdom, faithfulness and economy applied by the official in making the expenditure. Today it is no longer sufficient that appropriations should be applied to purposes approved, it is more important that these should be avoided.

Functions of The Audit

In brief, the functions of audit are to see that:

(i) Expenditure is not beyond the amount of allotment;

(ii) All legal and other formalities provided by the financial rules were completed before the expenditure was incurred;

(iii) Extravagance has been avoided;

(iv) Money has been wisely spent;

(v) Supporting vouchers and receipts show the same amount as is shown in the records;

(vi) The cannons of financial propriety were observed while the expenditure was made;

(vii) All the money has been collected which was to be collected in accordance with the Finance Act.

From the functions of Audit enumerated above it may be concluded that audit is an important watchdog maintained by the legislature to prevent fraud in expenditure and to ensure economy and wisdom in public expending. It may also be borne in mind that audit is the servant of the legislature. The Auditor-General, who is the head of the Audit Department, submits his Report to the Legislature which studies it and takes necessary steps against officials responsible for unauthorized and unwise expenditure. Osber Peaks call him as the "guide, philosopher and friend". It need hardly be emphasized that the Auditor-General should be independent of any executive control if he is to discharge his functions without any fear or favour. It is very important that public money should be properly spent and that utmost care should be taken to prevent fraud or embezzlement.

Thus,"auditing is an analysis of proposed or past expenditures with respect not only to their legality but also to their desirability. Accounting data provides much of the information upon which audits are made. Auditors examine expenditure vouchers and other documents showing proposed or past financial transactions."

ASPECTS OF AUDIT CONDUCTED OF THE APPROPRIATION ACCOUNTS IN INDIA

Audit has acquired a crucial importance in the process of financial administration of parliamentary democracies. This is employed as a tool of parliamentary control over public expenditure in order to ensure that the funds voted by the legislature are utilised by the executive organ only for 'approved purposes and with due regard to considerations of economy and efficiency.' The audit of appropriation accounts can be analysed from the following standpoints.

(1) Audit of Accountancy. The auditor of public accounts keeping the point of accountancy in his mind is expected to perform the same functions as those of an auditor of a private commercial accounts. Here the purpose is to satisfy about the accuracy and comprehensiveness of accounts,"to ensure that all revenues and receipts collected by the government are accounted for under the proper heads, that all expenditure and disbursements are supported by proper authorisations, vouched for and correctly categorized, and that final account gives a complete and true picture of the financial transactions it is supposed to." This also includes checking frauds and technical errors.

In India the process of audit of the government accounts is continuous, and it proceeds alongwith cash transactions to the extent it is possible. The process is not postponed 'till the year is over and the final accounts of the year are completed.

(2) Audit of Authority. "Closely allied to appropriation audit" writer Durell, "and necessarily bound up with it, it is the audit of authority or administrative unit : the examination of expenditure with a view to seeing that it is supported by the requisite authority in each case." The Audit and Accounts Order provides that the Comptroller and Auditor-General will ascertain whether the expenditure conforms to the authority. Accouding to Basil Chubb,"The House appropriates the grants, but the expenditure, even though made on the service for which it is appropriated, is not valid unless incurred under proper authority. The provision made by Parliament (Legislature) for a service detailed in the estimates is not in itself any authority for carrying out that service, if it is a service for which treasury authority is required. The audit of authority is therefore an important function of the Comptroller and Auditor-General, and it is his duty to report to the House any unauthorized expenditure for which treasury sanction is unobtainable; and he would normally recommend it for disallowance,but in special circumstances he would use his discretion as to admitting charges which are unauthorized, subject to the review of the Public Accounts Committee, whose attention would be drawn to them in his report."

Constitutional provisions provide the source and the basis of all audit and authorities and under these the comptroller and Auditor-General must keep a watch and be assured that "all expenditures incurred should be in strict conformity with the relevant provisions of the Constitution and of the laws made thereunder, and should also conform to the financial rules and regulations framed by a competent authority, supported by sanction accorded by a competent authority. In conducting the audit in respect of the audit of authority, the auditor performs quasi-judicial functions, in that he has to apply the rules and orders as they stand, irrespective of the position of the person against whom they are enforced. He may not relax or waive the rules, except where he is specially empowered to do so."

The Auditor comments upon in his Audit Report about the Cases where expenditure had been done in the absence of the approval of a competent authority, and also the cases where the expenditure has been done in excess of such authority, as noticed by the auditor in the course of audit of authority. This is done to bring such irregularities to the attention of the legislature and the Public Accounts Committee.

(3) Audit of Appropriation Accounts and Finance Accounts. Audit of appropriation is the most important part of statutory audit. It is the most significant duty of the public auditor to ensure that grants are appropriated for the purpose for which they are provided by the legislature. As Durell has put it, "The appropriation of the grants to specific purposes is the expression of the will of Parliament, which becomes law on the passing of the Appropriation Act. Deviations therefrom consequently diminish parliamentary control, even though specially legislated for in certain cases, because Parliament can only be able to give an ex-post facto sanction to them. The strictness with which appropriation is applied is the measure of parliamentary control. No grants may be exceeded without fresh parliamentary authority accorded by a supplementary estimate or an excess grant, except in those special cases in which the Treasury (Finance Ministry/ Department) is empowered to exercise temporarily, modified powers of virement (reappropriation), subject to final approval by the House. The money must be spent within the time for which it was granted, and no sums are chargeable against the grants which do not actually come in course of payment within the financial year, a natural sequence of this condition being that any unspent surplus must be surrendered. Every amount charged in the account must be supported by proof of payment, the Comptroller and Auditor General being the subjudge of the sufficiency of evidence of payment."

It is essential that audit of Appropriation Accounts is comprehensive and complete. In this regard it is suggested that 'a test audit cannot be substituted for a through audit.' Every act of disbursement must be verified as per entries in the books right upto its proper head of service to ensure that the wishes of the legislature is duly carried out. 'These intentions are expressed in the estimates as finally granted by the legislature.' In this way the estimates, constitute the basis for the appropriation audit.

There are two main objectives of the audit of appropriation accounts. These are: *(i)* 'defective budgeting' and *(ii)* 'keeping expenditures within the scope of grants sanctioned by the legislature'. In case of defective budgeting, the auditor must review and comment upon the following:

(i) Amount of expenditure that has exceeded the voted grants;

(ii) Charged appropriation without sanction of supplementary grants and appropriations;

(iii) To check that supplementary grants have been obtained during the year but 'having proved unnecessary eventually';

(iv) To find out the amount of money which have been surrendered unutilized and also reappropriations which have proved to be excess.

Regarding the 'keeping expenditures within the scopes of grants sanctioned by the legislature', the auditor must comment upon the following matters:

(i) The moneys mentioned as having been spent against a particular grant must not exceed the amount so granted. The authority permitting such expenditure should not sanction amounts exceeding what is available under the grant;

(ii) The expenditure has been incurred for the purposes which are set out in the demands for grants;

(iii) That the expenditure mentioned against a particular grant 'must be of such a character so as to entitle itself to be recorded as such;'

(iv) There has been no new expenditure on any new service which was not considered at the time of passing the budget.

As it has already been stated that under the provisions of the Constitution, the expenditure charged upon the Consolidated Fund of India is 'required to be shown separately from that which has been voted, and also that expenditure on revenue account is to be shown separately from capital expenditure.' "It is, therefore, an important function of Audit to verify that no expenditure is classified as 'charged on the Consolidated Fund' except no expenditure is classified as voted which should be 'charged'."

The allocation between revenue expenditure and capital expenditure is very important for the classification of expenditure to avoid confusion."It should be borne in mind that the decision whether expenditure shall be met from current revenues or from borrowed moneys rests with the executive subject to the approval of the legislature. It is, however the duty of Audit to bring to notice occasions on which the classification of expenditure between revenue and capital or its distribution between current revenues or loan funds appears to be contrary to the dictates of sound and prudent financial administration. The financial and accounting conception of capital expenditure is imported from commercial theory and practice and an essential feature is that expenditure of a capital nature is not met from the revenue or profits of a concern. The essential purpose of the opening of capital heads of account is to facilitate the exhibition of financial results of any special undertaking on the basis of generally accepted commercial or in some more simple coventional manner, either that the cost of a service may be ascertained or that the full financial implication of any policy may be made clear." It has been seen the executive often decides to finance capital expenditure from revenue accounts in this regard it is said that it too should be properly recorded.

Finance Accounts. The auditor's report on finance Accounts relates to the salient features of current revenues and expenditures, the financial performance of important public works, the debt position distinguishing between productive debt and unproductive debt and the arrangements for redemption of such debts including comments from their adequacy or not." The auditor's report comprises a review of the balances of Public Debt, Deposits, and Remittance heads and this review seeks to achieve the objective of: "*(a)* showing a comprehensive enumeration of the balances under all Debt, Deposit, and Remittance Heads; and *(b)* examining and setting out the correct state of account under each head."

(4) Audit of Propriety. An expenditure should be in order, properly vouched expenditure, must carry the sanction of a proper authority, and also the rules have been observed both by the disbursing and sanctioning officers, must be met from the grants sanctioned by the legislature and properly recorded. 'Notwithstanding all these formalities having been observed regularly, cases involving extravagance and waste may arise. Such expenditures are termed as improper expenditures.' In the similar way there may be 'improper use of stocks and stores.'

Sound financial administration makes it imperative that a review of the expenditure from the angle of propriety is also made. Since audit is an instrument of financial control, and the auditor must report all cases of extravagence and waste to the legislature. "This is known as 'higher audit' and require a considerable amount of fact and discretion on the part of the auditor. The principle underlying such an audit is that 'every government official must exercise the same care in respect of expenditure of public moneys as a person of ordinary prudence would exercise in respect of expenditure of his own money'." In such cases the auditor must go beyond the vouchers and scrutinizes those aspects of expenditure which fall beyond the formal audit.

To ensure propriety at this level, the Auditor considers the following points:

"(a) no expenditure should ordinarily be sanctioned which would benefit the personal cause of the authority sanctioning such an expenditure directly or indirectly; and

(b) No money should ordinarily be spent which would benefit a particular person or section of the society unless either the amount of expenditure involved is insignificant, or a claim could be established in the court of law, or it is in conformity with a policy or custom."

In this respect the functions of the comptroller and Auditor General has not been precisely defined. Durell opined that such functions of the comptroller and Auditor General fall within the range of the 'discretionary review', and the limits of such review the governed more by usage and precedent than enactment. "This practice of drawing attention to cases of extravagance is a good instance of a development of procedure arising out of the system provided by Parliament, but not specifically legislated for."

❐